BOOK OF LISTS

BOOK OF LISTS
BOOK OF LISTS
BOOK OF LISTS
BOOK OF LISTS
BOOK OF LISTS
BOOK OF LISTS

Christopher Rigby

BARDFIELD
PRESS

First published by Bardfield Press in 2005
Copyright © 2005 Miles Kelly Publishing Ltd

Bardfield Press is an imprint of
Miles Kelly Publishing Ltd
Bardfield Centre, Great Bardfield, Essex, CM7 4SL

4 6 8 10 9 7 5 3

Editorial Director Belinda Gallagher
Art Director Jo Brewer
Design Layout Ian Paulyn, Louisa Leitao
Picture Research Manager Liberty Newton
Picture Researcher Laura Faulder
Production Elizabeth Brunwin
Scanning and Reprographics
Anthony Cambray, Mike Coupe, Ian Paulyn
Proofreader Margaret Berrill

British Library Cataloguing-in-Publication Data
A catalogue record for this book is available from the British Library

ISBN 1-84236-622-X

Printed in China

www.mileskelly.net
info@mileskelly.net

CONTENTS

PEOPLE 22–111

SCIENCE 112–195

TV & FILM 196–249

MUSIC 250–299

ART & LITERATURE 300–333

SPORT 334–369

HISTORY 370–395

GEOGRAPHY 396–435

MISCELLANEOUS 436–511

BOOK OF LISTS

PEOPLE

FIRSTS 24

10 FAMOUS PEOPLE WITH A
FEAR OF FLYING 25

10 WRITERS WHO WERE MANIC
DEPRESSIVES. 25

10 FAMOUS PEOPLE WHO SUFFERED
FROM DYSLEXIA. 26

10 FAMOUS DIABETICS 26

CELEBRITIES AND THEIR TATTOOS. 27

FAMOUS PEOPLE AND THEIR PETS 28

10 FEMALE WINNERS OF
THE 'REAR OF THE YEAR' AWARD. 29

10 MALE WINNERS OF
THE 'REAR OF THE YEAR' AWARD. 29

UNUSUAL MIDDLE NAMES OF 50
FAMOUS PEOPLE. 30

10 FAMOUS PEOPLE WHO LIVED
TO THE AGE OF 100 31

10 FAMOUS PEOPLE WHO DIED
BEFORE THE AGE OF 30 31

10 FAMOUS PEOPLE WITH TWIN SIBLINGS 32

10 FAMOUS PEOPLE WHO ARE
PARENTS OF TWINS 32

50 FAMOUS VEGETARIANS 33

10 FAMOUS PEOPLE BORN ON
CHRISTMAS DAY 34

10 FAMOUS AMERICANS BORN ON
THE 4TH OF JULY 34

LIKE SISTER AND BROTHER. 35

10 FAMOUS PEOPLE WHO SUFFERED FROM
EPILEPSY 36

10 CELEBRITIES WHO INSURED PARTS OF
THEIR BODY 36

UNUSUAL NAMES OF CELEBRITIES'
CHILDREN 37

EPONYMOUSLY SPEAKING. 38

60 FAMOUS PEOPLE WITH
ROSES NAMED AFTER THEM 40

THE WIT AND WISDOM OF OSCAR WILDE 41

THE WIT AND WISDOM OF WOODY ALLEN. 42

THE WIT AND WISDOM OF WC FIELDS. 42

10 BEASTLY QUOTES 43

THAT'S MY DOG
50 historical and fictional dogs
and their owners 44

10 RELIGIONS AND THEIR FOUNDERS 46

CATHEDRALS AND THEIR SAINTS 46

10 FAMOUS FOLLOWERS OF KABBALAH 47

10 FAMOUS SCIENTOLOGISTS 47

10 FAMOUS JEHOVAH'S WITNESSES. 48

CONTENTS

10 FAMOUS BUDDHISTS 48

20 FAMOUS PEOPLE WHO ARE
THE SUBJECTS OF LONDON STATUES 49

20 FAMOUS PEOPLE WITH STATIONS NAMED
AFTER THEM ON THE PARIS METRO 49

TILL DIVORCE US DO PART
20 Famous people and their spouses 50

10 WINNERS OF THE PIPE SMOKER
OF THE YEAR AWARD 52

10 FILM STARS WHO HAVE BEEN VOTED 'SEXIEST
MAN ALIVE' BY PEOPLE MAGAZINE 52

SHIP AHOY 53

A PRESIDENTIAL PARADE 54

20 FAMOUS PEOPLE WHO DIED IN
AN AIR CRASH 56

20 FAMOUS PEOPLE WHO DIED
IN A ROAD ACCIDENT 56

10 FAMOUS PEOPLE WITH ONE EYE 57

10 FAMOUS PEOPLE WHO ARE
LEFT-HANDED 57

50 HISTORICAL / FICTIONAL HORSES
AND THEIR OWNERS 58

FAMOUS NAMES IN COCKNEY
RHYMING SLANG 60

BORN IN THE USA 62

BORN IN THE UK 64

PATRON SAINTS OF PROFESSIONS 66

BEASTLY NICKNAMES 67

PRESIDENTIAL NICKNAMES 68

NICKNAMES OF BRITISH PRIME MINISTERS 69

10 FAMOUS PEOPLE WHO HAVE BEEN
DEPICTED ON BRITISH STAMPS 70

10 FAMOUS PEOPLE WHO HAVE BEEN
DEPICTED ON AMERICAN STAMPS 70

FASHION FACTS 71

BOYS' NAMES AND THEIR MEANINGS 72

GIRLS' NAMES AND THEIR MEANINGS 74

MEANINGS OF SURNAMES 76

10 FAMOUS PEOPLE WHO USED TO
BE TEACHERS 77

10 FAMOUS PEOPLE WHO QUALIFIED
AS DOCTORS 77

10 FAMOUS OXFORD GRADUATES 78

10 FAMOUS CAMBRIDGE GRADUATES 78

COLLECTIVELY SPEAKING 78

FAMOUS COLLECTORS 79

DINING WITH THE STARS
Restaurants owned by celebrities 80

20 PEOPLE BORN UNDER THE STAR
SIGN OF AQUARIUS 81

20 PEOPLE BORN UNDER THE STAR
SIGN OF PISCES 81

BOOK OF LISTS

20 PEOPLE BORN UNDER THE STAR
SIGN OF ARIES 82

20 PEOPLE BORN UNDER THE STAR
SIGN OF TAURUS 82

20 PEOPLE BORN UNDER THE STAR
SIGN OF GEMINI 83

20 PEOPLE BORN UNDER THE STAR
SIGN OF CANCER 83

20 PEOPLE BORN UNDER THE STAR
SIGN OF LEO 84

20 PEOPLE BORN UNDER THE STAR
SIGN OF VIRGO 84

20 PEOPLE BORN UNDER THE
STAR SIGN OF LIBRA 85

20 PEOPLE BORN UNDER THE
STAR SIGN OF SCORPIO 85

20 PEOPLE BORN UNDER THE
STAR SIGN OF SAGITTARIUS 86

20 PEOPLE BORN UNDER THE
STAR SIGN OF CAPRICORN 86

10 FAMOUS PEOPLE BORN IN INDIA 87

10 FAMOUS PEOPLE BORN IN GERMANY 87

ONE SMALL STEP FOR MAN
The 12 men who have
walked on the Moon 88

SPACE FIRSTS 88

THE ROYAL FAMILY 89

THE SIX PARTS OF THE CORONATION 89

THE QUEEN'S CORGIS 90

STAR SIGNS OF THE ROYAL FAMILY 90

PAPAL PARAPHERNALIA 91

OFFICIAL TITLES OF THE POPE 91

10 PRODUCTS THAT HAVE BEEN
ENDORSED BY FOOTBALLERS 92

10 PRODUCTS THAT HAVE
BEEN ENDORSED BY DAVID BECKHAM 92

A BEAUTY QUEEN PAGEANT
Celebrities who are former
beauty queens 93

THE FULL NAMES OF FAMOUS PEOPLE
KNOWN BY ONE-WORD NAMES 94

BEFORE THEY WERE FAMOUS
Former occupations of famous people 96

20 FAMOUS PEOPLE WHO HAVE ATTENDED
YALE UNIVERSITY 98

20 FAMOUS PEOPLE WHO HAVE ATTENDED
HARVARD UNIVERSITY 98

10 FAMOUS WOMEN WHO WERE
TEENAGE BRIDES 99

10 FAMOUS MEN WHO MARRIED
TEENAGE BRIDES 99

THOROUGHFARES AROUND THE
WORLD NAMED AFTER PEOPLE 100

CONTENTS

10 FAMOUS PEOPLE WHO HAVE
SUFFERED FROM A STAMMER 101

MOUNTAINEERING FIRSTS 102

AVIATION FIRSTS 103

INITIAL THOUGHTS
Famous people with initial
letters as part of their name 104

PRIZE GUYS
Famous awards named after people 106

10 WINNERS OF THE NOBEL PEACE PRIZE 107

35 PEOPLE WHO HAVE BEEN NAMED
TIME MAGAZINE 'MAN OF THE YEAR' 108

TIME MAGAZINE 'MAN OF THE
20TH CENTURY' 109

THE YEAR THEY DIED 110

SCIENCE

RAINING CATS 114

. . . AND DOGS 115

PRIZE GUYS
A selection of Nobel Prize winners
CHEMISTRY 116

MEDICINE 116

PHYSICS 117

ENOUGH TO DRIVE YOU BATTY 118

MYTHS ABOUT BATS 118

SPECIES OF BAT 119

ENDANGERED SPECIES 120

10 ADDITIONAL ENDANGERED SPECIES 120

DID YOU KNOW? 121

ANIMAL PHOBIAS 122

MORE PHOBIAS 123

THE BEAUFORT SCALE (WINDS) 124

THE RICHTER SCALE (EARTHQUAKES) 124

ELEMENTS NAMED AFTER PEOPLE 125

ELEMENTS NAMED AFTER PLACES 125

BEASTLY SYMBOLS 126

ANIMAL ADJECTIVES 127

MORSE CODE 128

COMPUTER ABBREVIATIONS 129

MEDICAL ABBREVIATIONS 130

THE HIDDEN MEANINGS OF
FLOWERS AND PLANTS 131

THE FEMALE OF THE SPECIES 132

COLLECTIVE NOUNS FOR CREATURES 133

THE PERCENTAGE OF GASES IN
THE AIR THAT WE BREATHE 134

THE SHAPE OF THINGS 135

A TO Z OF 'OLOGIES' 136

BOOK OF LISTS

ELEPHANTS ON PARADE 137

SO THAT'S WHAT IT'S CALLED 138

ACUPUNCTURE POINTS 139

HOW LOUD?
Decibel levels of everyday noises 140

YOUNG AT HEART 141

TYPES OF CLOUD 142

RAINBOW MNEMONIC 142

ODDS OF BEING STRUCK BY LIGHTNING 142

NATURE'S SIGNS THAT ARE SAID TO
SIGNAL IMPENDING RAIN 143

HURRICANES 144

NAMES FOR HURRICANES IN 2005 144

NAMES FOR HURRICANES IN 2006 145

NAMES FOR HURRICANES IN 2007 145

10 TYPES OF LIGHTNING 146

TEMPERATURE CONVERSIONS 146

WEATHER FACTS 147

10 SEAS ON THE MOON 149

NAMES FOR MONTHLY FULL MOONS 149

A TO Z SELECTION OF BREEDS AND SPECIES . . 150

ALTERNATIVE NAMES FOR ANIMALS
AND PLANTS 152

CHEMICAL NAMES FOR EVERYDAY ITEMS 154

10 HOUSEHOLD INVENTIONS 155

10 SIMPLE INVENTIONS WE COULD
NOT DO WITHOUT 155

ANIMAL SIMILES 156

FLOWER POWER 157

STATE FLOWERS OF THE USA 158

HOME SWEET HOME 160

ANIMAL ETYMOLOGY 161

MEANINGS OF DINOSAUR NAMES 162

HUMAN BODY 163

ANIMAL KINGDOM 163

WEIGHTS OF ANIMALS' BRAINS 164

HOW MANY – HUMAN BODY? 165

HOW MANY – ANIMAL KINGDOM? 165

DOCTORS AND DISEASES 166

COMMON NAMES FOR DISEASES
AND CONDITIONS 167

A BONY BUNCH 168

PARTS OF THE HEART 169

HEARTBEAT 169

CALORIES BURNED IN EVERYDAY ACTIVITIES . . 170

BIRDS OF A FEATHER 171

OSTRICH ODDITIES 171

10 FLIGHTLESS BIRDS 171

STATE BIRDS OF THE USA 172

INSECT INFO 173

CONTENTS

BEETLEMANIA 173

SOMETHING FISHY 174

SHARK ATTACK 175

UNDER THE SEA 175

FUN WITH NUMBERS. 176

WHAT ARE THE ODDS?. 177

WHAT'S YOUR IQ? 178

FAMOUS PEOPLE WITH HIGH IQS 178

ESTIMATED IQ OF PEOPLE OF THE PAST 179

RECORD-BREAKERS IN NATURE. 180

HOW HARD?. 181

HOW HOT?. 182

SOME CHILLIES AND THEIR RATINGS 182

BIRTH FLOWERS 183

BIRTHSTONES 183

PEOPLE OF THE PAST WITH
    FATHERLY NICKNAMES 184

ALLOY, ALLOY, ALLOY. 185

THE CHEMICAL FORMULAE OF
    EVERDAY ITEMS 185

FAMOUS PEOPLE AND THEIR CATS 186

THE RAT PACK. 187

20 SPECIES OF RAT. 187

PRODUCTS OF PLANTS 188

GEMS 189

10 FAMOUS GEMS. 189

ASTRONOMY GLOSSARY 190

ASTRONOMERS ROYAL 191

HALLEY'S COMET. 191

ORIGINS OF DOG BREED NAMES. 192

IMPERIAL MEASURES 193

MYTHICAL BEASTS 194

NATIVE AMERICAN ANIMAL SYMBOLS. 195

FILM & TV

FILM FIRSTS 198

THE MAGNIFICENT SEVEN
    The 7 actors who played the original
    Magnificent Seven characters 200

THE 7 DESTINATIONS OF THE 'ROAD' FILMS
    STARRING BOB HOPE, BING CROSBY AND
    DOROTHY LAMOUR 201

THE FIRST 7 *CARRY ON* FILMS 201

THE 7 DEADLY SINS DEPICTED IN THE
    1995 FILM *SEVEN* STARRING BRAD
    PITT AND MORGAN FREEMAN. 201

SNOW WHITE'S 7 DWARFS 202

7 NAMES THAT WERE REJECTED BY
    WALT DISNEY FOR THE 7 DWARFS 202

BOOK OF LISTS

7 WOMEN WHO HAVE KISSED HARRISON FORD ON SCREEN 203

7 WOMEN WHO HAVE KISSED CLARK GABLE ON SCREEN 203

7 WOMEN WHO HAVE KISSED JACK NICHOLSON ON SCREEN 203

MOVIE STAR NICKNAMES
The nicknames of 30 film stars 204

MAY THE FORCE BE WITH YOU
The 'Star Wars' episodes 206

STAR WARS: THE TRIVIA 207

THE JEDI CODE OF HONOUR 207

10 TV PROGRAMMES LATER MADE INTO FILMS . 208

10 FILMS LATER MADE INTO TV PROGRAMMES 208

10 FILMS ADAPTED FROM SHAKESPEARE'S PLAYS 209

10 STEPHEN KING STORIES ADAPTED INTO FILMS 209

AN INNUENDO-LADEN LIST OF 'CARRY ON' CHARACTERS 210

THE BOND GIRLS 211

10 ACTORS WHO HAVE PLAYED SHERLOCK HOLMES 212

10 ACTORS WHO HAVE PLAYED DR WATSON . . . 212

THE THREE MUSKETEERS
6 ACTORS WHO HAVE PLAYED ARAMIS 213

6 ACTORS WHO HAVE PLAYED ATHOS 213

6 ACTORS WHO HAVE PLAYED PORTHOS 213

6 ACTORS WHO HAVE PLAYED D'ARTAGNAN . . . 213

10 ACTORS WHO HAVE PLAYED ROBIN HOOD . . 214

10 ACTORS WHO HAVE PLAYED TARZAN 214

10 ACTORS WHO HAVE PLAYED COUNT DRACULA 215

10 ACTORS WHO HAVE PLAYED DRACULA'S NEMESIS, VAN HELSING 215

TIME FOR THE TAGLINES 216

10 FAMOUS NAMES FROM THE WORLD OF FILMS WHO DIED IN 2000 218

10 FAMOUS NAMES FROM THE WORLD OF FILMS WHO DIED IN 2001 218

10 FAMOUS NAMES FROM THE WORLD OF FILMS WHO DIED IN 2002 219

10 FAMOUS NAMES FROM THE WORLD OF FILMS WHO DIED IN 2003 219

30 ACTORS WHO HAVE RECEIVED A KNIGHTHOOD 220

10 ACTRESSES WHO HAVE BEEN CREATED A DAME 220

THE GOLDEN RASPBERRIES
These films have been awarded the worst film 'Razzie': 221

10 NOTABLE ACTORS WHO WON THE WORST ACTOR 'RAZZIE' 222

CONTENTS

10 NOTABLE ACTRESSES WHO WON WORST
ACTRESS 'RAZZIE'. 223

30 FAMOUS FILM STARS WHO NEVER
WON AN OSCAR 224

30 CLASSIC MOVIES THAT FAILED TO
WIN AN OSCAR. 225

FILMS THAT HAVE WON 11 OSCARS 226

FILMS THAT HAVE WON 10 OSCARS 226

FILMS THAT HAVE WON 9 OSCARS 226

FILMS THAT HAVE WON 8 OSCARS 227

FILMS THAT HAVE WON
7 OSCARS 227

WHAT'S IN A NAME?
The real names of 30 male movie stars: . 228

WHAT'S IN A NAME?
The real names of 30 female
movie stars 230

10 ACTORS WHO HAVE DRESSED AS
WOMEN ON FILM 232

10 ACTORS WHO HAVE APPEARED IN
FULL-FRONTAL NUDE SCENES ON FILM 232

FOLLOW MY LEADER
20 famous leaders who have
been played on film 233

40 FAMOUS PEOPLE OF THE PAST
PLAYED ON FILM 234

40 FILM STARS AND 40 CITIES 236

10 ACTORS WHO STARRED IN THE FILM
THE GREAT ESCAPE 238

THE LAST WORDS SPOKEN IN 20
FAMOUS FILMS. 239

BOND TRIVIA 240

10 FILM STARS WHO FOLLOWED IN
A PARENT'S FOOTSTEPS. 242

10 PAIRS OF SILVER SCREEN SIBLINGS 242

THE AMERICAN FILM INSTITUTE'S TOP
10 MALE SCREEN LEGENDS 243

THE AMERICAN FILM INSTITUTE'S TOP
TEN FEMALE SCREEN LEGENDS 243

THE AMERICAN FILM INSTITUTE'S TOP
100 FILMS OF THE 20TH CENTURY 244

TV FIRSTS 246

TV ADDRESSES 247

10 TV SITCOMS SET IN NEW YORK 248

10 TV SITCOMS SET IN LONDON 248

THE THEMES AND THE SINGERS 249

MUSIC

MUSIC FIRSTS. 252

FAMOUS PEOPLE WHO HAVE PERFORMED
IN BANDS AND POP GROUPS 254

BOOK OF LISTS

THE FAB FOUR
THE BEATLES' UK NO.1 HIT SINGLES....... 255

8 BEATLES SONGS THAT WERE NO.1 IN
THE USA BUT NOT IN THE UK 255

30 FAMOUS FACES ON THE ALBUM COVER
OF 'SERGEANT PEPPER'S LONELY HEARTS
CLUB BAND' 256

LENNON & McCARTNEY COMPOSITIONS
THAT WERE NO. 1 HITS FOR OTHER ACTS ... 257

OTHER SONGS GIVEN AWAY BY THE BEATLES .. 257

10 ROCK AND ROLL SUICIDES............. 258

10 POP STARS WHO WERE SHOT DEAD...... 258

THE FIRST 10 INDUCTEES IN THE US
ROCK AND ROLL HALL OF FAME 259

THE FIRST 10 BRITISH GROUPS TO BE
INDUCTED INTO THE US ROCK AND
ROLL HALL OF FAME 259

DERIVATIONS OF POP GROUP NAMES....... 260

REAL NAMES OF 50 MALE POP STARS 262

REAL NAMES OF 30 FEMALE POP STARS 264

FORMER NAMES OF 40 POP GROUPS....... 266

10 POP HITS BY FOOTBALL CLUBS 268

10 POP HITS BY CHILDREN'S CHARACTERS ... 269

20 ACTORS WHO HAVE HAD CHART HITS 270

30 FAMOUS PEOPLE MENTIONED IN THE
LYRICS OF THE BILLY JOEL HIT
'WE DIDN'T START THE FIRE' 271

TRIBUTE TUNES........................ 272

10 RECORDS THAT WERE BANNED
BY THE BBC 273

UK NO.1 HITS AT CHRISTMAS 274

ROCKING ALL OVER THE WORLD
Pop groups named after places 276

22 NO. 2 HITS 277

10 SINGERS WHO TOPPED THE CHARTS
AS A TEENAGER 278

10 SINGERS WHO TOPPED THE CHARTS
PAST THEIR 50TH BIRTHDAY 279

NO. 1 HITS THAT ASKED A QUESTION 280

SONGS THAT WON A 'BEST
SONG' OSCAR 281

10 SINGERS BORN IN WALES 282

10 SINGERS BORN IN SCOTLAND 282

10 SINGERS BORN IN IRELAND 283

10 SINGERS BORN IN LONDON 283

IT TAKES TWO 284

THREE'S A CROWD 286

MUSICAL INSTRUCTIONS................. 287

A NIGHT AT THE OPERA................. 288

THE ALTERNATIVE TITLES OF 10
GILBERT & SULLIVAN OPERETTAS........ 290

THE ALTERNATIVE NAMES OF
10 SYMPHONIES..................... 291

CONTENTS

BACKING BANDS 292

RECORD LABELS 294

THE 9 UK NO. 1 HITS OF ABBA 295

THE 8 UK NO. 1 HITS OF THE
ROLLING STONES 295

THE 7 UK NO. 1 HITS OF
MICHAEL JACKSON 296

THE 8 UK NO. 1 HITS OF TAKE THAT 297

THE 9 UK NO. 1 HITS OF THE SPICE GIRLS 296

THE 7 UK NO. 1 HITS OF
GEORGE MICHAEL 297

THE MUSICALS OF ANDREW
LLOYD WEBBER 298

THE FINAL RESTING PLACES OF
POP STARS 299

ART & LITERATURE

PROFILE OF VINCENT VAN GOGH 302

10 PAINTINGS BY VINCENT VAN GOGH 302

PROFILE OF REMBRANDT 303

10 PAINTINGS BY REMBRANDT 303

PROFILE OF PABLO PICASSO 304

10 PAINTINGS BY PICASSO 304

PROFILE OF L S LOWRY 305

10 PAINTINGS BY LOWRY 305

PROFILE OF JOHN CONSTABLE 306

10 PAINTINGS BY JOHN CONSTABLE 306

ART FOR ART'S SAKE
20 famous paintings and
20 famous painters 307

STATUESQUE
20 statues and sculptures 308

OPENING LINES OF FAMOUS NOVELS 310

WHAT THE DICKENS
A Charles Dickens timeline 312

10 ACTORS WHO HAVE PORTRAYED
EBENEZER SCROOGE 313

10 ACTORS WHO HAVE PORTRAYED FAGIN 313

A DICKENSIAN JOB CENTRE 314

TO BE OR NOT TO BE
A profile of William Shakespeare 316

40 WORDS INVENTED BY WILLIAM
SHAKESPEARE 317

KENNETH BRANAGH MEETS
WILLIAM SHAKESPEARE
Henry V. 318

Othello 318

Love's Labour's Lost 318

Much Ado About Nothing 319

Hamlet 319

'JUNGLE BOOK' ANIMALS 320

BOOK OF LISTS

ANIMALS OF BEATRIX POTTER. 321

A HARRY POTTER GLOSSARY. 322

THE GOOD BOOK
The 10 most-mentioned animals
in the Bible 324

BIBLE FACTS 324

NOMS DE PLUME 325

10 AUTHORS THAT HAVE BEEN
DEPICTED ON UK STAMPS 326

10 AUTHORS THAT HAVE BEEN
DEPICTED ON US STAMPS 326

WATCHING THE DETECTIVES 327

NOVEL-TITLE CHARACTERS 328

NURSERY RHYME ORIGINS 330

CLOSING LINES OF FAMOUS NOVELS 332

SPORT

SPORTING FIRSTS 336

10 TROPHIES NAMED AFTER PEOPLE 337

AUTOBIOGRAPHICAL
The autobiographies of 30
sports stars. 338

30 FAMOUS PEOPLE AND THE FOOTBALL
TEAMS THEY SUPPORT 340

9 FOREIGN FOOTBALLERS WHO HAVE
BEEN VOTED 'FOOTBALLER OF THE
YEAR' IN ENGLAND 341

MAGNIFICENT SEVENS
7 Famous Olympians. 342

7 EVENTS IN THE HIGHLAND GAMES. 343

7 FAMOUS PEOPLE WHO COULD HAVE
BEEN FOOTBALLERS 343

SHIRT SPONSORS OF PREMIERSHIP
FOOTBALL TEAMS 2004–2005 344

GAMES AND SPORTS AND
THEIR INVENTORS. 345

THE BBC 'SPORTS PERSONALITY
OF THE YEAR' 346

PATRON SAINTS OF SPORT AND LEISURE 347

THE NICKNAMES OF SOME
SCOTTISH FOOTBALL CLUBS 348

THE NICKNAMES OF 30 SPORTS STARS 350

BEASTLY NICKNAMES OF SPORTING TEAMS
American Football. 352

Baseball. 352

Basketball 352

Cricket 352

Ice Hockey 353

Rugby League 353

Association Football 353

CONTENTS

THE NICKNAMES OF 20 NON-LEAGUE
  FOOTBALL CLUBS 2004–2005 354

HOWZAT?
  A CRICKET GLOSSARY 355

THE 10 WAYS OF BEING GIVEN OUT
  AT CRICKET 356

WISDEN'S TOP 10 CRICKETERS OF
  THE 20TH CENTURY 356

HORSES FOR COURSES
  The venues for 20 famous horse races . . 357

SPORTING ACRONYMS AND INITIALS 358

THE 2004 FORMULA ONE SEASON 360

THE 18 HOLES OF THE AUGUSTA
  GOLF COURSE 361

A GOLF GLOSSARY 362

JUDO TERMS 363

HOW MANY IN A SIDE? 364

180!!!
  A darts glossary 365

SCRABBLE POINTS 366

BINGO SLANG 367

10 CLUBS THAT HAVE WON THE FA CUP
  THAT ARE NOT LIKELY TO WIN IT AGAIN 368

12 FOUNDER MEMBERS OF THE
  FOOTBALL LEAGUE 368

THE FORMER NAMES OF 20 FOOTBALL
  CLUBS 369

HISTORY

THE 12 LABOURS OF HERCULES 372

THE 12 DISCIPLES OF JESUS 373

THE 12 TRIBES OF ISRAEL (NAMED AFTER
  THE SONS OF JACOB) 373

THE 10 COMMANDMENTS 374

FOUNDING FATHERS 375

GODS AND GODDESSES 376

13 PREDICTIONS OF NOSTRADAMUS 378

10 VICE PRESIDENTS THAT BECAME
  PRESIDENT OF THE USA 380

10 BRITISH CHANCELLORS WHO BECAME
  PRIME MINISTER 380

10 HISTORICAL NOVELS 381

10 NOVELS SET DURING WORLD WAR II 381

NICKNAMES OF PEOPLE OF THE PAST 382

ASSASSINATIONS THAT SHOOK THE WORLD . . . 383

EXECUTIONS THROUGH HISTORY 384

HISTORICAL EVENTS IN YEARS ENDING
  WITH A 6 385

BATTLE STATIONS
  Historical battles pre 20th century 386

FOUNDING DATES OF NEWSPAPERS 388

BOOK OF LISTS

BIRTH AND DEATH OF 20
 FAMOUS AMERICANS 389

THE WISDOM OF CONFUCIUS 390

THE WISDOM OFWINSTON CHURCHILL 391

THE THINGS THEY SAID 392

20 IN LINE TO THE BRITISH THRONE IN 2005 . . 393

COLLECTIVELY SPEAKING 394

GEOGRAPHY

PLACES NAMED AFTER PEOPLE 398

WHAT TIME IS IT? 400

CITIES BUILT ON 7 HILLS 401

FORMERLY KNOWN AS 402

XL ROMAN PLACE NAMES 404

BIRDS AND BEASTS ON FLAGS 406

ZIP CODES OF US STATES 408

STATE NICKNAMES 410

UNUSUAL LAWS AROUND THE WORLD 412

TOP 10 HIGHEST MOUNTAINS 413

TOP 10 LONGEST MOUNTAIN RANGES 413

TOP 10 LARGEST COUNTRIES 414

TOP 10 LARGEST ISLANDS 414

TOP 10 LARGEST SEAS 415

TOP 10 LARGEST LAKES 415

MOTTOS AROUND THE WORLD 416

10 PLACES NAMED AFTER
 GEORGE WASHINGTON 417

FIRST 10 STATES SET UP IN THE USA 417

UNUSUAL DAYS CELEBRATED IN THE USA 418

CITY NICKNAMES 420

TOP 10 US STATES FOR POPULATION 422

BOTTOM 10 US STATES FOR POPULATION 422

THE 10 HIGHEST WATERFALLS IN
 THE WORLD 423

TOP 10 MOST SPOKEN LANGUAGES IN
 THE WORLD 423

HOW TO SAY HELLO IN 40 DIFFERENT
 LANGUAGES 424

PAST AND PRESENT CAPITALS 425

WHAT'S IN A NAME?
 The meanings of the names
 of countries 426

THE MEANINGS OF THE NAMES OF TOWNS,
 CITIES AND STATES 428

TOP 10 MOST HIGHLY POPULATED
 COUNTRIES IN THE WORLD 430

WORLD POPULATION LANDMARKS 430

CONTENTS

10 COUNTRIES THAT JOINED
THE EU IN MAY 2004 430

15 COMPANIES FOUNDED IN GERMANY 431

20 COMPANIES FOUNDED IN JAPAN 431

SYMBOLS ON FLAGS 432

FLAGS THAT DEPICT A UNION JACK 433

AIRPORTS NAMED AFTER PEOPLE 434

INTERNATIONAL AIRPORTS OF
30 CAPITAL CITIES 435

MISCELLANEOUS

CELEBRITY UNICEF AMBASSADORS 438

ACCORDING TO A 2004 SURVEY OF
9 TO 15 YEAR OLDS THESE WERE THE
MOST POPULAR JOBS: 439

ACCORDING TO THE SAME SURVEY THESE
WERE THE LEAST POPULAR JOBS: 439

20 FAMOUS PEOPLE WHO WERE 40 IN 2004 . . . 440

20 FAMOUS PEOPLE WHO WERE 50 IN 2004 . . . 441

WHERE THERE'S A WILL
Wills of the famous 442

SECRET IDENTITIES OF SUPER HEROES 444

10 MEMBERS OF THE HOLE IN THE
WALL GANG 445

10 MEMBERS OF THE GREAT TRAIN
ROBBERS' GANG 445

20 SAINTS' DAYS 446

20 TITLES HELD BY QUEEN ELIZABETH II 447

THE LAST 20 POPES 448

TOP 10 RANKS OF THE BRITISH ARMY 449

TOP 10 RANKS OF THE ROYAL NAVY 449

TOP 10 RANKS OF THE ROYAL AIR FORCE 449

JOBS IN THE HOUSEHOLD OF HENRY VIII 450

20 PEOPLE WHO SUFFERED FROM
ATTENTION DEFICIT DISORDER 451

STARS IMMORTALISED ON HOLLYWOOD'S
WALK OF FAME 452

10 PEOPLE WHO RECEIVED STARS ON
HOLLYWOOD'S WALK OF FAME IN 2004 453

IMPRINTS LEFT IN THE CEMENT OF
GRAUMAN'S CHINESE THEATRE ON
HOLLYWOOD BOULEVARD 453

20 FAMOUS PEOPLE BURIED AT
WESTMINSTER ABBEY 454

R.I.P. 455

EPITAPHS ON GRAVESTONES
AND MEMORIALS 455

20 ENTERTAINERS WHO HAVE RECEIVED
THE PRESIDENTIAL MEDAL OF FREEDOM . . . 456

10 POLITICIANS WHO HAVE RECEIVED THE
PRESIDENTIAL MEDAL OF FREEDOM 457

BOOK OF LISTS

10 NON-AMERICANS WHO HAVE RECEIVED
THE PRESIDENTIAL MEDAL OF FREEDOM... 457

THE TOP 10 FILM DUOS WITH THE BEST
ON-SCREEN CHEMISTRY FROM A SURVEY
BY THE ROYAL SOCIETY OF CHEMISTRY 458

THE TOP 10 DUOS OF ALL TIME IN A 2004 POLL
OF UK WOOLWORTHS CUSTOMERS....... 458

THE 20 MOST INFLUENTIAL HAIRSTYLES OF
ALL TIME IN A 2004 POLL BY MORPHY
RICHARDS........................... 459

20 INDUCTEES INTO CANADA'S HALL
OF FAME........................... 460

10 FOUNDING MEMBERS OF THE UK MUSIC
HALL OF FAME 2004................... 461

10 SINGERS WHO FEATURED ON THE BAND
AID SINGLE, 'DO THEY KNOW IT'S CHRISTMAS'
IN 2004 461

THE JACKSON 10....................... 462

KEEPING UP WITH THE JONESES........... 463

20 SCATHING COMMENTS MADE BY SIMON
COWELL TO POP STAR WANNABES........ 464

10 SPORTING COMMENTATING GAFFES BY
MURRAY WALKER..................... 465

ISLAND CAPITALS 466

PRISONS AROUND THE WORLD............ 468

PRISONS IN THE UK.................... 469

PRISONS IN LONDON.................... 469

TOWERS AROUND THE WORLD 470

10 OLDEST CITIES IN THE UK 471

10 TOWNS GRANTED CITY STATUS IN
THE 20th CENTURY 471

ADDRESSES OF FAMOUS BUILDINGS 472

LIFE'S A BEACH 473

TOP 50 PLACES TO SEE BEFORE YOU DIE
ACCORDING TO A 2002 BBC SURVEY...... 474

QUOTES FROM PRIME MINISTERS.......... 476

10 UNUSUAL POLITICAL PARTIES
These parties contested seats in the
2001 UK General Election 477

10 UNUSUAL MANIFESTO POINTS
The Monster Raving Loony party put
forward these policies in the 2001
General Election..................... 477

ETIQUETTE AROUND THE WORLD........... 478

HANGOVER CURES..................... 479

20 ROLES TURNED DOWN BY 20
MOVIE STARS....................... 480

TITLES AND POSTS HELD BY ENTERTAINERS... 481

EATING DISORDERS.................... 482

CHRISTMAS DISHES AROUND THE WORLD 483

THE PC WORLD 484

TEXTING ABBREVIATIONS................ 485

WORDS ACROSS THE OCEAN
American counterparts of
English words:...................... 486

PROVERBIALLY SPEAKING 488

MYTHS AND LEGENDS
Origins of superstitions 490

GHOSTLY GOINGS ON.................... 492

HOW TO REPEL OR KILL A VAMPIRE 494

10 ACTORS OF VAMPIRES ON FILM......... 494

WEDDING-DAY SUPERSTITIONS
10 good omens on a wedding day....... 495

CHOOSE YOUR WEDDING DAY CAREFULLY..... 495

10 ARGONAUTS
The following accompanied Jason on
his quest for the Golden Fleece 496

10 KNIGHTS OF KING ARTHUR'S
ROUND TABLE...................... 496

TAROT CARDS 497

22 TRUMP CARDS OF THE MAJOR ARCANA ... 497

12 DAYS OF CHRISTMAS................. 498

WHAT THE GIFTS OF THE 12 DAYS OF
CHRISTMAS REPRESENT............... 498

IF AT FIRST YOU DON'T SUCCEED 499

A SUIT OF ARMOUR..................... 500

THE TITANIC.......................... 501

10 PASSENGERS WHO SURVIVED THE
SINKING 501

HOW MANY? 502

FAN CLUBS 503

10 FAN CLUBS OF ELVIS PRESLEY.......... 503

'WOOD' YOU BELIEVE IT?................. 504

ALL THE THREES 505

SCREEN FAREWELLS
The last cinema releases of some
famous movie stars 506

THE COCKTAIL MENU.................... 508

CHAMPAGNE BOTTLE SIZES.............. 509

HOW TO SAY GOODBYE IN 30 LANGUAGES 510

LAST WORDS OF 20 FAMOUS PEOPLE........ 511

PEOPLE

Find out what Sean Connery has tattooed on his arm,
the name of Kevin Costner's restaurant, Jackie Chan's
job before going into films, Tony Blair's nickname, the
patron saint of firemen, who was once Miss Manila.
Here are lists about the famous, from the present-day
to the long-ago, on their medical conditions, their
pets' names, their siblings, their witticisms, their
beliefs, their marriages and even their untimely
deaths. People, especially the famous, are always
fascinating, but even more so when they are
compared in lists with their sometimes weird and
always wonderful counterparts.

BOOK OF LISTS

FIRSTS

27BC	Roman Emperor	Augustus
AD32	Pope	St Peter
597	Archbishop of Canterbury	Augustine
1547	Tsar of Russia	Ivan IV (The Terrible)
1721	British Prime Minister	Sir Robert Walpole
1789	First Lady of the USA	Martha Washington
1837	Monarch to live in Buckingham Palace	Queen Victoria
1896	Olympic gold medal winner	James B Connolly of the USA for the hop, step and jump
1906	American to win a Nobel Peace Prize	Theodore Roosevelt
1930	Air hostess	Ellen Church of United Airlines
1947	Person to break the sound barrier	US test pilot Chuck Yeager
1951	Miss World	Kiki Haakonson, Miss Sweden
1960	Female Prime Minister	Sirmavo Bandaranaike of Ceylon
1962	Guest on Johnny Carson's Tonight Show	Joan Crawford
1963	Woman to receive a $1 million fee for a film	Elizabeth Taylor (Cleopatra)
1964	Man to appear on the cover of Playboy	Peter Sellers
1967	Person to appear on the cover of *Rolling Stone* magazine	John Lennon
1978	Test-tube baby	Louise Brown
1987	Woman in the Rock And Roll Hall of Fame	Aretha Franklin
1993	Female US Secretary of State	Madeleine Allbright

PEOPLE

10 FAMOUS PEOPLE WITH A FEAR OF FLYING

Ronald Reagan

- Muhammed Ali
- Dennis Bergkamp
- Cher
- Aretha Franklin
- Whoopi Goldberg
- Glenda Jackson
- Michael Jackson
- Stanley Kubrick
- Ronald Reagan
- Joanne Woodward

10 WRITERS WHO WERE MANIC DEPRESSIVES

- Hans Christian Andersen
- Robert Burns
- TS Eliot
- F Scott Fitzgerald
- Ernest Hemingway
- Victor Hugo
- John Keats
- Robert Louis Stevenson
- Mark Twain
- Virginia Woolf

Robert Burns

BOOK OF LISTS

10 FAMOUS PEOPLE WHO SUFFERED FROM DYSLEXIA

- Fred Astaire
- Richard Branson
- Winston Churchill
- Tom Cruise
- Walt Disney
- Thomas Alva Edison
- Magic Johnson
- Jay Leno
- Pablo Picasso
- Henry Winkler

Fred Astaire

10 FAMOUS DIABETICS

Mae West

- Lionel Bart
- Halle Berry
- Johnny Cash
- Paul Eddington
- Billie Jean King
- Mary Tyler Moore
- Harry Secombe
- Luther Vandross
- Mae West
- Jane Wyman

PEOPLE

CELEBRITIES AND THEIR TATTOOS

Jennifer Aniston .... Small heart on her stomach

Sean Bean .... Blade in honour of his favourite football team Sheffield Utd

David Beckham ...... Several tattoos, including a large crucifix on his back

Victoria Beckham ... The initials DB on her wrist

Halle Berry .... Flower on her right buttock

David Bowie .... Lizard on his ankle

Mel C .... Her tattoos run into double figures and include a phoenix on her back and the word Angel on her stomach

Eric Cantona .... Head of a Native American on his chest

Sean Connery .... Scotland Forever on his arm, a design he hides when filming

Johnny Depp .... Winona Forever, for his then girlfriend Winona Ryder. When the pair split, Depp changed it to Wino Forever

Angelina Jolie .... Asian tiger on her back

Ronan Keating ...... Chinese symbol on his right shoulder

Diego Maradona .... The revolutionary Che Guevara on his upper right arm

Ian McKellen .... He and eight of his *Lord of the Rings* co-stars sport a tattoo with an Elvish design meaning, 'The Nine' symbolizing the nine members of the Fellowship of the Ring

Helen Mirren .... Small Indian symbol on her left hand that signifies 'Equality'

Oliver Reed .... Eagles talons on the most intimate part of his anatomy

Julia Roberts .... Butterfly on her lower back

Mike Tyson .... Tattoos that depict Che Guevara, Arthur Ashe and Chairman Mao

Robbie Williams ..... Various designs including lyrics from the Beatles hit, 'All You Need is Love'

BOOK OF LISTS

FAMOUS PEOPLE AND THEIR PETS

Frank Bruno	Siamese cat called Samson
Robert Burns	Ewe called Mailie
Jim Carrey	Iguana called Houston
George Clooney	Pot-bellied pig called Max
Leslie Grantham	Pink flamingo adopted at London Zoo
Michael Jackson	Chimp called Bubbles, snake called Muscles, llama called Louie
Angelina Jolie	Rat called Harry
John F Kennedy	Cat called Tom Kitten
John Lennon	Cat called Elvis
George Orwell	Goat called Muriel
Elvis Presley	Chimpanzee called Scatter
Adam Sandler	Bulldog called Meatball
William Shatner	Doberman called Kirk
Britney Spears	Yorkshire terrier called Baby
Sylvester Stallone	Boxer called Gangster
Robert Louis Stevenson	Donkey called Modestine
Mark Twain	Cat called Beelzebub
Mike Tyson	Tigers called Kenya and Storm
Rudolph Valentino	Lion called Zela
Venus Williams	Yorkshire terrier called Pete, named after Pete Sampras

Rudolph Valentino

PEOPLE

10 FEMALE WINNERS OF THE 'REAR OF THE YEAR' AWARD

- Alex Best
- Charlotte Church
- Ulrika Jonsson
- Felicity Kendal
- Sarah Lancashire
- Elaine Paige
- Su Pollard
- Claire Sweeney
- Denise Van Outen
- Barbara Windsor

Barbara Windsor

10 MALE WINNERS OF THE 'REAR OF THE YEAR' AWARD

Gary Barlow

- John Altman
- Gary Barlow
- Michael Barrymore
- Richard Fairbrass
- Aled Haydn-Jones
- Ronan Keating
- Graham Norton
- Frank Skinner
- Robbie Williams
- Scott Wright

BOOK OF LISTS

UNUSUAL MIDDLE NAMES OF 50 FAMOUS PEOPLE

Alden	Gene Hackman	**Maitland**	James Stewart
Alick	Frankie Howerd	**Marcellus**	Cassius Clay
Alois	Arnold Schwarzenegger	**Marwood**	John Cleese
Baines	Lyndon B Johnson	**Mathieson**	Kenny Dalglish
Bonaventure	Spencer Tracy	**McLauren**	Robin Williams
Bruno Nero	Lawrence Dallaglio	**McNichol**	Donald Sutherland
Bysshe	Percy Shelley	**Milhous**	Richard Nixon
Carandini	Christopher Lee	**Mungo**	Hugh Grant
Carson	Macauley Culkin	**Nesta**	Bob Marley
Columcille	Mel Gibson	**Newbold**	Sebastian Coe
Coverley	Ludovic Kennedy	**Paradine**	David Frost
Curran	Gene Kelly	**Reagan**	Eddie Murphy
DeForest	Humphrey Bogart	**Robard**	Howard Hughes
Earl	Jimmy Carter	**Rolihlahla**	Nelson Mandela
Elias	Walt Disney	**Scudamore**	Michael Redgrave
Ernald	Oswald Mosley	**Selden**	Robert Duvall
Golightly	Robson Green	**St Auburn**	Garfield Sobers
Houghton	Katharine Hepburn	**St John**	Richard Harris
Hunter Fisher	Willie Carson	**Tiffany**	Richard Gere
Ira	Russell Crowe	**Villiers**	Mia Farrow
Ivanhoe	Emile Heskey	**Vogel**	Kurt Russell
King	Nick Nolte	**Whipper**	Alan Wells
Klapka	Jerome K Jerome	**Wolf**	Alan Arkin
Livingstone	Chris Eubank	**Wilton**	Peter Cushing
Mackintosh	Michael Foot	**Yolande**	Susannah York

PEOPLE

10 FAMOUS PEOPLE WHO LIVED TO THE AGE OF 100

- Irving Berlin
- George Burns
- Lord Alfred Denning
- Bob Hope
- Rose Kennedy (mother of John F Kennedy)
- Grandma Moses
- The Queen Mother
- Hal Roach
- Manny Shinwell
- Thomas Sopwith, designer of the Sopwith Camel

Bob Hope

10 FAMOUS PEOPLE WHO DIED BEFORE THE AGE OF 30

River Phoenix

- Marc Bolan aged 29
- Anne Frank aged 15
- Jimi Hendrix aged 27
- Buddy Holly aged 22
- Joan of Arc aged 19
- Janis Joplin aged 27
- Brandon Lee aged 28
- Lee Harvey Oswald aged 24
- River Phoenix aged 23
- Otis Redding aged 26

10 FAMOUS PEOPLE WITH TWIN SIBLINGS

Alanis Morissette

Montgomery Clift	Twin sister Roberta
Henry Cooper	Twin brother George
Jerry Hall	Twin brother Terry
Linda Hamilton	Twin sister Leslie
Alanis Morissette	Twin brother Wade
Elvis Presley	Twin brother Jesse (died at birth)
Isabella Rossellini	Twin sister Isotta
Kiefer Sutherland	Twin sister Rachel
Justin Timberlake	Twin sister Laura (died at birth)
Will Young	Twin brother Rupert

10 FAMOUS PEOPLE WHO ARE PARENTS OF TWINS

Fern Britton	Jack and Henry
Bing Crosby	Dennis and Phillip
Geena Davis	Kian and Kaiis
Robert De Niro	Aaron and Julian
James Doohan	Christopher and Montgomery
Mel Gibson	Christian and Edward
Lee Majors	Dane and Trey
William Shakespeare	Hamnet and Judith
James Stewart	Judy and Kelly
Margaret Thatcher	Carol and Mark

Margaret Thatcher

PEOPLE

50 FAMOUS VEGETARIANS

- Bryan Adams
- Brigitte Bardot
- Drew Barrymore
- Kim Basinger
- Linda Blair
- Orlando Bloom
- Chelsea Clinton
- John Denver
- Danny DeVito
- David Duchovny
- Albert Einstein
- Uri Geller
- Richard Gere
- Robin Gibb
- Sir John Gielgud
- Josh Harnett
- Woody Harrelson
- Dustin Hoffman
- Michael Jackson
- Martin Kemp
- KD Lang
- Paul McCartney
- Sir Ian McKellen
- Hayley Mills
- Demi Moore

- Mary Tyler Moore
- Martina Navratilova
- Paul Newman
- Gwyneth Paltrow
- Guy Pearce
- Pink
- Brad Pitt
- Natalie Portman
- Pythagoras
- Julia Sawalha
- Peter Sellers
- William Shatner
- George Bernard Shaw
- Percy Bysshe Shelley
- Alicia Silverstone
- Heather Small
- Leo Tolstoy
- Shania Twain
- Lindsay Wagner
- Richard Wagner
- Dennis Weaver
- HG Wells
- John Wesley
- Kate Winslet
- Reece Witherspoon

Albert Einstein

BOOK OF LISTS

10 FAMOUS PEOPLE BORN ON CHRISTMAS DAY

1642 . . . . Sir Isaac Newton
1867 . . . . Charles Pathé, creator of Pathé News
1889 . . . . Wallace DeWitt, founder of *Reader's Digest*
1899 . . . . Humphrey Bogart
1918 . . . . Anwar Sadat
1923 . . . . Noele Gordon
1945 . . . . Kenny Everett
1949 . . . . Sissy Spacek
1954 . . . . Annie Lennox
1954 . . . . Robin Campbell of UB 40

Sir Isaac Newton

10 FAMOUS AMERICANS BORN ON THE 4TH OF JULY

1804 . . . . Nathaniel Hawthorne, author of *The Scarlet Letter*
1810 . . . . Phineus T Barnum
1872 . . . . Calvin Coolidge
1900 . . . . Louis Armstrong
1902 . . . . Meyer Lansky, mobster
1911 . . . . Mitch Miller, singer
1927 . . . . Neil Simon
1938 . . . . Bill Withers
1946 . . . . Ron Kovik, Vietnam War veteran who inspired the film *Born on the 4th of July*
1962 . . . . Pam Shriver, tennis star

Louis Armstrong

34

PEOPLE

LIKE SISTER AND BROTHER

Andrews Sisters	Laverne, Maxine and Patty
The Bee Gees	Barry, Robin and Maurice Gibb
Beverley Sisters	Babs, Joy and Teddy
The Brontës	Anne, Emily, Charlotte and brother Bramwell
The Cheeky Girls	Gabriella and Monica Irimia
The Corrs	Andrea, Sharon, Caroline and brother Jim
Brothers Grimm	Jakob and Wilhelm
Hanson	Isaac, Taylor and Zachary
The Isley Brothers	O'Kelly, Ronald and Rudolph
The Jackson Five	Jackie, Jermaine, Marlon, Michael and Tito
Marx Brothers	Chico (Leonard), Groucho (Julius), Gummo (Milton), Harpo (Adolph) and Zeppo (Herbert)
The Nolans	Anne, Bernadette, Coleen, Denise, Linda and Maureen
The Osmonds	Alan, Donny, Jay, Jimmy, Merrill, Wayne and sister Marie
The Proclaimers	Charlie and Craig Reid
The Righteous Brothers	Bobby Hatfield and Bill Medley
Sister Sledge	Debra, Kathy, Joni and Kim
Sparks	Ron and Russell Mael
The Von Trapp children	Brigitta, Gretl, Liesl, Louisa, Marta, Friedrich and Kurt
The Walker Brothers	Scott Engel, Gary Leeds and John Maus
Warner Brothers	Albert, Harry, Jack and Sam

BOOK OF LISTS

10 FAMOUS PEOPLE WHO SUFFERED FROM EPILEPSY

- Alexander the Great
- Napoleon Bonaparte
- Richard Burton
- Julius Caesar
- Agatha Christie
- Danny Glover
- Hannibal
- Alfred Nobel
- William Shakespeare
- Vincent Van Gogh

Napoleon Bonaparte

10 CELEBRITIES WHO INSURED PARTS OF THEIR BODY

Marlene Dietrich

Fred Astaire. . . . . Legs for $650,000

Jamie Lee Curtis. . . . . Legs for $1 million

Marlene Dietrich. . . . . Voice for $1 million

Ken Dodd . . . . Teeth for £4 million

Jimmy Durante . . . . Nose for $50,000

Michael Flatley . . . . Legs for £25 million

Betty Grable. . . . . Legs for $1 million

Dolly Parton. . . . . Breasts for $600,000

Egon Ronay . . . . Taste buds for £250,000

Bruce Springsteen . . . . . . Voice for $6 million

UNUSUAL NAMES OF CELEBRITIES' CHILDREN

Woody Allen . . . . Satchel

Gillian Anderson . . . . Piper Maru

Mel B . . . . Phoenix Chi

Kim Basinger . . . . Ireland

Toni Braxton . . . . Denim and Diezel

Christie Brinkley . . . . Sailor Lee

Courtney Cox . . . . Coco Riley

Michael J Fox . . . . Aquinnah, Esme Annabelle and Schuyler

Madonna . . . . Lourdes and Rocco

Demi Moore & Bruce Willis . . . . Rumer Glenn, Scout Larue, Tallulah Belle

Demi Moore & daughters

Nick Nolte . . . . Brawley King

Jamie Oliver . . . . Poppy Honey and Daisy Boo

Gwyneth Paltrow . . . . Apple

Jonathan Ross . . . . Betty Kitten, Harvey Kirby and Honey Kinney

Will Smith . . . . Jaden Christopher Syre, William C Trey III and Willow Camille Reign

Sylvester Stallone . . . . Sage Moonblood, Seargoah, Sophia Rose, Scarlet Rose and Sistene Rose

John Travolta . . . . Ella Bleu and Jett

Paula Yates & Bob Geldof . . . . Fifi Trixibelle, Peaches Honeyblossom and Pixie

Paula Yates & Michael Hutchence . . . Heavenly Hiraani Tiger Lily

BOOK OF LISTS

EPONYMOUSLY SPEAKING

EPONYM	NAMED AFTER
Adidas	Adi Dassler
Alzheimer's disease	Alois Alzheimer
Apple Charlotte	Queen Charlotte, wife of King George III
Avocado	Jorge-Luis Avocado
Becquerel (unit of radioactivity)	Antoine Henri Becquerel
Beef stroganoff	Count Pavel Alexandrovich Stroganov
Bessemer converter	Henry Bessemer
Biro pen	Laszlo Biro
Braille alphabet	Louis Braille
Bunsen burner	Robert Bunsen
Caesar salad	Caesar Candini, Italian restaurateur
Celsius temperature scale	Anders Celsius
Cointreau	Adolphe & Edouard Cointreau
Colt revolver	Samuel Colt
Diesel engine	Rudolf Diesel
Dolby surround system	Ray Dolby
Fahrenheit temperature scale	Gabriel Fahrenheit
Farad (unit of capacitance)	Michael Faraday
Fuchsia	Leonard Fuchs
Galvanization	Luigi Galvani
Garibaldi biscuit	Giuseppe Garibaldi
Geiger counter	Hans Geiger

Avocado

PEOPLE

EPONYMOUSLY SPEAKING

EPONYM	NAMED AFTER
Guillotine	Joseph Ignace Guillotin
Harley Davidson	William Harley & Arthur Davidson
Harvey Wallbanger	Californian surfer Tom Harvey
Hodgkin's disease	Thomas Hodgkin
Jacuzzi bath	Roy Jacuzzi
Leotard	Jules Leotard
Mesmerism	Franz Mesmer
Moog synthesizer	Robert Moog
Morse code	Samuel Morse
Newton (unit of force)	Isaac Newton
Peach melba	Dame Nellie Melba
Richter scale	Charles Richter
Salchow (ice-skating jump)	Ulrich Salchow
Sandwich	John Montagu, 11th Earl of Sandwich
Saxophone	Adolph Sax
Shrapnel	Henry Shrapnel
Sousaphone	John Philip Sousa
20th Century Fox	William Fox
Volt	Alessandro Volta
Winchester rifle	Oliver F Winchester
Zeppelin airship	Franz Zeppelin

Sandwich

60 FAMOUS PEOPLE WITH ROSES NAMED AFTER THEM

- Julie Andrews
- Lucille Ball
- Ingrid Bergman
- Clara Bow
- Benjamin Britten
- George Burns
- Barbara Bush
- Maria Callas
- Jacques Cartier
- Bobby Charlton
- Chevy Chase
- Geoffrey Chaucer
- Patsy Cline
- Christopher Columbus
- Bing Crosby
- Catherine Deneuve
- Charles Dickens
- Christian Dior
- Edward Elgar
- Henry Fonda
- Henry Ford
- Judy Garland
- Cary Grant

- Audrey Hepburn
- Bob Hope
- Tony Jacklin
- Don Juan
- Penelope Keith
- Grace Kelly
- John F Kennedy
- Angela Lansbury
- Peggy Lee
- Gina Lollabrigida
- Sophia Loren
- Joanna Lumley
- Mary Queen of Scots
- James Mason
- Paul McCartney
- Michelangelo
- Marilyn Monroe
- Wolfgang Amadeus Mozart
- Audie Murphy
- Richard Nixon
- Rosie O'Donnell
- Dolly Parton
- Anna Pavlova

- Pele
- Edith Piaf
- Pablo Picasso
- Mary Pickford
- Marco Polo
- Charlotte Rampling
- Rembrandt
- LeAnne Rimes
- Ginger Rogers
- William Shakespeare
- Johann Strauss
- Barbra Streisand
- Elizabeth Taylor
- John Wayne

PEOPLE

THE WIT AND WISDOM OF OSCAR WILDE

'**The difference** between literature and journalism is that journalism is unreadable and literature is unread'

'**Morality is simply the attitude** we adopt toward people whom we generally dislike'

'**The world is a stage**, but the play is badly cast'

'**I never put off** till tomorrow what I can do the day after'

'**Ambition** is the last refuge of failure'

'**A cynic** is a man who knows the price of everything and the value of nothing'

'**One man's poetry** is another man's poison'

'**The old believe everything**, the middle-aged suspect everything and the young know everything'

'**Women are meant** to be loved, not to be understood'

'**Experience is simply** the name we give our mistakes'

Oscar Wilde

BOOK OF LISTS

THE WIT AND WISDOM OF WOODY ALLEN

'**I don't want** to achieve immortality through my work. I want to achieve it by not dying'

'**I am not afraid** of death. I just don't want to be there when it happens'

'**The lion and the calf** shall lie down together, but the calf won't get much sleep'

'**Sex alleviates** tension. Love causes it'

'**Basically my wife** was immature. I'd be in the bath and she'd come in and sink my boats'

'**If you want to** make God laugh, tell him your future plans'

'**94.5%** of all statistics are made up'

'**I don't think** my parents liked me. They put a live teddy bear in my crib'

'**I tended to place** my wife under a pedestal'

'**You can live to be a hundred** if you give up all the things that make you want to live to be a hundred'

THE WIT AND WISDOM OF WC FIELDS

'**Start off** every day with a smile and get it over with'

'**Horse sense** is the thing a horse has which keeps it from betting on people'

'**The best thing** to break is a contract'

'**Anyone who hates dogs** and small children can't be all bad'

'**Hollywood** is the gold cap on the tooth that should have been pulled out years ago'

'**Thou shalt not covet** thy neighbour's house unless they have a well stocked bar'

'**Women are like elephants.** I like to look at them but I wouldn't want to own one'

'**It was a woman** that drove me to drink. I never had the courtesy to thank her'

'**I am free of all prejudices.** I hate everybody equally'

'**I exercise extreme self control.** I never drink anything stronger than gin before breakfast'

10 BEASTLY QUOTES

Aristotle . . . . 'One swallow does not make a summer'

Louis Armstrong . . . . 'All music is folk music. I ain't never heard a horse sing a song'

GK Chesterton . . . . 'Do not free a camel of the burden of his hump, you may be freeing him from being a camel'

Winston Churchill . . . . . . 'I like pigs. Dogs look up to us. Cats look down on us. Pigs treat us as equals'

Walt Disney . . . . 'I loved Mickey Mouse more than any woman I have ever known'

Alfred Hitchcock . . . . 'Actors should be treated like cattle'

Abraham Lincoln . . . . 'No matter how much cats fight, there always seems to be plenty of kittens'

Plato . . . . 'A dog has the soul of a philosopher'

Harry S Truman . . . . 'You want a friend in Washington? Get a dog'

Mark Twain . . . . 'If a man could be crossed with a cat, it would improve the man but deteriorate the cat'

Winston Churchill

THAT'S MY DOG
50 historical and fictional dogs and their owners

DOG	OWNER
Ace	Bruce Wayne
Argos	Ulysses
Astro	The Jetsons
Barney	George W Bush
Boatswain	Lord Byron
Bolivar	Donald Duck
Braveheart	Inch High, Private Eye
Buck	The Bundys (*Married With Children*)
Buddy	Bill Clinton
Bullet	Roy Rogers
Bullseye	Bill Sikes (*Oliver Twist*)
Captain	George Washington
Cavall	King Arthur
Checkers	Richard Nixon
Cinders	Casey Jones
Diamond	Isaac Newton
Duke	The Beverly Hillbillies
Eddie	Martin Crane (*Frasier*)
Einstein	Dr Brown (*Back To The Future*)
Flash	The Dukes of Hazzard
Flush	Elizabeth Barrett Browning
Freeway	The Harts (*Hart To Hart*)
Gnasher	Dennis the Menace
Hamlet	Sir Walter Scott
Jack	Laura Ingalls Wilder

Argos & Ulysses

PEOPLE

THAT'S MY DOG
50 historical and fictional dogs and their owners

DOG	OWNER
Wessex	Thomas Hardy
Jeep	Popeye
Jip	Abraham Lincoln
Keeper	Emily Brontë
K9	Dr Who
Krypto	Superboy
Luath	Robert Burns
Mafia	Marilyn Monroe
Mathe	Richard II
Muttley	Dick Dastardly
Nana	The Darlings (*Peter Pan*)
Pearl	Beryl the Peril
Pyrites	Alexander the Great
Pluto	Mickey Mouse
Prince	Barbie doll
Reckless	The Waltons
Sandy	Little Orphan Annie
Santa's Little Helper	The Simpsons
Scamper	The Secret Seven
Snowy	Tin Tin
Tiger	The Brady Bunch
Timmy	The Famous Five
Toto	Dorothy Gale (*The Wizard of Oz*)
Truffles	George & Mildred Roper
Urian	Anne Boleyn

Muttley & Dick Dastardly

BOOK OF LISTS

10 RELIGIONS AND THEIR FOUNDERS

RELIGION	FOUNDED BY
Christian Science	Mary Baker Eddy
Islam	Mohammed
Jehovah's Witness	Charles Taze Russell
Hari Krishna	Swami Prabhupada
Kabbalah	Moses de Leon
Mormon	Joseph Smith
Scientology	Lafayette Ronald Hubbard
Sikhism	Guru Nanak
The Shakers	Mother Ann Lee
Zionism	Theodore Herzi

CATHEDRALS AND THEIR SAINTS

CATHEDRAL	DEDICATED TO
Bath	St Peter and St Paul
Coventry	St Michael
Hereford	St Mary and St Ethelbert
St Basil's, Moscow	St Basil
Manchester	St Nicholas
Norwich	St John the Baptist
Nottingham	St Barnabas
Prague	St Vitus
Swansea	St Joseph
Westminster Abbey	St Peter

St Basil's Cathedral

PEOPLE

10 FAMOUS FOLLOWERS OF KABBALAH

Elizabeth Taylor

- Madonna
- Britney Spears
- Elizabeth Taylor
- Demi Moore
- Goldie Hawn
- Barbra Streisand
- Winona Ryder
- Mick Jagger
- Diane Keaton
- Gwyneth Paltrow

10 FAMOUS SCIENTOLOGISTS

- Kirstie Alley
- John Travolta
- Sonny Bono
- Isaac Hayes
- Tom Cruise
- Sharon Stone
- Patrick Swayze
- Mimi Rogers
- Courtney Love
- Priscilla Presley

Tom Cruise

BOOK OF LISTS

10 FAMOUS JEHOVAH'S WITNESSES

Janet Jackson

- Michael Jackson
- Prince
- George Benson
- Naomi Campbell
- Hank Marvin
- Janet Jackson
- Mickey Spillane
- Venus Williams
- Evelyn Mandela
- Dwight D Eisenhower

10 FAMOUS BUDDHISTS

- Joanna Lumley
- David Bowie
- Richard Gere
- Ruby Wax
- Patti Smith
- Steven Seagal
- Oliver Stone
- Penelope Cruz
- Jackie Chan
- Tina Turner

David Bowie

PEOPLE

20 FAMOUS PEOPLE WHO ARE THE SUBJECTS OF LONDON STATUES

- Richard the Lionheart
- Charlie Chaplin
- The Duke of Wellington
- Charles II
- Horatio Nelson
- Oliver Cromwell
- Sir Thomas More
- Francis Bacon
- John F Kennedy
- Isambard Kingdom Brunel
- Queen Victoria
- William Shakespeare
- Prince Albert
- Henry VIII
- Captain James Cook
- Mary Queen of Scots
- Elizabeth I
- Michael Faraday
- Winston Churchill
- Boadicea

Charles II

20 FAMOUS PEOPLE WITH STATIONS NAMED AFTER THEM ON THE PARIS METRO

- Charles de Gaulle
- Francois Mitterand
- Pablo Picasso
- Colonel Fabien
- Louis Pasteur
- Franklin D Roosevelt
- St Paul
- Victor Hugo
- George V
- Georges Clemenceau
- Michelangelo
- Phillip II
- Pierre Curie
- Simon Bolivar
- St George
- Alexandre Dumas
- Francis Xavier
- Emile Zola
- Voltaire
- Cardinal Richelieu

BOOK OF LISTS

TILL DIVORCE US DO PART
20 Famous people and their spouses

Louis Armstrong . . . .Daisy Parker, Lillian Hardin, Alpha Smith, Lucille Wilson

Brigitte Bardot . . . . . .Roger Vadim, Jacques Charrier, Gunter Sachs, Bernard d'Omale

Roseanne Barr . . . . . .Bill Pentland, Tom Arnold, Benjamin Thomas

Nicolas Cage . . . . . . .Patricia Arquette, Lisa Marie Presley, Alice Kim

Glenn Campbell . . . . .Diane Kirk, Billie Jean Nunley, Sarah Davies, Kimberly Woollen

Joan Collins . . . . . . .Maxwell Reed, Anthony Newley, Ronald S Kass, Peter Holm,
Percy Gibson

Joan Crawford . . . . . .James Wetton, Douglas Fairbanks Jnr, Franchot Tone, Phillip Terry,
Alfred Steele

Tony Curtis . . . . .Janet Leigh, Christine Kaufmann, Leslie Allen, Lisa Deutsch,
Jill Vandenberg

Clark Gable . . . . .Josephine Dillon, Maria Franklin Printiss Lucas Langham,
Carole Lombard, Sylvia Ashley, Kay Spreckles

Zsa Zsa Gabor . . . . .Burhan Belge, Conrad Hilton,
George Sanders, Herbert Hunter,
Joshua S Cosden Jnr, Jack Ryan,
Michael O'Hara Felipe De Alba,
Frederic von Anhalt

Rex Harrison . . . . . . .Collette Thomas, Lilli Palmer,
Kay Kendall, Rachel Roberts,
Elizabeth Harris, Mercia Tinker

Stan Laurel . . . . .Lois Neilson, Virginia Ruth Rogers,
Vera Shuvalova, Ida Kitaeva

Elizabeth Taylor

TILL DIVORCE US DO PART
20 Famous people and their spouses

Jerry Lee Lewis .....Dorothy Barton, Jane Mitcham, Myra Gail Brown, Kerrie McCarver, Shawn Michelle Stevens

Jennifer Lopez ......Ojani Noa, Christopher Judd, Marc Anthony

Liza Minnelli ....Jack Haley Jnr, Mark Gero, David Gest

Mickey Rooney ......Carolyn Mitchell, Marge Lane, Carolyn Hockett, Jan Chamberlin Ava Gardner, Betty Jane Rase, Martha Vickers, Elaine Davis

Paul Simon ....Peggy Harper, Carrie Fisher, Edie Brickell

Frank Sinatra ....Nancy Barbato, Ava Gardner, Mia Farrow, Barbara Marx

Elizabeth Taylor .....Nicky Hilton, Michael Wilding, Michael Todd, Eddie Fisher Richard Burton, John Warner, Larry Fortensky

Tammy Wynette .....George Richey, Michael Tomlin, George Jones, Don Chapel Euple Byrd

Rex Harrison

10 WINNERS OF THE PIPE SMOKER OF THE YEAR AWARD

- Harold Wilson
- Rod Hull
- Eric Morecambe
- Henry Cooper
- JB Priestly
- Stephen Fry
- Trevor Baylis
- Malcolm Bradley
- Tony Benn
- Freddie Trueman

Harold Wilson

10 FILM STARS WHO HAVE BEEN VOTED 'SEXIEST MAN ALIVE' BY PEOPLE MAGAZINE

George Clooney

- Pierce Brosnan
- Ben Affleck
- George Clooney
- Brad Pitt
- Harrison Ford
- Tom Cruise
- Patrick Swayze
- Richard Gere
- Sean Connery
- Johnny Depp

PEOPLE

SHIP AHOY

THE SAILOR	THE SHIP
Roald Amundsen	Fram
Blackbeard	Queen Anne's Revenge
Christopher Columbus	Santa Maria
Captain James Cook	Endeavour
Charles Darwin	HMS Beagle
Francis Drake	Golden Hind (originally Pelican)
Edward Heath	Morning Cloud
Thor Heyerdahl	Kon Tiki raft
Henry VIII	Mary Rose (Henry's flagship)
Jason and the Argonauts	Argo
William Kidd	Adventure Galley
Ellen MacArthur	Kingfisher
Ferdinand Magellan	Victoria
Henry Morgan	Oxford
Horatio Nelson	HMS Victory
Popeye	Olive
Walter Raleigh	Ark
Robert Falcon Scott	Discovery
Ernest Shackleton	Nimrod

Santa Maria

BOOK OF LISTS

A PRESIDENTIAL PARADE

John Adams was the first US President to live in the White House

One state, ten lakes and thirty-three counties in the USA are named after George Washington

John Tyler was the first US President to marry whilst in office.

The only President to be married in the White House was Grover Cleveland, who tied the knot with Frances Folsom in 1886

James Buchanan was the only US President to be a bachelor

Ulysses F Grant

PEOPLE

A PRESIDENTIAL PARADE

The smallest US President was James Madison who stood 5ft 4ins tall (163cm)

The tallest US President was Abraham Lincoln who stood 6ft 4ins tall (193cm)

The heaviest US President at 136kg (300lbs) was William Howard Taft, who had to order a new bathtub for the White House after he got stuck in the old one

President Calvin Coolidge died of a heart attack in 1933, shortly after completing a jigsaw puzzle of George Washington

Franklin D Roosevelt was the only US President to serve four terms of office

James K Polk was the first US President in office to have his photograph taken

John F Kennedy and William Taft are the only Presidents to be buried at the Arlington National Cemetery

President William McKinley always wore a red carnation in his lapel for good luck. In 1901 he was assassinated

William Henry Harrison was the first US President to die in office

Richard Nixon was the first President to visit all fifty states of the USA

Ulysses F Grant was arrested during his presidential term and fined $20 for exceeding the Washington speed limit on his horse

Franklin Pierce was the first US President to install a Christmas tree in the White House

In 1892, Benjamin Harrison became the first US President to attend a baseball game

Rutherford B Hayes was the first US President to have a telephone installed in the White House

Theodore Roosevelt was the first US President to fly in an aeroplane

BOOK OF LISTS

20 FAMOUS PEOPLE WHO DIED IN AN AIR CRASH

- Patsy Cline
- Hanse Cronje
- John Denver
- Amelia Earhart
- Duncan Edwards
- Yuri Gagarin
- Graham Hill
- Buddy Holly
- Leslie Howard
- Amy Johnson
- John F Kennedy Jnr
- Carole Lombard
- Rocky Marciano
- Glenn Miller
- Ricky Nelson
- Otis Redding
- Will Rogers
- Charles Rolls
- Payne Stewart
- Ritchie Valens

Amelia Earhart

20 FAMOUS PEOPLE WHO DIED IN A ROAD ACCIDENT

- Dodi Al-Fayed
- Duane Allman
- Ian Bannen
- Marc Bolan
- Eddie Cochran
- Laurie Cunningham
- James Dean
- Diana, Princess of Wales
- Isadora Duncan
- Princess Grace of Monaco
- Ben Hollioake
- TE Lawrence
- Desmond Llewellyn
- Lisa 'Left Eye' Lopes
- Linda Lovelace
- Jayne Mansfield
- Margaret Mitchell
- General George Patton
- Jackson Pollock
- Cozy Powell

TE Lawrence

PEOPLE

10 FAMOUS PEOPLE WITH ONE EYE

- Horatio Nelson
- Peter Falk
- Joe Davis
- Rex Harrison
- Leo McKern
- Sammy Davis Jnr
- Gordon Banks
- James Thurber
- Hannibal

Horatio Nelson

- Theodore Roosevelt, lost the sight of one eye following a boxing accident

10 FAMOUS PEOPLE WHO ARE LEFT-HANDED

Judy Garland

- Queen Victoria
- Paul McCartney
- Bill Clinton
- Osama Bin Laden
- Leonardo da Vinci
- Judy Garland
- David Gower
- Marcel Marceau
- Whoopi Goldberg
- Monica Seles

BOOK OF LISTS

50 HISTORICAL / FICTIONAL HORSES AND THEIR OWNERS

HORSE	OWNER
Al Borak	Mohammed
Appy	The Virginian
Arion	Hercules
Babieca	El Cid
Barrique	Sir Lancelot
Black Agnes	Mary Queen of Scots
Black Bess	Dick Turpin
Blackie	Chief Sitting Bull
Brown Beauty	Paul Revere
Bucephalus	Alexander the Great
Buttermilk	Dale Evans
Candy	Wyatt Earp
Champion	Gene Autry
Champion	Ricky North
Cincinnati	Ulysses S Grant
Copenhagen	The Duke of Wellington
Diablo	The Cisco Kid
Duke	John Wayne
Fauvel	Richard the Lionheart
Hercules	Steptoe and Son
Incitatus	Caligula
Isham	Buffalo Bill
Kanthaka	Buddha
Lamri	King Arthur
Little Sorrel	Stonewall Jackson
Magnolia	George Washington

Dick Turpin / Black Bess

PEOPLE

50 HISTORICAL / FICTIONAL HORSES AND THEIR OWNERS

HORSE	OWNER
Marengo	Napoleon Bonaparte
Marsala	Giuseppe Garibaldi
Mr Ed	Wilbur Post
Old Bob	Abraham Lincoln
Pegasus	Bellerophon
Rising Sun	Elvis Presley
Rocky	Tex Tucker
Rosinante	Don Quixote
Satan	Calamity Jane
Scout	Tonto
Shadowfax	Gandalf the wizard
Silver	Lone Ranger
Sleipner	Odin
Sorrell	William III
Target	Annie Oakley
Tony	Tom Mix
Topper	Hopalong Cassidy
Tornado	Zorro
Traveler	Robert E Lee
Trigger	Ernie (fastest milkman)
Trigger	Roy Rogers
Vic	General George Custer
White Surrey	Richard III
Xanthus	Achilles

El Cid

FAMOUS NAMES IN COCKNEY RHYMING SLANG

NAME	SLANG FOR
Adam and Eve	Believe
Aristotle	Bottle
Acker Bilk	Milk
Lionel Blair	Chair
Tony Blairs	Flares
Bo Peep	Sleep
Billy Bunter	Punter
Cain and Abel	Table
Conan Doyle	Boil
The Duke of Kent	Rent
Errol Flynn	Chin
Farmer Giles	Piles
Lillian Gish	Fish
Darren Gough	Cough
David Gower	Shower
Damon Hill	Pill
Jack the Ripper	Kipper
Ronan Keating	Meeting
Ned Kelly	Belly
Rosie Lee	Tea
Vera Lynn	Gin
John Major	Wager

Aristotle

FAMOUS NAMES USED IN COCKNEY RHYMING SLANG

NAME	SLANG FOR
Tom Mix	Fix
Ruby Murray	Curry
Harvey Nichol	Pickle
Gregory Peck	Cheque
Vincent Price	Ice
Arthur Rank	Bank
Claire Rayners	Trainers
Richard the Third	Bird
Barney Rubble	Trouble
Barnaby Rudge	Judge
Walter Scott	Pot
Ayrton Senna	Tenner
Tommy Steele	Eel
Janet Street-Porter	Quarter
Tom Thumb	Rum
Pete Tong	Wrong
Frankie Vaughan	Prawn
Alan Whickers	Knickers

Ned Kelly

BOOK OF LISTS

BORN IN THE USA

Alabama	Jesse Owens, Lionel Richie, Helen Keller
Alaska	Margaret Bell, Vitus Bering, Scott Gomez
Arizona	Stevie Nicks, Geronimo, Linda Ronstadt
Arkansas	Johnny Cash, Bill Clinton, Alan Ladd
California	Drew Barrymore, Richard Nixon, Clint Eastwood
Colorado	John Kerry, Tim Allen, Jack Dempsey
Connecticut	Glenn Close, George Bush Jnr, Benjamin Spock
Delaware	Elisabeth Shue, Howard Pyle, Rutherford Hayes
Florida	Wesley Snipes, Jim Morrison, Faye Dunaway
Georgia	Oliver Hardy, Jimmy Carter, Julia Roberts
Hawaii	Nicole Kidman, Harold Sakata, Bette Midler
Idaho	Ezra Pound, Lana Turner, Gutzon Borglum
Illinois	Harrison Ford, Ronald Reagan, Walt Disney
Indiana	James Dean, Janet Jackson, Steve McQueen
Iowa	John Wayne, Johnny Carson, Elijah Wood
Kansas	Dennis Hopper, Charlie Parker, Buster Keaton
Kentucky	George Clooney, Johnny Depp, Abraham Lincoln
Louisiana	Louis Armstrong, Harry Connick Jnr, Britney Spears
Maine	Stephen King, Liv Tyler, John Ford
Maryland	Ed Norton, Babe Ruth, Frank Zappa
Massachusetts	Matt Damon, John F Kennedy, Bette Davis
Michigan	Burt Reynolds, Madonna, Sonny Bono
Minnesota	Judy Garland, Charles Schulz, Bob Dylan
Mississippi	Elvis Presley, Oprah Winfrey, Jim Henson
Missouri	Kathleen Turner, TS Eliot, Jesse James

PEOPLE

Montana	David Lynch, Evel Knievel, Gary Cooper
Nebraska	Marlon Brando, Dick Cheney, Henry Fonda
Nevada	Andre Agassi, Ben Alexander, Patricia Nixon
New Hampshire	Alan Shepard, Mary Baker Eddy, Franklin Pierce
New Jersey	Danny DeVito, Michael Douglas, Jerry Lewis
New Mexico	John Denver, Demi Moore, Conrad Hilton
New York	Al Capone, Tom Cruise, Billy Joel
North Carolina	Julianne Moore, Billy Graham, Roberta Flack
North Dakota	Peggy Lee, Angie Dickinson, Louie L'Amour
Ohio	Halle Berry, Clark Gable, Doris Day
Oklahoma	Brad Pitt, Ron Howard, Garth Brooks
Oregon	Dick Fosbury, Tonya Harding, Matt Groening
Pennsylvania	Charles Bronson, Richard Gere, Bill Cosby
Rhode Island	Nathaniel Greene, Bobby Hackett, George Cohan
South Carolina	James Brown, Dizzy Gillespie, Chris Rock
South Dakota	Hubert Humphrey, Cheryl Ladd, Chief Crazy Horse
Tennessee	Morgan Freeman, Dolly Parton, Quentin Tarantino
Texas	Joan Crawford, Roy Orbison, Steve Martin
Utah	Donny Osmond, Loretta Young, Butch Cassidy
Vermont	Calvin Coolidge, Brigham Young, Chester Arthur
Virginia	Patsy Cline, George Washington, Arthur Ashe
Washington	Kurt Cobain, Bing Crosby, Bill Gates
West Virginia	Pearl Buck, Mary Lou Retton, Chuck Yeager
Wisconsin	Spencer Tracy, Orson Welles, Joseph McCarthy
Wyoming	Jackson Pollock, Chief Washakie, Patricia MacLachlan

BOOK OF LISTS

BORN IN THE UK

Bedfordshire . . . . Ronnie Barker, John Bunyan, Samuel Whitbread

Berkshire . . . . Kate Winslet, Tracey Ullman, Mike Oldfield

Buckinghamshire . . . . . Terry Pratchett, Tim Rice, Nick Beggs

Cambridgeshire . . . . Olivia Newton John, Henry Royce, Stephen Fry

Cheshire . . . . Lewis Carroll, Michael Owen, Christopher Isherwood

Cornwall . . . . William Golding, Kirstin Scott Thomas, Captain William Bligh

Cumbria . . . . Stan Laurel, William Wordsworth, Fletcher Christian

Derbyshire . . . . Arthur Lowe, Joe Davis, Robert Lindsay

Devon . . . . Francis Drake, Agatha Christie, Captain Robert Falcon Scott

Dorset . . . . Matthew Pinsent, Thomas Hardy, The Tolpuddle Martyrs

Durham . . . . Wendy Craig, Alan Price, Elizabeth Barrett Browning

Essex . . . . Nick Berry, Noel Edmonds, Alan Davies

Hampshire . . . . Benny Hill, Nicholas Lyndhurst, Peter Sellers

Kent . . . . David Frost, Mick Jagger, Boy George

Lancashire . . . . Peter Kay, Julie Goodyear, Ian McKellen

Leicestershire . . . . John Merrick, Gary Lineker, Graham Chapman

Lincolnshire . . . . Michael Foale, Isaac Newton, Margaret Thatcher

Norfolk . . . . Horatio Nelson, Elizabeth Fry, Diana Princess of Wales

Northamptonshire . . . . . Richard III, Francis Crick, John Dryden

Northumberland . . . . . . Robson Green, Catherine Cookson, Jackie Milburn

Nottinghamshire . . . . . . Richard Beckinsale, DH Lawrence, William Booth

Oxfordshire . . . . Winston Churchill, Hugh Laurie, Lester Piggott

PEOPLE

Shropshire . . . . Billy Wright, Charles Darwin, Robert Clive

Staffordshire . . . . Izaak Walton, Robbie Williams, Samuel Johnson

Suffolk . . . . John Mills, Thomas Gainsborough, Benjamin Britten

Surrey . . . . Julie Andrews, Richard Briers, Laurence Olivier

Sussex . . . . Harry Enfield, Percy Bysshe Shelley, Simon Cowell

Warwickshire . . . . Felicity Kendal, Rupert Brooke, Jeremy Brett

Wiltshire . . . . Joseph Fiennes, Christopher Wren, Billie Piper

Yorkshire . . . . Judi Dench, Ben Kingsley, Frankie Howerd

Agatha Christie

PATRON SAINTS OF PROFESSIONS

PROFESSION	PATRON SAINT
Astronomers	Dominic
Beekeepers	Ambrose
Blacksmiths	Dunstan
Bricklayers	Stephen
Butchers	Anthony the Abbot
Carpenters	Joseph
Dancers	Vitus
Dentists	Apollonia
Doctors	Luke
Firemen	Florian
Fishermen	Peter
Grocers	Michael
Journalists	Francis of Sales
Librarians	Jerome
Musicians	Cecilia
Scientists	Albert
Secretaries	Genesius
Singers	Gregory
Tax collectors	Matthew
Teachers	Gregory
Undertakers	Dismas
Writers	Paul

St Paul

BEASTLY NICKNAMES

Anne of Cleves . . . . The Flanders Mare

Ian Botham . . . . Guy the Gorilla

Christopher Chataway . . . . . . The Red Fox

William Cody . . . . Buffalo Bill

Freddie Davies . . . . Parrot Face

Eddie Edwards . . . . The Eagle

Harold I . . . . Harefoot

Rene Lacoste . . . . The Crocodile

Niki Lauda . . . . The Clockwork Mouse

Charles Lindbergh . . . . The Lone Eagle

Nat Lofthouse . . . . The Lion of Vienna

John Merrick . . . . The Elephant Man

Jim Morrison . . . . The Lizard King

Eric Moussambani . . . . Eric the Eel

Jack Nicklaus . . . . The Golden Bear

Greg Norman . . . . The Great White Shark

Jesse Owens . . . . The Ebony Antelope

Charlie Parker . . . . Bird

Edith Piaf . . . . The Little Sparrow

Nancy Reagan . . . . The Smiling Mamba

Richard I . . . . The Lionheart

Erwin Rommel . . . . The Desert Fox

Barry White . . . . The Walrus of Love

Richard I

BOOK OF LISTS

PRESIDENTIAL NICKNAMES

PRESIDENT	NICKNAME
Chester Arthur	Elegant Arthur
James Buchanan	Ten Cent Jimmy
Grover Cleveland	The Veto President
Bill Clinton	The Comeback Kid
Calvin Coolidge	Silent Cal
Dwight D Eisenhower	Ike
James Garfield	The Preacher President
Benjamin Harrison	The Centennial President
Andrew Jackson	Old Hickory
Andrew Johnson	The Tennessee Tailor
James Madison	The Father of the Constitution
William McKinley	The Idol of Ohio
Richard Nixon	Tricky Dicky
Franklin Pierce	Young Hickory
Ronald Reagan	The Gipper
Theodore Roosevelt	Teddy
William Howard Taft	Big Bill
Zachary Taylor	Old Rough and Ready
Martin Van Buren	The Little Magician
George Washington	The Father of His Country

Bill Clinton

PEOPLE

NICKNAMES OF BRITISH PRIME MINISTERS

PRIME MINISTER	NICKNAME
Herbert Asquith	The Sledgehammer
Arthur James Balfour	Bloody Balfour
Tony Blair	Bambi
Andrew Bonar Law	The Unknown Prime Minister
James Callaghan	Sunny Jim
George Canning	The Zany of Debate
Neville Chamberlain	The Coroner
Winston Churchill	Winnie
Benjamin Disraeli	Dizzy
William Gladstone	The Grand Old Man
George Grenville	The Gentle Shepherd
David Lloyd George	The Welsh Wizard
Harold Macmillan	Supermac
Viscount Palmerston	Lord Cupid
Henry Pelham	King Henry the Ninth
William Pitt the Elder	The Great Commoner
Earl Russell	The Widow's Mite
Margaret Thatcher	The Iron Lady
Robert Walpole	Sir Blustering
Arthur Wellesley	The Iron Duke

Tony Blair

BOOK OF LISTS

10 FAMOUS PEOPLE WHO HAVE BEEN DEPICTED ON BRITISH STAMPS

- Charles Babbage
- Robert the Bruce
- Edward Elgar
- Sir Walter Raleigh
- Freddie Mercury
- Robert Falcon Scott
- Joseph Lister
- Florence Nightingale
- Lord Baden-Powell
- Henry Morton Stanley

Sir Walter Raleigh

10 FAMOUS PEOPLE WHO HAVE BEEN DEPICTED ON AMERICAN STAMPS

- Wyatt Earp
- Louis Armstrong
- Davy Crockett
- Alexander Graham Bell
- Babe Ruth
- Elvis Presley
- Albert Einstein
- Buzz Aldrin
- Otis Redding
- Harry Houdini

Buzz Aldrin

PEOPLE

FASHION FACTS

Bikini . . . . .Invented by Louis Reard and named after the Bikini atoll

Bloomers . . . . .Named after Amelia Jenks Bloomer, a women's rights campaigner

Burberry . . . . .Founded by and named after 21-year-old Thomas Burberry

Cardigan . . . . .Named after James Thomas Burdenell, the 7th Earl of Cardigan

DKNY . . . . .Fashion chain, named after Donna Karan and New York

Doc Marten . . . . . . .Invented in Germany by Dr Klaus Maertens, who developed the boots after injuring his ankle in a skiing accident

Dolly Varden . . . . . . .Large hat, named after a female character in *Barnaby Rudge*

Gladstone bag . . . . . .Large bag named after British Prime Minister William Gladstone

Kipper tie . . . . .Named after its inventor, the fashion designer Michael Fish

Mackintosh . . . . .Invented by and named after the Scottish engineer Charles Macintosh

Mini skirt . . . . .Invented by Mary Quant

The New Look . . . . . .1947 fashion range created by Christian Dior

Nylon . . . . .Invented by Iowa-born scientist Wallace Carothers and named after New York and London

Pantyhose . . . . .Invented in 1959 by Allen Gant of North Carolina

Stetson . . . . .Invented by a 19th-century hat-maker called John Batterson Stetson

Tam o'Shanter . . . . .Scottish hat named from a character in a Robert Burns poem

Top hat . . . . .Invented and first worn by a London haberdasher called John Hetherington. He was arrested for wearing a tall structure designed to frighten timid people

Trilby . . . . .Hat named after the eponymous heroine of an 1894 Guy du Maurier novel

Velcro . . . . .Invented by Swiss engineer George de Mestral in 1948

Zip . . . . .Originally known as a clasp locker, it was patented by Whitcomb Judson in 1893

BOOK OF LISTS

BOYS' NAMES AND THEIR MEANINGS

Aaron	Exalted	**Eamon**	Protector
Abraham	Father of a multitude	**Ebenezer**	Rock of help
Adolph	Wolf	**Edward**	Happy guardian
Adrian	Dark or rich	**Elvis**	All-wise
Alan	Handsome	**Eric**	Honourable ruler
Alastair	Protector of men	**Felix**	Happy and prosperous
Alvin	Noble friend	**Fergal**	Man of valour
Austin	Venerable	**Francis**	Free man
Barry	Spearlike	**Gareth**	Gentle
Basil	Kinglike	**Geoffrey**	Divinely peaceful
Benjamin	Son of my right hand	**Gregory**	Vigilant
Brendan	Raven	**Henry**	Ruler of the home
Calvin	Little bald one	**Humphrey**	Protector of the peace
Cedric	Chief	**Ian**	God is gracious
Christopher	Bearing Christ	**Isaac**	The laughing one
Chuck	Manly	**James**	The supplanter
Clarence	Luminous	**Jasper**	The treasurer
Cuthbert	Brilliant	**Kenneth**	Handsome and fair
Damian	Tame	**Leonard**	Brave as a lion
Darius	Wealthy	**Magnus**	The great one
David	Beloved	**Mark**	Warlike
Dennis	Wild	**Marvin**	Friend of the sea
Donovan	Dark warrior	**Maurice**	Dark-skinned

PEOPLE

BOYS' NAMES AND THEIR MEANINGS

Orson / Little Bear

Nicholas	Victory of the people
Nigel	Black-haired
Noel	Christmas
Orson	Little bear
Otto	Prosperous
Paul	Small
Patrick	Nobleman
Peter	Rock
Phillip	Lover of horses
Placido	Calm
Quentin	Fifth-born child
Raymond	Wise protector
Reginald	Powerful ruler
Richard	Brave and strong
Robert	Famous

Simon	Listener
Solomon	Wise and peaceful
Stavros	Crowned
Sylvester	From the forest
Terence	Tender
Timothy	Honouring God
Vernon	Youthful
Vincent	Conqueror
Virgil	Strong
Wilbur	Resolute one
Wilfred	Peacemaker
Xavier	Bright
Yusif	Wealthy
Ziggy	Get rid of anger

Noel / Christmas

BOOK OF LISTS

GIRLS' NAMES AND THEIR MEANINGS

Abigail	Father's joy
Adele	Noble
Agatha	Kind
Agnes	Pure
Alison	Light of the sun
Andrea	Strong
Anne	Grace
Barbara	Stranger
Beatrice	She who brings joy
Bridget	Spirited
Caitlin	Pure
Camille	Virginal
Caroline	Free person
Catherine	Pure
Charlotte	Womanly
Clare	Bright and famous
Clementine	Merciful
Deborah	Industrious woman
Diana	The divine one
Edith	Prosperity
Eileen	Light of the sun
Enid	A pure soul
Farrah	Beautiful

Felicity	Lucky
Fiona	The fair one
Florence	Blossoming
Genevieve	Woman of the people
Heidi	Noble and kind
Hilary	The cheerful one
Irene	Peace
Yoko	Positive
Jennifer	Fair and soft
Jessica	Wealthy
Kimberley	From the meadow
Lara	Cheerful
Leela	Playful
Lola	Sorrow
Lucille	Light
Lynne	Pretty
Mabel	Lovable
Marie	Bitter
Nadine	Hope
Natalie	Born at Christmas
Olga	Holy one
Penelope	The weaver
Phoebe	Radiant

GIRLS' NAMES AND THEIR MEANINGS

Ria . . . . Of the river

Ruth . . . . Beautiful and compassionate

Samantha . . . . She who listens

Sandra . . . . The defender

Sonia . . . . Wisdom

Stacey . . . . She who will rise again

Teresa . . . . The harvester

Ulrika . . . . Wolf ruler

Uma . . . . Peace

Valerie . . . . Strong

Virginia . . . . Pure

Vivien . . . . Full of life

Winifred . . . . A peaceful friend

Winona . . . . First-born daughter

Eileen / Light of the Sun

BOOK OF LISTS

MEANINGS OF SURNAMES

Abbott . . . . Chief ruler of an abbey

Anderson . . . . . . Son of Andrew

Barker . . . . A tanner of leather

Becker . . . . Derived from the German for 'baker'

Braddock . . . . . . Derived from the Old English for 'broad dock'

Campbell . . . . . . Derived from the Gaelic for 'crooked mouth'

Clinton . . . . Derived from Clinton in Northamptonshire meaning 'settlement on the summit'

Cooper . . . . Barrel-maker

Crawford . . . . . . Derived from the Gaelic for 'crossing of blood'

Cunningham . . . . From Scottish dialect meaning 'rabbit's home'

Dalton . . . . From the Old English for 'valley town'

Docherty . . . . Derived from an ancient word meaning 'obstructive'

Fairclough . . . . . From the Old English for 'fair cliff'

Fleming . . . . From the French for 'from Flanders'

Fraser . . . . From the word fraises, the French word for 'strawberry'

Irving . . . . From a Scottish place name meaning 'green water'

Lambert . . . . From the German for 'bright land'

Mancini . . . . From the Italian for 'left-handed'

Morgan . . . . From the Welsh for 'born of the sea'

Prescott . . . . Priest's cottage

Quigley . . . . Old English nickname for an agile person

Rigby . . . . From the Norse for 'ridge farm'

Roosevelt . . . . . . Derived from the Dutch for 'rose field'

Smith . . . . From the Old English word *smid* meaning 'worker in metal'

Webster . . . . Alternative Old English name for a weaver

PEOPLE

10 FAMOUS PEOPLE WHO USED TO BE TEACHERS

HG Wells

- Russell Harty
- JRR Tolkien
- Jim Bowen
- JK Rowling
- Anita Roddick
- HG Wells
- Tom O'Connor
- Desmond Tutu
- Dawn French
- Gareth Hale

10 FAMOUS PEOPLE WHO QUALIFIED AS DOCTORS

- Roger Bannister
- Che Guevara
- Anton Chekhov
- Arthur Conan Doyle
- Harry Hill
- Somerset Maugham
- Graeme Garden
- WG Grace
- Jonathan Miller
- David Owen

Che Guevara

BOOK OF LISTS

10 FAMOUS OXFORD GRADUATES

- Bill Clinton
- Rowan Atkinson
- Iris Murdoch
- Imran Khan
- Oscar Wilde
- Kingsley Amis
- Tony Benn
- Robin Day
- Stephen Hawking
- Keith Chegwin

10 FAMOUS CAMBRIDGE GRADUATES

Charles Darwin

- Stephen Fry
- Peter Cook
- Tony Slattery
- David Baddiel
- Emma Thompson
- David Frost
- Clive James
- John Cleese
- Charles Darwin
- William Wordsworth

COLLECTIVELY SPEAKING

COLLECTOR OF

Bank notes . . . . Notaphilist

Beer mats . . . . Tegestologist

Birds' eggs . . . . Oologist

Butterflies . . . . Lepidopterist

Cheese labels . . . . Fromologist

COLLECTOR OF

Coins . . . . Numismatist

Key rings . . . . Copoclephile

Matchbox labels . . . . Phillumenist

Postcards . . . . Deltiologist

Teddy bears . . . . Arctophilist

FAMOUS COLLECTORS

COLLECTOR

Michael Aspel	Georgian silver
Dan Aykroyd	Police badges
Michael Caine	Galle glass
Jamie Lee Curtis	Photographs
Sarah Michelle Geller	Antique books
Tom Hanks	Antique typewriters
Elton John	Art deco
Freddie Mercury	Stamps
Bob Monkhouse	Silent movies
Demi Moore	Dolls
Prince Rainier of Monaco	Stamps
Jonathan Ross	Comic books
Donna Summer	Silver pillboxes
Ivana Trump	Women's compacts
John Wayne	Dolls

Demi Moore / Dolls

BOOK OF LISTS

DINING WITH THE STARS
Restaurants owned by celebrities

Ben Affleck & Matt Damon	The Continental
Dan Aykroyd	House of Blues
Stephen Baldwin	Luahn
Kevin Costner	Clubhouse
Robert De Niro & Christopher Walken	Ago
Cameron Diaz	Bambu
Robert Duval	The Railstop
Peter Fonda	Thunder Roadhouse
Woody Harrelson	02
Don Johnson	Ana Mandara
Jennifer Lopez	Madres
Kelly McGillis	Kelly's Caribbean Bar, Grill & Brewery
Paul Newman	Hampton's
Jamie Oliver	Fifteen
Arnold Schwarzenegger	Schazi On Main
Wesley Snipes	China One
Steven Spielberg	Dive!
Justin Timberlake	Chi
Steven Tyler & Joe Perry	Mount Blue
Bill Wyman	Sticky Fingers

PEOPLE

20 PEOPLE BORN UNDER THE STAR SIGN OF AQUARIUS

- Joy Adamson
- Jennifer Aniston
- Jack Benny
- Humphrey Bogart
- Lewis Carroll
- Natalie Cole
- Geena Davis
- James Dean
- Neil Diamond
- Charles Dickens
- Christian Dior
- WC Fields
- Abraham Lincoln
- Paul Newman
- Yoko Ono
- Ronald Reagan
- Babe Ruth
- John Travolta
- Oprah Winfrey
- Virginia Woolf

Abraham Lincoln

20 PEOPLE BORN UNDER THE STAR SIGN OF PISCES

- Drew Barrymore
- Harry Belafonte
- Alexander Graham Bell
- Michael Caine
- Karen Carpenter
- Johnny Cash
- Glenn Close
- Kurt Cobain
- Cindy Crawford
- Billy Crystal
- George Harrison
- Ron Howard
- Jon Bon Jovi
- Liza Minnelli
- David Niven
- Kurt Russell
- Neil Sedaka
- Elizabeth Taylor
- Bruce Willis
- Joanne Woodward

Bruce Willis

20 PEOPLE BORN UNDER THE STAR SIGN OF ARIES

- Johann Sebastian Bach
- Alec Baldwin
- Warren Beatty
- Marlon Brando
- Casanova
- Charlie Chaplin
- Joan Crawford
- Russell Crowe
- Leonardo da Vinci
- Doris Day
- Daniel Day-Lewis
- Celine Dion
- David Frost
- Sir John Gielgud
- Elton John
- Steve McQueen
- Leonard Nimoy
- Sarah Jessica Parker
- Diana Ross
- Andrew Lloyd Webber

Johann Sebastian Bach

20 PEOPLE BORN UNDER THE STAR SIGN OF TAURUS

- Fred Astaire
- Cher
- George Clooney
- Perry Como
- Oliver Cromwell
- Bing Crosby
- Salvador Dali
- Queen Elizabeth II
- Ella Fitzgerald
- Margot Fonteyn
- Katharine Hepburn
- Janet Jackson
- Grace Jones
- Sugar Ray Leonard
- Karl Marx
- Jack Nicholson
- Florence Nightingale
- William Shakespeare
- Shirley Temple
- Uma Thurman

Florence Nightingale

PEOPLE

20 PEOPLE BORN UNDER THE STAR SIGN OF GEMINI

- Tim Allen
- Mel Blanc
- George W Bush
- Eric Cantona
- Joan Collins
- Courtney Cox
- Tony Curtis
- Johnny Depp
- Arthur Conan Doyle
- Michael J Fox
- Judy Garland
- Bob Hope
- Tom Jones
- Nicole Kidman
- Paul McCartney
- Marilyn Monroe
- Laurence Olivier
- Brooke Shields
- Kathleen Turner
- Gene Wilder

Nicole Kidman

20 PEOPLE BORN UNDER THE STAR SIGN OF CANCER

- Pamela Anderson
- Louis Armstrong
- Louis Bleriot
- Mel Brooks
- Yul Brynner
- Tom Cruise
- Harrison Ford
- Jerry Hall
- Tom Hanks
- Debbie Harry
- Anjelica Huston
- Janet Leigh
- Gina Lollabrigida
- Nelson Mandela
- George Orwell
- Carly Simon
- Sylvester Stallone
- Meryl Streep
- Donald Sutherland
- Robin Williams

George Orwell

BOOK OF LISTS

20 PEOPLE BORN UNDER THE STAR SIGN OF LEO

- Ben Affleck
- Neil Armstrong
- Lucille Ball
- Antonio Banderas
- Napoleon Bonaparte
- Fidel Castro
- Coco Chanel
- Bill Clinton
- Robert De Niro
- David Duchovny
- Amelia Earhart
- Dustin Hoffman
- Whitney Houston
- Jennifer Lopez
- Madonna
- Yves St Laurent
- Pete Sampras
- George Bernard Shaw
- Andy Warhol
- Mae West

Coco Chanel

20 PEOPLE BORN UNDER THE STAR SIGN OF VIRGO

- Lauren Bacall
- Agatha Christie
- Sean Connery
- Harry Connick Jnr
- Jimmy Connors
- Roald Dahl
- Cameron Diaz
- Greta Garbo
- Richard Gere
- Jesse James
- Gene Kelly
- Stephen King
- DH Lawrence
- Keanu Reeves
- Claudia Schiffer
- Peter Sellers
- Charlie Sheen
- Mother Teresa
- Shania Twain
- HG Wells

Greta Garbo

PEOPLE

20 PEOPLE BORN UNDER THE STAR SIGN OF LIBRA

- Julie Andrews
- Brigitte Bardot
- Jackie Collins
- Matt Damon
- Michael Douglas
- Dwight D Eisenhower
- George Gershwin
- Julio Iglesias
- John Lennon
- Martina Navratilova
- Admiral Nelson
- Gwyneth Paltrow
- Luciano Pavarotti
- Christopher Reeve
- Mickey Rooney
- Will Smith
- Bruce Springsteen
- Sting
- Sigourney Weaver
- Oscar Wilde

Will Smith

20 PEOPLE BORN UNDER THE STAR SIGN OF SCORPIO

- Richard Burton
- Prince Charles
- John Cleese
- Marie Curie
- Bo Derek
- Danny DeVito
- Sally Field
- Jodie Foster
- Bill Gates
- Whoopi Goldberg
- Rock Hudson
- Grace Kelly
- Calvin Klein
- Burt Lancaster
- Pablo Picasso
- Julia Roberts
- Roy Rogers
- Winona Ryder
- Martin Scorsese
- Dylan Thomas

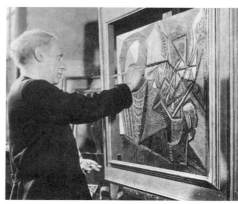

Pablo Picasso

BOOK OF LISTS

20 PEOPLE BORN UNDER THE STAR SIGN OF SAGITTARIUS

- Christina Aguilera
- Louisa May Alcott
- Woody Allen
- Jane Austen
- Beethoven
- Kenneth Branagh
- Winston Churchill
- Noel Coward
- Jamie Lee Curtis
- Sammy Davis Jnr
- Charles de Gaulle
- Joe DiMaggio
- Walt Disney
- Jimi Hendrix
- Bette Midler
- Brad Pitt
- Frank Sinatra
- Tina Turner
- Mark Twain
- Andy Williams

Noel Coward

20 PEOPLE BORN UNDER THE STAR SIGN OF CAPRICORN

- Mohammed Ali
- David Bowie
- Louis Braille
- Kevin Costner
- John Denver
- Cary Grant
- Oliver Hardy
- Stephen Hawking
- J Edgar Hoover
- Janis Joplin
- Martin Luther King
- Rudyard Kipling
- AA Milne
- Kate Moss
- Richard Nixon
- Dolly Parton
- Maggie Smith
- Rod Stewart
- Denzel Washington
- Tiger Woods

J Edgar Hoover

PEOPLE

10 FAMOUS PEOPLE BORN IN INDIA

- Vivien Leigh
- Pete Best
- Paddy Ashdown
- Joanna Lumley
- Engelbert Humperdinck
- Kim Philby
- Cliff Richard
- Spike Milligan
- George Orwell
- Julie Christie

Joanna Lumley

10 FAMOUS PEOPLE BORN IN GERMANY

Anne Frank

- Gyles Brandeth
- Bruce Willis
- John McEnroe
- Dr Ruth
- Anne Frank
- Henry Kissinger
- Peter Alliss
- Claudia Schiffer
- Albert Einstein
- Martin Lawrence

BOOK OF LISTS

ONE SMALL STEP FOR MAN
The 12 men who have walked on the Moon

- Neil Armstrong
- Charles Peter Conrad
- Alan Shepard
- David Scott
- John Young
- Eugene Cernan
- Edwin 'Buzz' Aldrin
- Charles Duke
- Harrison Schmitt
- Alan Bean
- Edgar Mitchell
- James Irwin

Buzz Aldrin

SPACE FIRSTS

Man in space	Yuri Gagarin	1961
American in space	Alan Shepard	1961
American to orbit the Earth	John Glenn	1962
Woman in space	Valentina Tereshkova	1963
Space walk	Alexei Leonov	1965
American woman in space	Sally Ride	1983
African American man in space	Guion 'Guy' Bluford	1983
British woman in space	Helen Sharman	1991
African American woman in space	Mae Jemison	1992
Woman to pilot a spacecraft	Eileen Collins	1995

PEOPLE

THE ROYAL FAMILY

Queen Elizabeth II was the 39th sovereign to be crowned at Westminster Abbey

In 1957, Queen Elizabeth II gave her first Christmas broadcast on live television

In 1972, Queen Elizabeth II received a Silver Wedding anniversary gift, in the shape of a seven-year-old elephant called Jumbo, from the President of Cameroon

Prince Charles was the first member of the Royal Family to donate blood

Princess Anne was the first member of the Royal Family to appear as a contestant on a television game show, when she featured alongside Emlyn Hughes in *A Question of Sport*

Queen Elizabeth II was the first member of the Royal Family to receive a gold disc for record sales. The CD 'Party At The Palace', marking her Golden Jubilee sold in excess of 100,000 copies in the first week of its release

Following the tragic death of Princess Diana, the re-worked Elton John hit 'Candle in the Wind' topped the Canadian singles charts for over a year

When Prince Andrew was born in 1960, Elizabeth II became the first reigning monarch to give birth to a child since Queen Victoria in 1857

At the age of 76, Queen Elizabeth II is the oldest monarch to have celebrated a Golden Jubilee

THE SIX PARTS OF THE CORONATION

- The Recognition
- The Anointing
- The Enthronement
- The Oath
- The Investiture (includes the crowning)
- The Homage

BOOK OF LISTS

THE QUEEN'S CORGIS

- Pharos
- Emma
- Holly
- Linnet
- Willow
- Susan
- Spark
- Fable
- Chipper
- Sugar
- Heather

Corgi

STAR SIGNS OF THE ROYAL FAMILY

Sophie Rhys Jones	Capricorn
Prince Andrew	Aquarius
Prince Edward	Pisces
Princess Eugenie	Aries
Queen Elizabeth II	Taurus
Prince William	Gemini
Princess Anne	Leo
Prince Harry	Virgo
Sarah Ferguson	Libra
Prince Charles	Scorpio

Sarah Ferguson

PEOPLE

PAPAL PARAPHERNALIA

The first Pope in an alphabetical list is Adeodatus and the last is Zosimus

A total of 26 Popes have been assassinated

The shortest serving Pope, Stephen II, served for just one day in AD752

The youngest Pope at the age of 12 was Pope Benedict IX

The white smoke from the Vatican Palace, that signals the election of a new Pope, is caused by the burning of the ballot papers

In 1982, Pope John Paul II became the first Pope to visit Britain

Nicholas Breakspeare was the only Englishman to be elected Pope, taking the papal name of Adrian IV

The last non-Italian Pope before Pope John Paul II was Dutchman Adrian VI in 1522

In the last millennium there were 205 Italian Popes, 19 French Popes, 14 Greek Popes, 8 Syrian Popes, 5 German Popes, 3 African Popes, 2 Spanish Popes, 1 Austrian Pope, 1 Palestinian Pope, 1 English Pope, 1 Dutch Pope and 1 Polish Pope

The three most common names for Popes are John (23 times), Gregory (16 times) and Benedict (16 times)

OFFICIAL TITLES OF THE POPE

- The Bishop of Rome
- The Holy Father
- The Vicar of Christ
- The Successor of St Peter
- Sovereign of the Vatican City
- Supreme Pontiff of the Universal Church
- The Prince of Apostles
- Patriarch of the West
- Primate of Italy
- Archbishop and Metropolitan of the Roman Province

10 PRODUCTS THAT HAVE BEEN ENDORSED BY FOOTBALLERS

BT . . . . Kenny Dalglish

Horlicks . . . . Les Ferdinand

The Guardian . . . . . . Eric Cantona

L'Oreal . . . . David Ginola

Kit Kat . . . . Roy Keane

Renault Clio . . . . Thierry Henry

Chicken Tonight . . . . Ian Wright

McDonalds . . . . Alan Shearer

Walkers Crisps . . . . Gary Lineker

Lucozade Sport . . . . Michael Owen

Michael Owen

10 PRODUCTS THAT HAVE BEEN ENDORSED BY DAVID BECKHAM

David Beckham

- Vodafone
- Police sunglasses
- Marks & Spencers clothes range
- Brylcreem
- Pepsi Cola
- Adidas
- Game Boy Advance
- Castrol engine oil
- Gillette
- Meiji Seika Kaisha's chocolate

PEOPLE

A BEAUTY QUEEN PAGEANT
Celebrities who are former beauty queens

CELEBRITY	TITLE HELD
Shakira Baksh (Mrs Michael Caine)	Miss Guyana
Halle Berry	Miss USA
Linda Carter	Miss USA
Faye Dunaway	Miss University of Florida (runner-up)
Zsa Zsa Gabor	Miss Hungary
Debbie Greenwood	Miss UK
Jerry Hall	Miss Texas
Dorothy Lamour	Miss New Orleans
Sophia Loren	Miss Italy
Imelda Marcos	Miss Manila
Wilnelia Merced (Mrs Bruce Forsyth)	Miss World
Marilyn Monroe	Miss California Artichoke Queen
Michelle Pfeiffer	Miss Orange County
Debbie Reynolds	Miss Burbank
Meg Ryan	Prom Queen at Bethel High School
Cybil Shepherd	Miss Teenage Memphis
Sissy Spacek	Homecoming Queen at Quitman High School
Sharon Stone	Miss Crawford County
Raquel Welch	Miss Maid of California
Vanessa Williams	Miss America

THE FULL NAMES OF FAMOUS PEOPLE KNOWN BY ONE-WORD NAMES

Aaliyah . . . . Aaliyah Dana Haughton

Bjork . . . . Bjork Gudmundsdottir

Bono . . . . Paul Hewson

Caprice . . . . Caprice Bourret

Cher . . . . Cherilyn LaPierre Sarkisian

Coolio . . . . Artis Ivey Junior

Dido . . . . Florian Cloud de Bounevialle Armstrong

Dion . . . . Dion DiMucci

Divine . . . . Harris Glenn Milstead

Donovan . . . . Donovan Leitch

Eminem . . . . Marshall Bruce Mathers

Enya . . . . Eithne Ni Bhraonain

Fish . . . . Derek Dick

Gabrielle . . . . Louisa Gabrielle Bobb

Jordan . . . . Katy Price

Lemmy . . . . Ian Kilminster

Liberace . . . . Wladziu Valentino Liberace

Limahl . . . . Christopher Hamill

Lulu . . . . Marie Lawrie

Madonna . . . . Madonna Veronica Louise Ciccone Ritchie

Melanie . . . . Melanie Safka

Bjork

PEOPLE

THE FULL NAMES OF FAMOUS PEOPLE KNOWN BY ONE-WORD NAMES

Moby	Richard Melville Hall
Mya	Mya Marie Harrison
Pele	Edson Arantes do Nascimento
Pink	Alecia Moore
Pocahontas	Rebecca Rolfe (married name)
Prince	Prince Rogers Nelson
Rasputin	Gregory Efimovich Rasputin
Raul	Raul Gonzalez Blanco
Rembrandt	Rembrandt Harmenszoon van Rijn
Ronaldo	Ronaldo Luiz Nazario de Lima
Sade	Helen Folasade Adu
Seal	Sealhenry Olusegun Olumide Samuel
Shaggy	Orville Burrell
Sting	Gordon Sumner
Tiffany	Tiffany Darwish
Topol	Chaim Topol
Twiggy	Lesley Hornby
Vangelis	Evangelos Odysseas Papathanassiou
Whigfield	Sannia Carlson
Yazz	Yasmin Evans
Zico	Artur Antunes Coimbra

Rasputin

BEFORE THEY WERE FAMOUS
Former occupations of famous people

Bank clerk. . . . . TS Eliot, Terry Wogan, Ronnie Barker

Barrister/lawyer . . . . Margaret Thatcher, Nelson Mandela, Jerry Springer, Clive Anderson

Bodyguards. . . . . Steven Seagal, Mr T

Bricklayers . . . . Jackie Chan, Freddie Starr, Sean Connery

Circus entertainers . . . . Yul Brynner as an acrobat, Burt Lancaster as a trapeze artist, Christopher Walken as a lion tamer, Bob Hoskins as a fire-eater

Mr T

PEOPLE

BEFORE THEY WERE FAMOUS
Former occupations of famous people

Cryptographers . . . . Walter Matthau, Buster Keaton

Electricians . . . . Rod Hull, David Jason

Hairdressers . . . . Sid James, Perry Como, Michael Barrymore, Danny DeVito

Journalists . . . . Neil Tennant, Ian Fleming, Karl Marx, Billy Wilder

Mail boys . . . . Jack Nicholson for MGM, Simon Cowell for EMI

Makeup artist for corpses . Whoopi Goldberg

McDonalds employees . . . . . . Sharon Stone, Andie McDowell

Models . . . . Lauren Bacall, Roger Moore, James Garner, Cameron Diaz, Grace Kelly, Courtney Cox

Piano-players . . . . Les Dawson, Jack Lemmon

Rat-catcher . . . . Warren Beatty

Salesmen . . . . Dustin Hoffman selling toys, Johnny Depp selling pens, Sir John Mills selling toilet paper

Secretaries . . . . Angie Dickinson, Jane Russell

Stand-up comedians . . . . Eddie Murphy, Robbie Coltrane, Jim Carrey

Trainee priests/monks . . . . . Tom Cruise, Dan Aykroyd, Tom Baker, Vincent Van Gogh

Truck-drivers . . . . Elvis Presley, Rock Hudson, Chevy Chase

Waitresses/waiters . . . . Kathy Bates, Sandra Bullock, Russell Crowe

Window-dressers . . . . John Inman, Paul Eddington

BOOK OF LISTS

20 FAMOUS PEOPLE WHO HAVE ATTENDED YALE UNIVERSITY

- Angela Bassett
- Jennifer Beals
- Dick Cheney
- Michael Cimono
- Bill Clinton
- Hillary Clinton
- Claire Danes
- Gerald Ford
- Sara Gilbert
- Holly Hunter
- David Hyde-Pierce
- John Kerry
- Samuel Morse
- Ed Norton
- Vincent Price
- Cole Porter
- Benjamin Spock
- Oliver Stone
- William Howard Taft
- Henry Winkler

20 FAMOUS PEOPLE WHO ATTENDED HARVARD UNIVERSITY

- John Quincy Adams
- Leonard Bernstein
- Benazir Bhutto
- Stockard Channing
- Jacques Chirac
- Michael Crichton
- TS Eliot
- Bill Gates
- Al Gore
- Fred Gwynne
- John F Kennedy
- Henry Kissinger
- Jack Lemmon
- John Lithgow
- Henry Wadsworth Longfellow
- Natalie Portman
- Franklin D Roosevelt
- Theodore Roosevelt
- Elisabeth Shue
- John Updike

PEOPLE

10 FAMOUS WOMEN WHO WERE TEENAGE BRIDES

Brigitte Bardot .... 18 years old when she married Roger Vadim

Joan Collins .... 19 years old when she married Maxwell Reed

Diana Dors .... 19 years old when she married Dennis Hamilton

Melanie Griffith .... 14 years old when she married Don Johnson for the first time

Janet Jackson . . . . . 18 years old when she eloped with James Debarge

Marilyn Monroe .... 16 years old when she married James Dougherty

Elizabeth Taylor .... 18 years old when she married Conrad Hilton Jnr

Shirley Temple ..... 17 years old when she married John Agar

Mae West .... 17 years old when she married Frank Wallace

Tammy Wynette .... 17 years old when she married Euple Byrd

10 FAMOUS MEN WHO MARRIED TEENAGE BRIDES

Mohammed Ali .... Married Belinda Boyd when she was 17 years old

Charlie Chaplin .... Married Oona O'Neil aged 17, Lita Grey aged 16 and
Mildred Harris aged 16

Gary Cooper .... Married Sandra Shaw when she was 19 years old

Macauley Culkin ... Married Rachel Miner when she was 17 years old

Chris Evans .... Married Billie Piper when she was 18 years old

Henry VIII .... Married Catherine Howard when she was 19 years old

Jerry Lee Lewis .... Married his 13-year-old cousin Myra Lewis

Roman Polanski ... Married Barbara Lass when she was 18 years old

Jonathan Ross ..... Married Jane Goldman when she was 18 years old

Bill Wyman .... Married Mandy Smith when she was 18 years old

BOOK OF LISTS

THOROUGHFARES AROUND THE WORLD NAMED AFTER PEOPLE

Alexandras, Athens . . . . Avenue named after Alexander the Great

Astaire Avenue, Culver City, California . . . Named after the legendary hoofer

Barbara Castle Way, Blackburn . . . . Named after the former MP for Blackburn

Bob Hope Drive, Burbank, California . . . . . Named after the famous comedian

Bogart Circle, Cerritos, California . . . . Named after the Hollywood star
Humphrey Bogart

Bond Street, London . . . . Named after Sir Thomas Bond, financial
controller of Queen Victoria's household

Carmen Miranda Square, Hollywood . . . . . Named after the Brazilian singer/actress

Chaplin Drive, San Fernando Valley . . . . . . Named after the silent-movie star
Charlie Chaplin

Downing Street, London . . . . Named after Sir George Downing,
a 17th-century politician

Gene Autry Way, California . . . . Leads to Anaheim stadium,
. . . . home of the California Angels

George Street, Sydney . . . . Named after King George III

Jack London Square, Oakland . . . . Named after the American author of
White Fang

Jefferson Street, San Francisco . . . . Named after Thomas Jefferson,
the third President of the USA. Other streets
named after Presidents in San Francisco
include Jackson Street, Washington Street,
Buchanan Street and Fillmore Street

Joey Ramone Place, New York . . . . Named after the lead singer of the Ramones

PEOPLE

Lombard Street, London	Named after Italian bankers who left Lombardy
Martin Luther King Boulevard, Michigan . .	Named after the Civil Rights leader
Matt Busby Way, Manchester	Named after Matt Busby, the Manchester United manager, and located at Old Trafford
Regent Street, London	Named after the Prince Regent, George Augustus Frederick
Shaftesbury Avenue, London	Named after Anthony Ashley Cooper, the 7th Earl of Shaftesbury
Sloane Square, London	Named after Sir Hans Sloane, an 18th-century physician

10 FAMOUS PEOPLE WHO HAVE SUFFERED FROM A STAMMER

- Harvey Keitel
- Winston Churchill
- Bruce Willis
- Isaac Newton
- Gareth Gates
- Marilyn Monroe
- Lewis Carroll
- King Charles I
- Charles Darwin
- King George VI

Isaac Newton

BOOK OF LISTS

MOUNTAINEERING FIRSTS

Climb Mont Blanc . . . . 1786 . . .Dr Michel Gabriel Paccard and
Jacques Balmat

Climb the Matterhorn . . . . 1865 . . .Edward Whymper

Climb Kilimanjaro . . . . 1889 . . .Hans Meyer and Ludwig Purtscheller

Climb Mount McKinley . . . . 1913 . . .Harry Karstens, Walter Harper and
Robert Tatum

Climb Mount Everest . . . . 1953 . . .Edmund Hillary and Tenzing Norgay

Climb K2 . . . . 1954 . . .Lino Lacedelli and Achille Compagnoni

Climb Kangchenjunga . . . . 1955 . . .George Band, Joe Brown,
Norman Hardie & Tony Streather

American to climb Everest . . . . 1963 . . .James Whittaker

Woman to climb Everest . . . . 1975 . . .Junko Tabei

Blind person to climb Everest . . . . . . 2000 . . .Erik Weihenmayer

Edmund Hillary and Tenzing Norgay

AVIATION FIRSTS

Balloon flight . . . . .1783 . . Jacques and Joseph Montgolfier

Manned plane flight . . . . .1903 . . The Wright Brothers

Cross-Channel flight . . . . .1909 . . Louis Bleriot

Woman to fly the Channel . . . . .1912 . . Harriet Quimby

Non-stop transatlantic flight . . . . .1919 . . John Alcock and Arthur Brown

Solo transatlantic flight . . . . .1927 . . Charles Lindbergh

Solo transatlantic flight by a woman . . . . . . .1932 . . Amelia Earhart

Round-the-world solo flight . . . . .1933 . . Wiley Post

Transatlantic helicopter flight . . . . .1952 . . Captain Vincent H McGovern and
First Lieutenant Harold W Moore

Transatlantic flight by hot air balloon . . . . . .1987 . . Richard Branson and
Per Lindstrand

Montgolfier Balloon

BOOK OF LISTS

INITIAL THOUGHTS
Famous people with initial letters as part of their name

NAME	STANDS FOR
F Murray Abraham	Fahrid
WH Auden	Wystan Hugh
Mel B	Brown
JM Barrie	James Matthew
HE Bates	Herbert Ernest
Mel C	Chisholm
GK Chesterton	Gilbert Keith
FW De Klerk	Frederick Willem
TS Eliot	Thomas Stearns
WC Fields	William Claude
F Scott Fitzgerald	Francis
CS Forester	Cecil Smith
EM Forster	Edward Morgan
Kenny G	Gorelick
WG Grace	William Gilbert
H Rider Haggard	Henry
J Edgar Hoover	John
AE Houseman	Alfred Edward
PD James	Phyllis Dorothy

BB King

PEOPLE

INITIAL THOUGHTS
Famous people with initial letters as part of their name

NAME	STANDS FOR
R Kelly	Robert
BB King	Blues Boy
KD Lang	Kathryn Dawn
DH Lawrence	David Herbert
TE Lawrence	Thomas Edward
CS Lewis	Clive Staples
AA Milne	Alan Alexander
JB Priestly	John Boynton
J Arthur Rank	Joseph
Franklin D Roosevelt	Delano
JK Rowling	Joanne Kathleen
JD Salinger	Jerome David
WH Smith	William Henry
JRR Tolkien	John Ronald Reuel
PL Travers	Pamela Lyndon
HG Wells	Herbert George
FW Woolworth	Frank Winfield
PG Wodehouse	Pelham Grenville
WB Yeats	William Butler

Franklin D Roosevelt

PRIZE GUYS
Famous awards named after people

Carnegie Medal . . . . . . Award for children's literature named in honour of Andrew Carnegie

César . . . . French counterpart of the Oscars, named after the sculptor César Baldacinni

Clio . . . . Advertising and design award named after the Greek muse Clio

Hugo Award for sci-fi named after Hugo Gernsback, the founder of the
and fantasy stories . . magazine *Amazing Stories*

Logie . . . . Australian TV award named after the inventor of television, John Logie Baird

Nobel Prize . . . . Named after the inventor of dynamite, Alfred Nobel

Pulitzer Prize . . . . Literary award named after the journalist Joseph Pulitzer

Stirling Prize . . . . British architecture award, named after the architect James Stirling

Tony . . . . US theatre award named after Antoinette Perry, the founder of the American Theatre Wing

Turner Prize . . . . Annual art award named after the painter JMW Turner

John Logie Baird

PEOPLE

10 WINNERS OF THE NOBEL PEACE PRIZE

1901. . . Jean Henri Dunant . . . . For founding the International Red Cross

1906. . . Theodore Roosevelt . . . . For initiating the treaty to end the Russo-Japanese War

1919. . . Woodrow Wilson . . . . For founding the League of Nations

1937. . . Viscount Cecil of Chelwood . . . Founder of the International Peace Campaign

1964. . . Martin Luther King . . . . Campaigning for civil rights

1977. . . Henry Kissinger . . . . For the Vietnam Peace Accord

1979. . . Mother Teresa . . . . For charity work amongst the poverty-stricken

1983. . Lech Wales . . . . Founder of Solidarity

1984. . . Desmond Tutu . . . . For fighting apartheid

1990. . . Mikhail Gorbachev . . . . For ending the Cold War

Mother Teresa

35 PEOPLE WHO HAVE BEEN NAMED *TIME* MAGAZINE 'MAN OF THE YEAR'

- Yasser Arafat
- Willy Brandt
- George Bush Jnr
- George Bush Snr
- Jimmy Carter
- Walter Chrysler
- Winston Churchill
- Bill Clinton
- Charles de Gaulle
- FW de Klerk
- John Dulles
- Dwight D Eisenhower
- Elizabeth II *
- King Faisal
- Mahatma Gandhi
- Mikhail Gorbachev
- Rudolph Giuliani
- Adolf Hitler
- Lyndon B Johnson
- John F Kennedy
- Ayatollah Khomeini

Mahatma Gandhi

PEOPLE

35 PEOPLE WHO HAVE BEEN NAMED *TIME* MAGAZINE 'MAN OF THE YEAR'

- Martin Luther King
- Henry Kissinger
- Nikita Krushchev
- Charles Lindbergh
- Jim Lovell
- Nelson Mandela
- Richard Nixon
- Pope John XIII
- Pope John Paul II
- Ronald Reagan
- Franklin D Roosevelt
- Anwar Sadat
- Haile Selassie
- Wallis Simpson *

Adolf Hitler

TIME MAGAZINE 'MAN OF THE 20TH CENTURY'

- Albert Einstein

* Examples where the title has been applied to both sexes

BOOK OF LISTS

THE YEAR THEY DIED

1968	Martin Luther King, Robert Kennedy, Yuri Gagarin, Jim Clark, Helen Keller
1969	Judy Garland, Rocky Marciano, Dwight D Eisenhower, Brian Jones, Boris Karloff
1970	Jimi Hendrix, Charles de Gaulle, Janis Joplin, Gypsy Rose Lee, Tammi Terrell
1971	Jim Morrison, Papa Doc Duvalier, Audie Murphy, Louis Armstrong, Igor Stravinsky
1972	Edward VIII, Maurice Chevalier, J Edgar Hoover, Margaret Rutherford, Harry S Truman
1973	Bruce Lee, Bobby Darin, JRR Tolkien, Noel Coward, Edward G Robinson
1974	Duke Ellington, Bud Abbott, Georges Pompidou, Jack Benny, Mama Cass Elliott
1975	Francisco Franco, PG Wodehouse, Aristotle Onassis, Graham Hill, Susan Hayward
1976	Agatha Christie, Sid James, Howard Hughes, Paul Robeson, Benjamin Britten
1977	Elvis Presley, Charlie Chaplin, Marc Bolan, Groucho Marx, Bing Crosby
1978	Robert Menzies, Robert Shaw, Keith Moon, Pope Paul VI, Pope John Paul I
1979	Sid Vicious, John Wayne, Mary Pickford, Josef Mengele, Richard Beckinsale
1980	John Lennon, Peter Sellers, Jesse Owens, Alfred Hitchcock, Joy Adamson
1981	Bill Haley, Anwar Sadat, Bob Marley, Bill Shankly, Natalie Wood
1982	Princess Grace, John Belushi, Arthur Lowe, Leonid Brezhnev, Giles Villeneuve
1983	Karen Carpenter, David Niven, Tennessee Williams, Gloria Swanson, Dennis Wilson

PEOPLE

THE YEAR THEY DIED

1984	Tommy Cooper, Richard Burton, Marvin Gaye, Eric Morecambe, Leonard Rossiter
1985	Rock Hudson, Phil Silvers, Orson Welles, Ricky Nelson, Yul Brynner
1986	James Cagney, Harold Macmillan, Ray Miland, Benny Goodman, Cary Grant
1987	Fred Astaire, Andy Warhol, Maria Von Trapp, Danny Kaye, Rudolf Hess
1988	Kenneth Williams, Roy Orbison, Franklin D Roosevelt, Kim Philby, Andy Gibb
1989	Lucille Ball, Salvador Dali, Mel Blanc, Irving Berlin, Emperor Hirohito
1990	Terry Thomas, Sammy Davis Jnr, Jim Henson, Ava Gardner, Rex Harrison
1991	Freddie Mercury, Michael Landon, Dr Seuss, Miles Davis, Graham Greene
1992	Benny Hill, Francis Bacon, Marlene Dietrich, Denholm Elliott, Isaac Asimov
1993	Audrey Hepburn, Bobby Moore, River Phoenix, Arthur Ashe, Frank Zappa
1994	Telly Savalas, Kurt Cobain, Richard Nixon, Burt Lancaster, John Candy
1995	Ginger Rogers, Kenny Everett, Peter Cook, Fred Perry, Paul Eddington
1996	George Burns, François Mitterrand, Jon Pertwee, Ella Fitzgerald, Rene Lacoste
1997	Princess Diana, Mother Teresa, Gianni Versace, Michael Hutchence, James Stewart
1998	Frank Sinatra, Catherine Cookson, Tammy Wynette, Carl Perkins, Sonny Bono
1999	Oliver Reed, Dusty Springfield, Stanley Kubrick, Joe DiMaggio, Dirk Bogarde
2000	John Gielgud, Charles Schulz, Ian Dury, Barbara Cartland, Alec Guinness
2001	Donald Bradman, George Harrison, Harry Secombe, Jack Lemmon, Perry Como
2002	John Thaw, Spike Milligan, Dudley Moore, Lonnie Donegan, Richard Harris
2003	Maurice Gibb, Bob Hope, Gregory Peck, Adam Faith, Barry White
2004	Ronald Reagan, Peter Ustinov, Estée Lauder, Brian Clough, Marlon Brando

SCIENCE

Bees have five eyes, Quentin Tarantino's IQ is 160, mother bats are known to adopt orphaned bats, a fear of horses is called hippophobia, the adjective from worm is the word vermian, the daffodil symbolizes deceit, SARS stands for Severe Accute Respiratory Syndrome. This is a miniscule sampling of facts from the many lists in this section, including animals and plants, human biology, science, scientists, inventions, mathematics, medicine, diseases, doctors, food, climate, astronomy, elements... the list goes on and on.

RAINING CATS . . .

Cats have 290 bones in their body, 10% of which are located in the tail

In Ancient Rome, the cat was a symbol of liberty

The correct term for cat's whiskers is the vibrissae

Ailurophobia is the morbid fear of cats, an affliction suffered by Julius Caesar

Cats have three eyelids on each eye. The extra third eyelid is called the haw

Sir Isaac Newton, a noted cat lover, invented the cat flap

According to folklore, if a cat sleeps with all four paws tucked under its body, it is a sign that cold weather is imminent

A cat's heart beats twice as fast as a human heart

Ancient Egyptians believed that cats were sacred animals. Egyptian families would shave off their eyebrows when the family cat passed away

The cheetah is the only member of the cat family with non-retractable claws

Mummified cat

SCIENCE

. . . AND DOGS

All domestic dog breeds are members of the family *Canis familiaris*, Latin for 'familiar wolf'

The chow is the only breed of dog with a black tongue

In Imperial China, commoners were not allowed to own Pekinese dogs

The Dalmatian is the only breed of dog that can contract gout

One of the world's oldest breeds is the saluki, originating in Mesopotamia around 3000BC

The bloodhound is the only animal whose evidence is admissible in a US court of law

In 1905, the first canine film star appeared in a movie entitled *Rescued By Rover.*

The name Rover, uncommon for dogs prior to the film, became a popular moniker for the family dog

The basenji and the dingo are the only members of the canine family that are unable to bark.

The basenji, also known as the African barkless dog, yodels as opposed to barking

Labrador retrievers were so named as they were originally bred to retrieve fishing nets

Ancient Romans employed ancestors of the rottweiler as attack and guard dogs. Following a successful invasion of Germany, the dog was introduced to the area of Rottweil, hence the name

Dingo

BOOK OF LISTS

PRIZE GUYS
A selection of Nobel Prize winners

CHEMISTRY RECIPIENT	AWARDED FOR
Sir William Ramsay	Discovery of inert gases
Ernest Rutherford	Research into the chemistry of radioactive substances
Harold Clayton Urey	Discovery of heavy hydrogen

MEDICINE RECIPIENT	AWARDED FOR
Frederick Banting & John Macleod	Discovery of insulin
Emil Behring	Serum to treat diphtheria
Francis Crick & James Watson	Discovery of DNA
Henrik Dam & Edward Doisy	Discovery of vitamin K
Alexander Fleming	Discovery of penicillin
Robert Koch	Discovering the cause of tuberculosis
Karl Landsteiner	Discovery of human blood types
Thomas Hunt Morgan	Research into the effects of chromosomes in hereditary diseases
Paul Herrmann Muller	Discovering the insecticide DDT
Ronald Ross	Research into malaria

SCIENCE

PRIZE GUYS
A selection of Nobel Prize winners

PHYSICS RECIPIENT	AWARDED FOR
James Chadwick	Discovery of the neutron
Marie & Pierre Curie	Research into radiation and discovery of radium
Albert Einstein	Research into theoretical physics
Dennis Gabor	Invention of the hologram
Gabriel Lippmann	Research into colour photography
Max Planck	Research into quantum physics
Wilhelm Rontgen	Discovery of x-rays

Albert Einstein

BOOK OF LISTS

ENOUGH TO DRIVE YOU BATTY

The bat is the only mammal capable of true flight

Mother bats are known to adopt orphaned bats

Bat droppings are called guano

Bats make up a quarter of all known animal species

The bumblebee bat, native to Thailand, is the world's smallest mammal

Bats are able to hibernate at will, by shutting down their metabolism system

Bats pollinate bananas

Bats belong to the order *chiroptera*, meaning, 'hand wing'

Bats hang upside down as their legs and feet are not strong enough to support their body and wings for great lengths of time

Vampire bat

MYTHS ABOUT BATS

Blind as a bat?	Bats actually posses acute eyesight and this, combined with their echolocation system, makes them proficient night hunters
Vampire bats feed on humans?	Such occurrences are vary rare, as bats do not like the taste of human blood
Bats are riddled with rabies?	Less than 1% of bats contract rabies
Vampire bats suck blood?	Vampire bats make a small cut with their sharp teeth then lap up the blood with their tongues
Bats are dirty creatures?	Bats are resistant to most diseases and groom constantly

SPECIES OF BAT

There are almost 1000 different species of bat worldwide including:

- Bulmer's fruit bat
- Dwarf dog-faced bat
- Nigerian free-tailed bat
- Black mastiff bat
- Hairless bat
- Angola hairy bat
- Rusty pipistrelle
- Soprano pipistrelle
- Hairy-winged bat
- Gloomy tube-nosed bat
- Nut-coloured yellow bat
- Lesser bamboo bat
- Greater bamboo bat
- Harlequin bat
- Canary big-eared bat
- New Zealand lesser short-tailed bat
- Least long-fingered bat
- Mouse-eared bat
- Robust yellow bat
- Singapore whiskered bat

BOOK OF LISTS

ENDANGERED SPECIES

In 2004, the World Wildlife Fund issued a Top 10 list of the world's animals and plants most at risk from illegal trading:

1 Great white shark
2 Humphead wrasse, a species of coral-reef fish
3 Ramin, a tropical hardwood
4 Tiger
5 Irawaddy dolphin
6 Elephant
7 Pig-nosed turtle
8 Yellow-crested cockatoo
9 Leaf-tailed gecko
10 Asian yew trees

Great white shark

10 ADDITIONAL ENDANGERED SPECIES

- Leatherback sea turtle
- Peregrine falcon
- Sperm whale
- Indiana bat
- Tiger salamander
- American burying beetle
- Dwarf wedgemussel
- Shortnose sturgeon
- Northern cricket frog
- Eskimo curlew

Sperm whale

SCIENCE

DID YOU KNOW?

David Beckham has a morbid fear of birds

Country and western star Lyle Lovett, ex-husband of Julia Roberts, has a morbid fear of cows

Hollywood movie star Nicole Kidman is afraid of butterflies

Alexander the Great, Benito Mussolini and Napoleon Bonaparte were all terrified of cats

Clint Eastwood, despite starring in numerous westerns, is allergic to horses

TV chef Ainsley Harriott shares a fear of snakes with the movie hero Indiana Jones

Famous arachnophobics include Johnny Depp, Wendy Richard and Andre Agassi

The actor Robson Green has a morbid fear of wasps

The film director Steven Spielberg is terrified of insects

The film stars Brad Pitt and Christian Ricci share a fear of sharks

Wolf spider

ANIMAL PHOBIAS

ANIMAL	PHOBIA	ANIMAL	PHOBIA
Mice	Musophobia	Otters	Lutraphobia
Animals	Zoophobia	Reptiles	Herpetophobia
Animal fur	Doraphobia	Sharks	Selacophobia
Ants	Myrmecophobia	Shellfish	Ostraconophobia
Bees	Apiphobia	Snakes	Ophidiophobia
Birds	Ornithophobia	Spiders	Arachnophobia
Bulls	Taurophobia	Termites	Isopterophobia
Cats	Ailurophobia	Toads	Bufonophobia
Chickens	Alektorophobia	Wasps	Spheksophobia
Dogs	Cynophobia	Wild animals	Agrizoophobia
Fish	Ichthyophobia	Worms	Helminthophobia
Frogs	Batrachophobia		
Horses	Hippophobia		
Insects	Entomophobia		
Lice	Pediculophobia		

Wasp

MORE PHOBIAS

PHOBIA	FEAR OF	PHOBIA	FEAR OF
Achulophobia	Darkness	Ergasiophobia	Surgery
Acrophobia	Heights	Gametophobia	Marriage
Agoraphobia	Open spaces	Geniophobia	Chins
Algophobia	Pain	Genuphobia	Knees
Anthrophobia	Flowers	Haematophobia	Blood
Astraphobia	Lightning	Homichiphobia	Fog
Belonephobia	Needles	Koniphobia	Dust
Blennophobia	Slime	Monophobia	Being alone
Brontophobia	Thunder	Odontophobia	Teeth
Carcinophobia	Cancer	Peladophobia	Bald people
Carnophobia	Meat	Phasmophobia	Ghosts
Catoptrophobia	Mirrors	Photophobia	Light
Cheimaphobia	Cold	Phyllophobia	Leaves
Chromophobia	Colour	Pogonophobia	Beards
Claustrophobia	Confined spaces	Potamophobia	Rivers
Clinophobia	Going to bed	Pyrophobia	Fire
Coitophobia	Sexual intercourse	Siderophobia	Stars
Demophobia	Crowds	Siderodromophobia	Travelling by train
Dendrophobia	Trees	Sitophobia	Food
Dipsophobia	Drinking	Tachophobia	Speed
Potophobia	Alcohol	Triskaidekaphobia	The number 13
Dromophobia	Crossing the road	Xenophobia	Foreigners

BOOK OF LISTS

THE BEAUFORT SCALE (WINDS)

0 Calm
1 Light air
2 Light breeze
3 Gentle breeze
4 Moderate breeze
5 Fresh breeze
6 Strong breeze

7 Near gale
8 Gale
9 Severe gale
10 Storm
11 Violent storm
12 Hurricane

THE RICHTER SCALE (EARTHQUAKES)

1 Instrumental
2 Feeble
3 Slight
4 Moderate
5 Rather strong
6 Strong

7 Very strong
8 Destructive
9 Ruinous
10 Disastrous
11 Very disastrous
12 Catastrophic

SCIENCE

ELEMENTS NAMED AFTER PEOPLE

ELEMENT	NAMED AFTER
Curium	Marie & Pierre Curie
Einsteinium	Albert Einstein
Fermium	Italian nuclear physicist Enrico Fermi
Gadolinium	Finnish chemist Johann Gadolin
Hahnium	German chemist Otto Hahn
Lawrencium	Physicist and Nobel Prize winner Ernest Lawrence
Mendelevium	Siberian chemist Dmitry Ivanovich Mendeleyev
Rutherfordium	New Zealand physicist Ernest Rutherford

**Marie &
Pierre Curie**

ELEMENTS NAMED AFTER PLACES

ELEMENT	NAMED AFTER
Berkelium	Berkeley University, California
Californium	California
Copper	Cyprus
Europium	Europe
Francium	France
Germanium	Germany
Holmium	Stockholm, from the Roman name Holmia
Polonium	Poland
Scandium	Scandinavia
Ytterbium	Swedish village of Ytterby

California

BEASTLY SYMBOLS

Bacardi logo	Bat
British Wildlife Trust	Badger
Canada	Beaver
Chile	Condor
Democratic Party (USA)	Donkey
Esso	Tiger
Ferrari	Prancing horse
HMV	Nipper the dog
Lacoste	Crocodile
Lloyds TSB	Black horse
MGM	Leo the lion

Giant Panda

Kiwi

New Zealand	Kiwi
Peugeot	Lion
Reader's Digest	Pegasus, the winged horse
Republican Party (USA)	Elephant
RSPB	Avocet
Suzuki	Rhinoceros
USA	Bald eagle
World Wildlife Fund	Giant panda
Zoo on an Ordnance Survey map	Elephant

ANIMAL ADJECTIVES

ANIMAL	ADJECTIVE
Ant	Formicine
Ape	Simian
Badger	Musteline
Bat	Pteropine
Bear	Ursine
Bee	Apiarian
Bluebird	Turdine
Bull	Taurine
Camel	Cameline
Cat	Feline
Cow	Bovine
Crab	Cancrine
Crow	Corvine
Deer	Cervine
Dog	Canine
Dolphin	Delphine
Dove	Columbine
Eagle	Aquiline
Ferret	Musteline
Fish	Piscine
Flea	Pulicine
Fox	Vulpine

Ant

Dolphin

Peacock

ANIMAL	ADJECTIVE
Frog	Ranine
Goat	Caprine
Goose	Anserine
Gull	Larine
Hare	Leporine
Kangaroo	Macropodine
Leopard	Pardine
Lion	Leonine
Lobster	Homarine
Magpie	Garruline
Mouse	Murine
Partridge	Perdicine
Peacock	Pavonine
Rabbit	Lapine
Rat	Murine
Sheep	Ovine
Snake	Anguine
Swan	Cygnine
Tiger	Tigrine
Wasp	Vespine
Wolf	Lupine
Worm	Vermian

MORSE CODE

A	Dot dash	**Q**	Dash dash dot dash
B	Dash dot dot dot	**R**	Dot dash dot
C	Dash dot dash dot	**S**	Dot dot dot
D	Dash dot dot	**T**	Dash
E	Dot	**U**	Dot dot dash
F	Dot dot dash dot	**V**	Dot dot dot dash
G	Dash dash dot	**W**	Dot dash dash
H	Dot dot dot dot	**X**	Dash dot dot dash
I	Dot dot	**Y**	Dash dot dash dash
J	Dot dash dash dash	**Z**	Dash dash dot dot
K	Dash dot dash		
L	Dot dash dot dot		
M	Dash dash		
N	Dash dot		
O	Dash dash dash		
P	Dot dash dash dot		

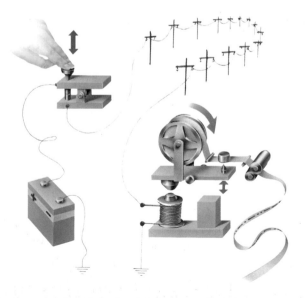

SCIENCE

COMPUTER ABBREVIATIONS

AAC . . . . advanced audio coding

AGP . . . . accelerated graphics port

AI . . . . artificial intelligence

AMD . . . . advanced micro devices

API . . . . application programming interface

BASIC . . . . . . beginners all-purpose symbolic instruction code

BBS . . . . bulletin board system

CAD . . . . computer aided design

CPU . . . . central processing unit

DOS . . . . disc operating system

FAQ . . . . frequently asked questions

GIGO . . . . garbage in garbage out

HTML . . . . . . hypertext markup language

HTTP . . . . . . hypertext transport protocol

IT . . . . information technology

LAN . . . . local area network

MMU . . . . . . memory management unit

PC . . . . personal computer

PDA . . . . personal digital assistant

RAM . . . . random access memory

ROM . . . . read only memory

WAN . . . . wide area network

WAP . . . . wireless application protocol

MEDICAL ABBREVIATIONS

ADD	attention deficit disorder
AIDS	acquired immune deficiency syndrome
BSE	bovine spongiform encephalopathy
CAT scan	computed axial tomography
CHF	congestive heart failure
CJD	Creutzfeldt-Jakob disease
CPR	cardiopulmonary resuscitation
DPT vaccine	diphtheria, pertussis, tetanus
DNA	deoxyribonucleic acid
DVT	deep-vein thrombosis
ECG	electrocardiogram
EMF	endomyocardial fibrosis
GHRF	growth-hormone releasing factor
HIV	human immunodeficiency virus
HRT	hormone replacement therapy
ICU	intensive care unit
IVF	in vitro fertilization
MMR vaccine	measles, mumps, rubella
MS	multiple sclerosis
REM	rapid eye movement
SARS	severe acute respiratory syndrome
SIDS	sudden infant death syndrome
TB	tuberculosis

DNA

SCIENCE

THE HIDDEN MEANINGS OF FLOWERS AND PLANTS

FLOWER	MEANING
Basil	Hatred
Cactus	Maternal love
Daffodil	Deceit
Daisy	Affection
Geranium	Melancholy
Honeysuckle	Bonds of love
Hyacinth	Benevolence
Larkspur	Levity
Laurel	Glory
Lavender	Distrust
Lily	Pride
Lily of the valley	Return of happiness
Narcissus	Selfishness
Nettle	Cruelty
Rose	Beauty
Saffron	Abuse
Snowdrop	Consolation
Sunflower	False riches
Tulip	Declaration of love
Weeping willow	Sadness

Sunflower / False riches

BOOK OF LISTS

THE FEMALE OF THE SPECIES

ANIMAL	FEMALE	ANIMAL	FEMALE
Alligator	Cow	Leopard	Leopardess
Badger	Sow	Lion	Lioness
Bear	Sow	Otter	Bitch
Bee	Queen & worker	Opossum	Jill
Camel	Cow	Peacock	Peahen
Canary	Hen	Pig	Sow
Cat	Queen	Rabbit	Doe
Coyote	Gyp	Rat	Doe
Deer	Doe & hind	Rhinoceros	Cow
Dog	Bitch	Salmon	Hen
Dolphin	Cow	Sandpiper	Reeve
Donkey	Jenny	Sheep	Ewe
Elephant	Cow	Squirrel	Doe
Ferret	Jill	Swan	Pen
Foal	Filly	Tiger	Tigress
Fox	Vixen	Wallaby	Jill
Giraffe	Cow	Whale	Cow
Goat	Nanny	Yak	Cow
Hedgehog	Sow	Zebra	Mare
Hippopotamus	Cow		
Horse	Mare		
Kangaroo	Doe		

SCIENCE

COLLECTIVE NOUNS FOR CREATURES

Antelope	Herd	**Geese**	Gaggle
Ant	Army or colony	**Goldfish**	Troubling
Ape	Shrewdness	**Gorilla**	Band
Ass	Pace	**Hare**	Down
Badger	Cete	**Hawk**	Cast
Bear	Sleuth or sloth	**Jellyfish**	Smuck
Beaver	Colony	**Kitten**	Kindle
Bee	Swarm or hive	**Lapwing**	Deceit
Bloodhound	Sute	**Lark**	Exaltation
Cat	Clowder	**Leopard**	Leap
Camel	Caravan	**Lion**	Pride
Chicken	Brood	**Magpie**	Tiding
Crocodile	Bask	**Mouse**	Nest
Crow	Murder	**Mole**	Labour
Deer	Herd	**Monkey**	Troop
Donkey	Drove	**Mosquito**	Scourge
Eagle	Convocation	**Mule**	Barren
Elephant	Herd	**Nightingale**	Watch
Falcon	Cast	**Owl**	Parliament
Ferret	Business	**Parrot**	Pandemonium
Finch	Charm	**Partridge**	Covey
Fox	Skulk	**Peacock**	Muster
Frog	Army	**Pheasant**	Nye

Geese / Gaggle

THE PERCENTAGE OF GASES IN THE AIR THAT WE BREATHE

Nitrogen	78.084%	Methane	0.0002%
Oxygen	20.94%	Helium	0.000524%
Argon	0.934%	Krypton	0.000114%
Carbon dioxide	0.0314%	Hydrogen	0.00005%
Neon	0.001818%	Xenon	0.0000087%

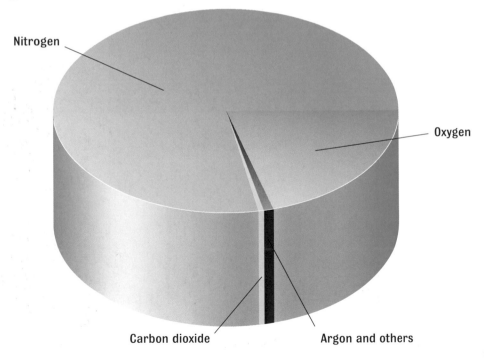

Nitrogen

Oxygen

Carbon dioxide

Argon and others

SCIENCE

THE SHAPE OF THINGS

3 sides . . . . . . Triangle		**12 sides** . . . . .Dodecagon	
4 sides . . . . . . Rectangle		**13 sides** . . . . .Triskaidecagon	
5 sides . . . . . . Pentagon		**14 sides** . . . . .Tetrakaidecagon	
6 sides . . . . . . Hexagon		**15 sides** . . . . .Pendedecagon	
7 sides . . . . . . Heptagon		**16 sides** . . . . .Hexdocagon	
8 sides . . . . . . Octagon		**17 sides** . . . . .Heptdecagon	
9 sides . . . . . . Nonagon		**18 sides** . . . . .Octdecagon	
10 sides . . . . . Decagon		**19 sides** . . . . .Enneadecagon	
11 sides . . . . . Undecagon		**20 sides** . . . . .Icosagon	

Triangle

Hexagon

Nonagon

Dodecagon

Pendedecagon

Octdecagon

BOOK OF LISTS

A TO Z OF 'OLOGIES'

OLOGY	STUDY OF	OLOGY	STUDY OF
Anemology	Wind	Oncology	Cancer
Anthropology	Mankind	Ornithology	Birds
Apiology	Bees	Oology	Eggs
Archaeology	Ancient remains	Orology	Mountains
Audiology	Sound	Palaeontology	Fossils
Bryology	Mosses	Pedology	Soil
Cardiology	Heart and heart disease	Petrology	Rocks
Conchology	Shells	Pomology	Fruit
Cosmology	Universe	Rhinology	Noses
Cryptology	Codes	Seismology	Earthquakes
Cytology	Cells	Somotology	Human characteristics
Dactylology	Fingerprints	Speleology	Caves
Dendrology	Trees	Tribology	Friction and lubrication
Entomology	Insects	Toxicology	Poisons
Ethology	Animal behaviour	Vexillology	Flags
Graphology	Handwriting	Vulcanology	Volcanoes
Haematology	Blood	Xenobiology	Non-terrestrial life
Limnology	Lakes	Zymology	Fermentation
Meteorology	Weather		
Mycology	Fungi		
Nephology	Clouds		
Nosology	Diseases		

ELEPHANTS ON PARADE

An elephant has an estimated 40,000 muscles in its trunk

An elephant is incapable of jumping

The maximum lifespan of an elephant is 70 years

Elephants are the only animals on Earth with four knees

The African elephant has the largest brain of any land mammal, four times larger than a human brain

Elephants sleep standing up

The sperm of a mouse is larger than the sperm of an elephant

An elephant's trunk has the capacity to hold two litres of water

September 22 is Elephant Appreciation Day

The average weight of the African male elephant is 4990kg, with females weighing 2720kg

Elephants are pachyderms, meaning 'thick-skinned'. Despite this their skin is so sensitive they are able to feel a fly landing on it

An elephant's tongue weighs an average 12kg

The gestation period of an elephant is 23 months

An African elephant has the largest ears in the animal kingdom. On average they measure 2m by 1.2m with each weighing up to 20kg

Elephants can smell water up to 5km away

The African elephant has four toes on its front feet and three toes on its rear feet

An elephant's trunk is so strong it can uproot a tree and so sensitive as to be able to turn the page of a book

An elephant never forgets. This old adage is based on the fact that elephants can remember the exact place where they were born and often return to their birthplace when they are about to die

BOOK OF LISTS

SO THAT'S WHAT IT'S CALLED

Axilla	Technical name for the armpit
Canthus	Corner where the upper and lower eyelids meet at each side of the eye
Coccyx	The four fused vertebrae at the bottom of the spine
Gastronemius	Calf muscle
Glabella	The gap between the eyebrows
Hallux	The big toe
Lachrymal glands	The glands responsible for secreting tears
Larynx	Technical name for the voice box
Lentigines	Medical name for freckles
Lunula	Crescent-shaped area at the base of fingernails
Myeloid tissue	Bone marrow
Naevus	Technical name for a mole
Pericardium	Muscular sac containing the heart
Philtrum	Groove under the nose down to the top lip
Sclera	The white of the eye
Septum	The structure dividing the nostrils
Serborric dermatitis	Technical name for dandruff
Ulnar nerve	Technical name for the funny bone
Vitreous humour	Fluid that fills the eyeball between the lens and the retina
Zygomatic bone	The cheek bone

Bone marrow

SCIENCE

ACUPUNCTURE POINTS

NAME	LOCATION	TREATS
Cheng Qi	Below the eyeball	Myopia
Chi Ze	Fold of the elbow	Asthma, coughs
He Gu	Between thumb and index finger	Hay fever, acne
Jing Ming	Corner of the eye	Blurred vision
Ji Quan	Armpit	Stiff shoulder
Lao Gong	Centre of the palm	Mouth ulcers
Lie Que	Above the wrist	Wind
Nei Guan	Tendons above the wrist	Angina, sea sickness
Quan Liao	Cheek	Neuralgia, toothache
Shang Yang	Index finger	Fever
Shao Shang	Thumb	Sore throat
Tai Yang	Temple	Toothache
Tianjing	Elbow	Migraine, depression, thyroid disorder
Tian Zong	Shoulder blade	Anxiety
Waiguan	Between the ulna and radius	Migraine
Xuehai	Knee	Premenstrual tension
Yangchi	Wrist	Dryness of the mouth
Yin Bai	Big toe	Insomnia
Yintang	At the end of the eyebrows	Stress
Yongkuan	Sole of the foot	Anxiety, rage, night sweats

BOOK OF LISTS

HOW LOUD?
Decibel levels of everyday noises

10 decibels . . . . . Normal breathing

15 decibels . . . . . Rustling leaves

20 decibels . . . . . The buzz of a mosquito

30 decibels . . . . . Whisper

50 decibels . . . . . Normal conversation

60 decibels . . . . . Singing birds

60 decibels . . . . . Sewing machine

70 decibels . . . . . Vacuum cleaner

70 decibels . . . . . Rush hour traffic

80 decibels . . . . . Garbage disposal unit

90 decibels . . . . . Motorbike

90 decibels . . . . . Hairdryer

90 decibels . . . . . Lawnmower

100 decibels . . . . . Chainsaw

110 decibels . . . . . Walkman on high volume

115 decibels . . . . . Ambulance or police siren

120 decibels . . . . . Rock concert

130 decibels . . . . . Shotgun fire

180 decibels . . . . . Rocket launch

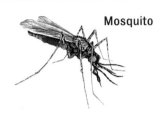

Mosquito

Rocket launch

Sustained exposure to noise levels exceeding
85 decibels can cause permanent damage
to hearing.

YOUNG AT HEART

ANIMAL	YOUNG	ANIMAL	YOUNG	ANIMAL	YOUNG
Antelope	Calf	Hamster	Pup	Oyster	Spat
Badger	Kit	Hare	Leveret	Pig	Piglet
Bat	Pup	Hawk	Eyas	Pigeon	Squab
Bear	Cub	Hippopotamus	Calf	Pilchard	Sardine
Beaver	Kitten	Hog	Shoat	Rabbit	Kit
Camel	Calf	Horse	Foal	Rhinoceros	Calf
Cat	Kitten	Jellyfish	Ephyra	Snail	Spat
Cod	Codling	Kangaroo	Joey	Spider	Spiderling
Cow	Calf	Lion	Cub	Squirrel	Kitten
Crane fly	Leatherjacket	Llama	Cria	Swan	Cygnet
Crocodile	Crocklet	Mosquito	Nymph	Sheep	Lamb
Deer	Fawn	Ostrich	Chick	Tiger	Cub
Dog	Puppy	Otter	Whelp	Whale	Calf
Duck	Duckling	Owl	Owlet	Zebra	Foal
Eagle	Eaglet				
Eel	Elver				
Elephant	Calf				
Fish	Fry				
Frog	Tadpole				
Giraffe	Calf				
Goat	Kid				
Goose	Gosling				

Joey

BOOK OF LISTS

TYPES OF CLOUD

Cirrus . . . . Feathery white clouds

Cirrocumulus . . . . . Small patchy white clouds

Cirrostratus . . . . . . Thin white sheets of clouds

Cumulus . . . . White puffy clouds

Stratus . . . . Low grey clouds

Nimbus . . . . Dark heavy rain clouds

Clouds

RAINBOW MNEMONIC

Richard Of York Gave Battle In Vain

Red, Orange, Yellow, Green, Blue, Indigo, Violet

ODDS OF BEING STRUCK BY LIGHTNING

800,000 – 1

Lightning never strikes the same place twice? Complete myth – Lightning often strikes the same spot several times during one storm

NATURE'S SIGNS THAT ARE SAID TO SIGNAL IMPENDING RAIN

- **Bats** fly lower
- **Frogs** emerge from the water croaking
- **Daisies** close their petals
- **Wolves** howl
- **Birds** sing more
- **Cattle** gather close together
- **Cats** sit with their tails to the fire
- **Roosters** crow before retiring to sleep
- **Fish** take bait more eagerly
- **Dolphins** swim closer to land

Howling wolf

BOOK OF LISTS

HURRICANES

Hurricanes have been given personal names since 1953, and these names are revised every six years by the World Meteorological Organisation.

NAMES FOR HURRICANES IN 2005

- Arlene
- Bret
- Cindy
- Dennis
- Emily
- Franklin
- Gert
- Harvey
- Irene
- Jose
- Katrina

- Lee
- Maria
- Nate
- Ophelia
- Philippe
- Rita
- Stan
- Tammy
- Vince
- Wilma

SCIENCE

NAMES FOR HURRICANES IN 2006

- Alberto
- Beryl
- Chris
- Debby
- Ernesto
- Florence
- Gordon
- Helene
- Isaac
- Joyce
- Kirk
- Leslie
- Michael
- Nadine
- Oscar
- Patty
- Rafael
- Sandy
- Tony
- Valerie
- William

NAMES FOR HURRICANES IN 2007

- Andrea
- Barry
- Chantal
- Dean
- Erin
- Felix
- Gabrielle
- Humberto
- Ingrid
- Jerry
- Karen
- Lorenzo
- Olga
- Pablo
- Rebekah
- Sebastien
- Tanya
- Melissa
- Noel
- Van
- Wendy

BOOK OF LISTS

10 TYPES OF LIGHTNING

- Anvil
- Ball
- Bead
- Cloud to air
- Cloud to cloud
- Cloud to ground
- Forked
- Ribbon
- Sheet
- Staccato

Forked lightning

TEMPERATURE CONVERSIONS

Fahrenheit to Celsius . . . . . .subtract 32, multiply by 5 and divide by 9

Celsius to Fahrenheit . . . . . .multiply by 9, divide by 5 and add 32

10 degrees Celsius . . . . .50 degrees Fahrenheit

20 degrees Celsius . . . . .68 degrees Fahrenheit

30 degrees Celsius . . . . .86 degrees Fahrenheit

40 degrees Celsius . . . . .104 degrees Fahrenheit

50 degrees Celsius . . . . .122 degrees Fahrenheit

Absolute zero . . . .−273.1 degrees Celsius / −459.6 degrees Fahrenheit

SCIENCE

WEATHER FACTS

The South Pole has no sunshine for 182 days per year

The first official hurricane warning was issued by William Reed, Governor of Jamaica in 1847

An estimated 16 million thunderstorms hit the planet every year, an average of 44,000 daily

Windiest place on Earth . . . . Port Merton, Antarctica

Wettest place on Earth . . . . Mount Waialeale, Hawaii, an average annual rainfall of 12 metres

Driest place on Earth . . . . Atacama Desert, Chile, virtually no recorded rainfall

Largest recorded snowfall in a day . . . . Silver Lake, Colorado, April 1921, 1.8m (74ins)

Largest recorded hailstones . . . . Bangladesh, April 14 1986, weighing 1kg each

Highest ever recorded temperature . . . 58 degrees C, (136 F), Al Aziziyah, Libya, 1922

Lowest ever recorded temperature . . . . −89.6 degrees C (−128.6F) Vostock Station, Antarctica, 1983

Hailstones

Near side of the Moon

SCIENCE

10 SEAS ON THE MOON

- Sea of Cleverness
- Sea of Clouds
- Sea of Islands
- Sea of Moisture
- Sea of Nectar
- Sea of Serenity
- Sea of Showers
- Sea of Tranquillity
- Sea of Vapours
- Sea of Waves

NAMES FOR MONTHLY FULL MOONS

January . . . . Moon after Yule	**July** . . . . Hay moon
February . . . . Wolf moon	**August** . . . . Green corn moon
March . . . . Lenten moon	**September** . . . . . .Harvest moon
April . . . . Egg moon	**October** . . . . Hunter's moon
May . . . . Milk moon	**November** . . . . . . .Beaver's moon
June . . . . Strawberry moon	**December** . . . . . . .Moon before Yule

BOOK OF LISTS

A TO Z SELECTION OF BREEDS AND SPECIES

Alligator.... American, Black Caiman, Caiman, Chinese

Bat .... Fruit bat, Long-nosed bat, Pipistrelle, Vampire

Cow........ Aberdeen Angus, Danish red, Jersey, Highland, Piedmont, Texas longhorn

Duck....... Goldeneye, Harlequin, Mallard, Pintail, Shoveller, Teal

Eagle ...... Bald, Golden, Harpy, Sea

Fox .... Arctic, Desert, Fennec, Red

Goat .... Alpine, Angora, Boer, Cashmere, Nubian, Toggenburg

Horse...... Appaloosa, Clydesdale, Falabella, Lipizzaner, Shetland, Shire, Westphalian

Iguana ..... Desert, Dwarf, Green, Land, Rhinoceros, Rock

Jellyfish.... Appalachian Mountain, Arctic lion's mane, Freshwater, Portuguese Man o'War

Kangaroo... Eastern grey, Red, Tree, Western grey

Llama ...... Alpaca, Guanaco, South American

Common caiman

SCIENCE

Monkey .... Capuchin, Guenon, Macaque, Spider, Squirrel

Newt .... Crested, Pamlate, Smooth

Owl .... Barking, Barn, Eagle, Elf, Morepork, Pygmy, Screech

Pig .... Berkshire, Large Black Devon, Tamworth, Wessex saddleback

Quail .... Button, Gambel, Pharaoh, Tennessee red

Rabbit ..... Angora, Netherland dwarf, Siberian, Swiss fox

Sheep ...... Cheviot, Lincoln, Oxford, Ryeland, Wiltshire horn

Turkey ..... Bourbon, Broad-breasted bronze, Narragansett, Royal palm

Vole .... Californian, Field, Orkney, Prairie, Water

Walrus ..... Atlantic, Pacific

Yak .... Pali, Plateau grassland, Valley

Zebra ...... Abyssinian, Grevy, Mountain, Plains

Barn owl

ALTERNATIVE NAMES FOR ANIMALS AND PLANTS

Aardvark . . . . .Ant bear

Antirrhinum . . . . .Snapdragon

Beluga . . . . .Russian sturgeon

Bluebell . . . . .Wild hyacinth

Bush baby . . . . .Galago

Carnation . . . . .Gillyflower

Courgette . . . . .Zucchini

Coyote . . . . .Prairie wolf

Deadly nightshade . . . . . .Belladonna

Delphinium . . . . .Larkspur

Dogfish . . . . .Rock salmon

Dromedary . . . . .Arabian camel

Dugong . . . . .Sea cow

Gladiolus . . . . .Sword lily

Gnu . . . . .Wildebeest

Groundhog . . . . .Woodchuck

Gypsophila . . . . .Baby's breath

Hedge sparrow . . . . .Dunnock

Kookaburra . . . . .Laughing jackass

Muntjac . . . . .Barking deer

Ocelot . . . . .Painted leopard

Okra . . . . .Gumbo or Ladies' fingers

Ounce . . . . .Snow leopard

Puffin

SCIENCE

ALTERNATIVE NAMES FOR ANIMALS AND PLANTS

Pangolin . . . . .Scaly ant-eater

Puffin . . . . .Sea parrot

Shrike . . . . .Butcherbird

Termite . . . . .White ant

Viper . . . . .Adder

Wolverine . . . . .Glutton

Yaffle . . . . .Green woodpecker

Groundhogs

CHEMICAL NAMES FOR EVERYDAY ITEMS

COMMON NAME	CHEMICAL NAME
Antifreeze	Ethylene glycol
Asbestos	Magnesium silicate
Aspirin	Acetylsalicylic acid
Baking powder	Sodium bicarbonate
Bleach	Sodium hypochlorite
Carbolic acid	Phenol
Caustic soda	Sodium hydroxide
Chalk	Calcium carbonate
Chloroform	Trichloromethane
Dry ice	Solid carbon dioxide
Epsom salts	Magnesium sulphate
Fool's gold	Iron pyrites
Heavy water	Deuterium oxide
Laughing gas	Nitrous oxide
Lime	Calcium oxide
Mothballs	Naphthalene
Plaster of Paris	Calcium sulphate
PVC	Polyvinyl chloride
Rust	Iron oxide
Salt	Sodium chloride
Saltpetre	Potassium nitrate
Sand	Silicon dioxide
TNT	Trinitrotoluene
Vinegar	Acetic acid
Vitamin C	Ascorbic acid
Washing soda	Sodium carbonate

Rust

SCIENCE

10 HOUSEHOLD INVENTIONS

Burglar alarm	Edwin Holmes	1858
Electric drill	Wilhelm Fein	1895
Electric razor	Jacob Schick	1931
Food processor	Kenneth Wood	1947
Gas fire	Philippe Lebon	1799
Linoleum	Frederick Watson	1860
Microwave oven	Percy Spencer	1945
Non-stick pan	Marc Gregoir	1954
Pressure cooker	Denis Papin	1679
Refrigerator	Alexander Twinning & James Harrison	1850

10 SIMPLE INVENTIONS WE COULD NOT DO WITHOUT

Aerosol	Erik Rotheim	1926
Aspirin	Heinrich Kolbe	1859
Cat's eyes	Percy Shaw	1933
Credit card	Ralph Scheider	1950
Elastic bands	Stephen Perry	1845
Instant coffee	Nestle	1937
Match	Robert Boyle	1680
Paper clip	Johann Vaaler	1900
Safety pin	Walter Hunt	1849
Safety razor	King Camp Gillette	1895

BOOK OF LISTS

ANIMAL SIMILES

- As angry as a hornet
- As bald as a coot
- As blind as a bat
- As brave as a lion
- As busy as a bee
- As crazy as a loon
- As dead as a dodo
- As drunk as a skunk
- As eager as a beaver
- As free as a bird
- As graceful as a gazelle
- As hairy as a gorilla
- As happy as a lark
- As hungry as a horse
- As lame as a duck
- As loose as a goose
- As mad as a March hare
- As meek as a lamb
- As naked as a jaybird
- As poor as a church mouse
- As proud as a peacock
- As quiet as a mouse
- As sick as a dog
- As slippery as an eel
- As slow as a snail
- As sly as a fox
- As snug as a bug in a rug
- As strong as an ox
- As stubborn as a mule
- As weak as a kitten
- As wise as an owl

As blind as a bat

SCIENCE

FLOWER POWER

COUNTRY	NATIONAL FLOWER	COUNTRY	NATIONAL FLOWER
Argentina	Ceibo	Luxembourg	Rose
Austria	Edelweiss	Malaysia	Hibiscus
Australia	Wattle	Mexico	Dahlia
Bangladesh	Water Lily	Monaco	Carnation
Barbados	Dwarf Poinciana	Nepal	Rhododendron
Belgium	Red poppy	Netherlands	Tulip
Brazil	Orchid	New Zealand	Kowhai
Bulgaria	Rose	Norway	Purple Heather
Canada	Maple leaf	Pakistan	Jasmine
Chile	Copihue	Portugal	Lavender
China	Peong	Russia	Camomile
Cuba	Butterfly flower	Scotland	Thistle
Denmark	Marguerite daisy	Singapore	Orchid
Egypt	Lotus	South Africa	Protea
England	Rose	Sweden	Linnea
Estonia	Cornflower	Switzerland	Edelweiss
Finland	Lily of the valley	Turkey	Tulip
France	Fleur de lys	Ukraine	Sunflower
Germany	Cornflower	USA	Rose
India	Lotus	Venezuela	Orchid
Ireland	Shamrock	Wales	Daffodil
Japan	Chrysanthemum	Zimbabwe	Flame lily

BOOK OF LISTS

STATE FLOWERS OF THE USA

Alabama . . . . .Camellia

Alaska . . . . .Forget-me-not

Arizona . . . . .Giant cactus

Arkansas . . . . .Apple blossom

California . . . . .Golden poppy

Colorado . . . . .Columbine

Connecticut . . . . . . .Mountain laurel

Delaware . . . . .Peach blossom

Florida . . . . .Orange blossom

Georgia . . . . .Cherokee rose

Hawaii . . . . .Hibiscus

Idaho . . . . .Lewis mock orange

Illinois . . . . .Violet

Indiana . . . . .Peony

Pine cone

Iowa . . . . Prairie rose

Kansas . . . . Sunflower

Kentucky . . . . Goldenrod

Louisiana . . . . Magnolia

Maine . . . . Pine cone

Maryland . . . . Black-eyed Susan

Massachusetts . . Trailing arbutus

Michigan . . . . Apple blossom

Minnesota . . . . . . Lady's slipper

Californian golden poppy

SCIENCE

STATE FLOWERS OF THE USA

Mississippi . . . . Magnolia

Missouri . . . . Hawthorn

Montana . . . . Bitterro

Nebraska . . . . Goldenrod

Nevada . . . . Sagebrush

New Hampshire . . . . . Purple lilac

New Jersey . . . . Violet

New Mexico . . . . Yucca

New York . . . . Rose

North Carolina . . . . . Dogwood

North Dakota . . . . . . Prairie rose

Ohio . . . . Carnation

Oklahoma . . . . Mistletoe

Lady's slipper

Oregon . . . . Oregon grape

Pennsylvania . . . . Mountain laurel

Rhode Island . . . . Violet

South Carolina . . Jessamine

South Dakota . . . Pasque

Tennessee . . . . . . Iris

Texas . . . . Bluebonnet

Utah . . . . Lily

Vermont . . . . Clover

Virginia . . . . Dogwood

Washington . . . . . Rhododendron

West Virginia . . . Rhododendron

Wisconsin . . . . . . Violet

Wyoming . . . . Indian paintbrush

Iris

BOOK OF LISTS

HOME SWEET HOME

ANIMAL	HOME
Ant	Formicary
Badger	Sett
Bat	Roost
Bear	Den
Beaver	Lodge
Bee	Apiary or hive
Eagle	Eyrie
Fox	Earth
Hare	Down or form
Lion	Den
Mole	Fortress
Otter	Holt
Penguin	Rookery
Rabbit	Burrow or warren
Snake	Nest
Squirrel	Drey
Termite	Mound
Tiger	Lair
Wasp	Vespiary
Wolf	Lair

Termite mound

SCIENCE

ANIMAL ETYMOLOGY

ANIMAL	NAME FROM
Aardvark	Dutch for 'earth pig'
Armadillo	Spanish word armado meaning 'armoured'
Budgerigar	Aboriginal for 'good cockatoo'
Dodo	Portuguese for 'stupid'
Giraffe	Latin name *camelopardalis* meaning 'leopard-like camel'
Hippopotamus	Greek words for horse (*hippo*) and river (*potamus*)
Koala	Aboriginal for 'no drink'
Orang-utan	Malay for 'man of the forest'
Porcupine	French for 'spiny pig'
Rhinoceros	Greek for 'nose horn'

Orang-utan

MEANINGS OF DINOSAUR NAMES

DINOSAUR NAME	MEANING
Brachiosaurus	Arm lizard
Brontosaurus	Thunder lizard
Diplodocus	Double-beamed
Ichthyosaurus	Fish lizard

Triceratops

Pterodactyl	Wing finger
Scelidosaurus	Limb lizard
Stegosaurus	Roof lizard
Triceratops	Three-horned face
Tyrannosaurus Rex	Tyrant lizard king
Velociraptor	Speedy thief

SCIENCE

HUMAN BODY

The tongue is the only muscle in the human body not attached at both ends

It takes 17 muscles to smile and 43 to frown

85% of the human brain is comprised of water

A sneeze can exceed speeds of 160km per hour

A baby in the womb acquires fingerprints at the age of three months

The smallest muscle in the human body is the stapedius, located in the middle ear

The strongest muscle in the human body is the masseter, at the back of the jaw

The rarest blood group in the world is A-H

The brain uses a quarter of all the body's oxygen

The hardest substance in the human body is enamel, the outer layer of a tooth

Stapedius

ANIMAL KINGDOM

Polar bear

The camel is the only mammal that possesses oval blood cells

An armadillo always gives birth to twins

The skin of a polar bear is black

The giraffe is the only mammal to be born with two horns

Rats are unable to vomit

The koala bear has fingerprints that are almost identical to those of humans

The tongue of a chameleon is almost twice the length of its body

A newborn kangaroo measures around 2.54cm (1ins) in length

Dogs and humans are the only animals with prostate glands

Only female mosquitoes bite

BOOK OF LISTS

WEIGHTS OF ANIMALS' BRAINS

ANIMAL	BRAIN WEIGHT
Baboon	140gm
Camel	680gm
Cat	30gm
Chimpanzee	420gm
Cow	500gm
Dog	72gm
Dolphin	1700gm
Frog	0.1gm
Giraffe	680gm
Horse	530gm
Human	1400gm
Kangaroo	56gm
Lion	240gm
Owl	2.2gm
Porcupine	25gm
Rabbit	12gm
Racoon	39gm
Rat	2gm
Sheep	140gm
Sperm whale	7800gm (the largest brain in the animal kingdom)

Human brain

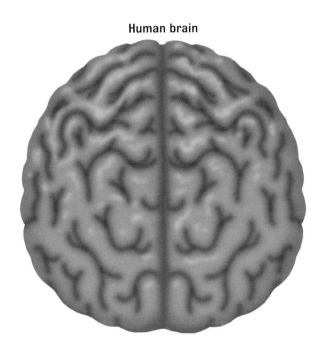

SCIENCE

HOW MANY – HUMAN BODY?

- Humans have 206 bones
- 300 bones as babies
- 33 vertebrae
- An average pulse rate of 70 to 80 beats per minute
- 3000 taste buds on their tongue
- 230 joints
- 100,000 hairs on an average scalp
- 23 pairs of chromosomes
- 365 acupuncture points
- 32 teeth in a full adult set, 12 molars, 8 pre-molars, 8 incisors, 4 canines

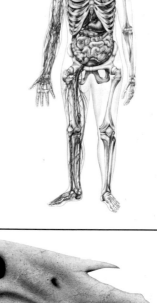

Human anatomy

HOW MANY – ANIMAL KINGDOM?

An ostrich has two toes on each foot

An elephant has four teeth

A cow has four stomachs

Bees have five eyes

Ants have five noses

Shrimps and lobsters both have ten legs

A male horse has 40 teeth, a female has 36

A crayfish has 200 chromosomes

A porcupine boasts over 30,000 quills

A giraffe has just seven bones in its neck, the same as humans

Horse teeth

BOOK OF LISTS

DOCTORS AND DISEASES

DOCTOR	SPECIALIZES IN
Cardiologist	Heart disease
Dermatologist	Skin
Gynaecologist	Female reproduction
Haematologist	Blood
Histologist	Cells and tissue
Nephrologist	Kidneys
Neurologist	Nervous system
Ophthalmologist	Eyes
Otologist	Ears
Paediatrician	Children

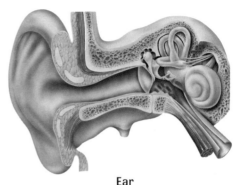

Ear

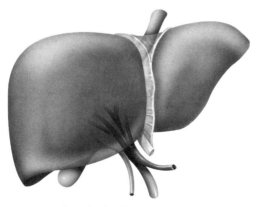

Liver

DISEASE	AFFECTS
Arthritis	Joints
Cirrhosis	Liver
Conjunctivitis	Eyes
Cystitis	Bladder
Dermatitis	Skin
Gingivitis	Gums
Hepatitis	Liver
Meningitis	Brain
Phlebitis	Veins
Pneumonia	Lungs

SCIENCE

COMMON NAMES FOR DISEASES AND CONDITIONS

BSE . . . . Mad-cow disease

Bursitis . . . . Housemaid's knee

Enuresis . . . . Bed-wetting

Epidemic parotitis . . . . Mumps

Epistaxis . . . . Nose bleed

Haemorrhoids . . . . Piles

Herpes Labialis . . . . Cold sore

Herpes Zoster . . . . Shingles

Hydrophobia . . . . Rabies

Hypermetropia . . . . Long-sightedness

Infantile osteomalacia . . . . . . Rickets

Infectious mononucleosis . . . Glandular fever

Myopia . . . . Short-sightedness

Pertussis . . . . Whooping cough

Pyrosis . . . . Heartburn

Rubella . . . . German measles

Rubeola . . . . Measles

Scrivener's palsy . . . . Writer's cramp

Somnambulism . . . . Sleep walking

Sydenham's Chorea . . . . St Vitus' Dance

Tinae Pedis . . . . Athlete's foot

Varicella . . . . Chickenpox

Variola . . . . Smallpox

Somnambulism

BOOK OF LISTS

A BONY BUNCH

Ankle bone	Talus
Bones of the arm	Upper arm humerus, lower arm radius and ulna
Breast bone	Sternum
Collar bone	Clavicle
Knee cap	Patella
Lower jaw bone	Mandible
Upper jaw bone	Maxilla
Shin bone	Tibia
Shoulder blade	Scapula
Skull	Cranium
Upper leg	Femur
Bones around the ankle	Tarsals
Bones in the foot	Metatarsals
Bones in the wrist	Carpals
Bones in the hand	Metacarpals
Fingers and toes	Phalanges

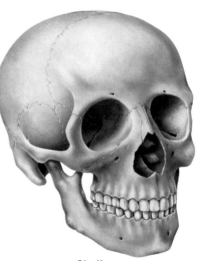

Skull

Longest bone in the human body	Femur
Smallest bone in the human body	Ossicles in the middle ear
Hardest bone in the human body	Jaw bone
Only bone not connected to another bone	Hyoid, located between mandible and the larynx
Last bone to mature	Clavicle

SCIENCE

PARTS OF THE HEART

- Aorta, the largest artery in the human body
- Anterior vena cava
- Posterior vena cava
- Left and right atrium (the upper chambers)
- Left and right ventricle (the lower chambers)
- Pulmonary artery
- Pulmonary vein
- Semilunar valve
- Atrioventricular valve
- Septum (wall dividing the two halves of the heart)

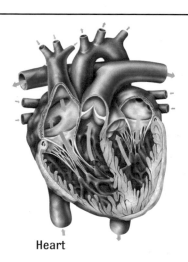

Heart

HEARTBEAT

Blue whale . . . . 5 to 6 beats per minute
Elephant . . . . .25 to 40
Horse . . . . .40 to 45
Puppy . . . . .120 to 160
Cat . . . . .160 to 220
Rabbit . . . . .200 to 210
Hamster . . . . .440 to 460
Mouse . . . . .600 to 700
Canary . . . . .960 to 1000
Hummingbird . . . . . .1200 to 1260

Hummingbird

CALORIES BURNED IN EVERYDAY ACTIVITIES

Kissing for one minute . . . . 30 calories

Sleeping . . . . 60 per hour

Watching television . . . . 75 per hour

Standing in a queue . . . . 100 per hour

Driving . . . . 120 per hour

Ironing clothes . . . . 150 per hour

Repairing the car . . . . 200 per hour

Gentle stroll . . . . 220 per hour

Cleaning the house . . . . 240 per hour

Climbing stairs . . . . 300 per hour

Digging the garden . . . . 360 per hour

Skating . . . . 360 per hour

Rock climbing . . . . 390 per hour

Mowing the lawn . . . . 400 per hour

Dancing . . . . 400 per hour

Playing tennis . . . . 420 per hour

Playing football . . . . 650 per hour

Swimming . . . . 720 per hour

Skipping with a rope . . . . 750 per hour

Jogging at 7 miles per hour . . . 920 per hour

Rock climbing

SCIENCE

BIRDS OF A FEATHER

Emus are unable to walk backwards

The first bird to be domesticated by man was the goose

The bones of a pigeon weigh less than its feathers

There are more chickens in the world than people

The swan is the only bird to possess a penis

Goose

OSTRICH ODDITIES

Ostrich fossils have been found dating back over 120 million years

The brain of an ostrich is smaller than its eye

An ostrich is the fastest animal on land on two legs

The ostrich is the only bird that gives us leather

Ostrich eggs are the largest eggs in the world and would take 40 minutes to hard boil

10 FLIGHTLESS BIRDS

- Ostrich
- Emu
- Kiwi
- Cassowary
- Rhea
- Penguin
- Kakapo
- Steamer duck
- Weka
- Calayan rail

BOOK OF LISTS

STATE BIRDS OF THE USA

STATE	BIRD	STATE	BIRD
Alabama	Yellowhammer	Montana	Western meadowlark
Alaska	Ptarmigan	Nebraska	Western meadowlark
Arizona	Cactus wren	Nevada	Bluebird
Arkansas	Mockingbird	New Hampshire	Purple finch
California	Valley quail	New Jersey	Goldfinch
Colorado	Lark bunting	New Mexico	Roadrunner
Connecticut	Robin	New York	Bluebird
Delaware	Blue hen chicken	North Carolina	Cardinal
Florida	Mockingbird	North Dakota	Western meadowlark
Georgia	Thrasher	Ohio	Cardinal
Hawaii	Hawaiian goose	Oklahoma	Scissortailed fly catcher
Idaho	Mountain bluebird	Oregon	Western meadowlark
Illinois	Cardinal	Pennsylvania	Grouse
Indiana	Cardinal	Rhode Island	Rhode Island red
Iowa	Goldfinch	South Carolina	Wren
Kansas	Western meadowlark	South Dakota	Pheasant
Kentucky	Cardinal	Tennessee	Mockingbird
Louisiana	Pelican	Texas	Mockingbird
Maine	Chickadee	Utah	Seagull
Maryland	Baltimore oriole	Vermont	Thrush
Massachusetts	Chickadee	Virginia	Cardinal
Michigan	Robin	Washington	Goldfinch
Minnesota	Loon	West Virginia	Cardinal
Mississippi	Mockingbird	Wisconsin	Robin
Missouri	Bluebird	Wyoming	Meadowlark

SCIENCE

INSECT INFO

The average lifespan of a dragonfly is 24 hours

The dragonfly is nicknamed the Devil's darning needle

The praying mantis is the only creature on the planet that is born with one ear

A caterpillar has over 2000 muscles in its body

The butterfly was originally called a flutterby

Mosquitoes are the world's deadliest creatures. The World Health Organization estimates that the diseases transmitted by their bites are responsible for over 2 million deaths each year

You are more likely to be bitten by a mosquito if you have blonde hair, wear blue clothes and eat bananas

The ant has the largest brain in the animal kingdom in proportion to the size of its body

The hum of a housefly is in the key of F

Spiders have eight legs, eight eyes and it is estimated that humans eat eight spiders in their lifetime during sleep

BEETLEMANIA

The heaviest insect in the animal kingdom is the Goliath beetle weighing over 110gms

The beetle is the largest order of animals on Earth with over 300,000 different species

A cockroach can survive for up to a week minus its head

Breeds of tropical cockroach can travel 50 times their body length in the space of a second, equivalent to an athlete running 100m in one second

Beetles taste like apples

SOMETHING FISHY

The age of a fish can be estimated by examining growth rings called ciruli on its scales

The female mackerel can lay up to half a million eggs at one time

Over 90% of all fish caught are caught in the Northern hemisphere

The Dwarf Gobi, at 8mm long, is the world's smallest vertebrate

A pregnant goldfish is known as a twit

Whale shark

SCIENCE

SHARK ATTACK

A shark's skeleton is comprised of cartilage

The largest shark at 15m long is the whale shark, the smallest at a mere 12.5cm is the dwarf shark

The great white shark can dislocate its own jaw to allow it to catch more fish

Sharkskin, known as shagreen, has in the past been used as sandpaper

The only species of freshwater shark are found in Lake Nicaragua in Central America

UNDER THE SEA

Dolphins always sleep with one eye open

The pupil of the eye of an octopus is rectangular

The giant squid is the world's largest invertebrate and also boasts the largest eyes in the animal kingdom, with a diameter of 40cm

The starfish has no brain and can turn itself inside out

A jellyfish has no brain, no eyes, no ears, no bones, no heart and consists of 95% water

The heart of a shrimp is located in its head

Oysters change sex annually

Starfish

The seahorse is the world's only species of animal whereby the male becomes pregnant

Large electric eels can produce shocks in excess of 650 volts of electricity

The whistle of the blue whale, at 188 decibels, is the loudest sound produced by any animal

BOOK OF LISTS

FUN WITH NUMBERS

The numbers on a roulette wheel add up to 666

The opposite side of a dice always adds up to 7

111, 222, 333, 444, 555, 666, 777, 888, 999 are all multiples of 37

1961 was the last year to read the same upside down as the right way up

The next year to read the same upside down as the right way up will be 6009

111111111 multiplied by 111111111 = 12345678987654321

There are 31,557,600 seconds in a year

Back in a jiffy? A jiffy is an actual period of time, equating to 1/100th of a second

There are only 12 letters in the Hawaiian alphabet

73,939,133 is a prime number, meaning that it is only divisible by 1 and itself. Remove the last number seven times and in each case the number remaining is a prime number. 7,393,913 is a prime number, 739,391 is a prime number and so on down to 7, which is a prime number

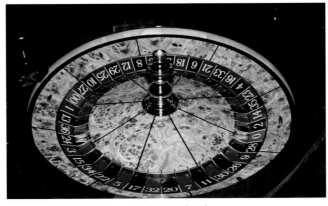

Roulette wheel

SCIENCE

WHAT ARE THE ODDS?

- Odds of giving birth to identical twins. . . . . 285 – 1
- Odds of giving birth to triplets . . . . 8100 – 1
- Odds of giving birth to quadruplets . . . . 729,000 – 1
- Odds of being struck by lightning . . . . 800,000 – 1
- Odds of being dealt a royal flush in poker . . . . . 649,739 – 1

Identical twins

Odds of winning the UK National Lottery

- The six main numbers . . . . 13,983,816 – 1
- Five numbers and bonus ball . . . . 2,330,636 – 1
- Five numbers . . . . 55,492 – 1
- Four numbers . . . . 1,033 – 1
- Three numbers. . . . . 57 – 1

Therefore you have more chance of being struck by lightning that winning the UK National Lottery Jackpot!

BOOK OF LISTS

WHAT'S YOUR IQ?

In 1916, Alfred Binet developed the IQ intelligence scale with the following guidelines

130 + ...Very superior

120 to 129 . . . . .Superior

110 to 119 . . . . .Above average

90 to 109 . . . . .Average

80 to 89 . . . . .Below average

70 to 79 . . . . .Borderline

Below 70 . . . . .Extremely low

FAMOUS PEOPLE WITH HIGH IQS

Madonna 140

Geena Davis 140

Al Gore 140

Hugh Hefner 152

Sharon Stone 154

Carol Vorderman . . .154

Clive Sinclair 159

Quentin Tarantino . . .160

Bill Gates 160

Jill St John 162

Bill Gates

SCIENCE

ESTIMATED IQ OF PEOPLE OF THE PAST

George Washington 118

Napoleon Bonaparte 145

Captain James Cook 160

Albert Einstein 160

Charles Darwin 165

Dr David Livingstone 170

Charles Dickens 180

Michelangelo 180

Sir Isaac Newton 190

Leonardo da Vinci 220

Leonardo da Vinci

Charles Darwin

RECORD-BREAKERS IN NATURE

Tallest land mammal . . . . Giraffe

Largest mammal . . . . Blue whale

Heaviest land mammal . . . . African elephant

Largest fish . . . . Whale shark

Largest land carnivore . . . . Polar bear

Largest feline . . . . Siberian tiger

Largest deer . . . . Alaskan moose

Largest rodent . . . . Capybara

Largest butterfly . . . . Queen Alexandra's bird wing

Largest bird . . . . Ostrich

Largest flower . . . . Rafflesia

Longest snake . . . . Reticulated python

Smallest horse . . . . Falabella

Smallest bird . . . . Bee hummingbird

Fastest land mammal . . . . Cheetah

Slowest land mammal . . . . Three-toed sloth

Most poisonous fish . . . . Stone fish

Most poisonous snake . . . . Gaboon viper

Most poisonous jellyfish . . . . . . Australian sea wasp

Loudest insect . . . . African cicada

Giraffes

SCIENCE

HOW HARD?

In 1812, Frederich Mohs devised the Mohs scale of hardness, 1 for the least hard and 10 for the hardest. He selected ten minerals available at the time to represent each level:

1   Talcum powder
2   Gypsum
3   Calcite
4   Fluorite
5   Apatite
6   Orthoclase
7   Quartz
8   Topaz
9   Corundum
10   Diamond

Talcum powder

Gypsum

Calcite

Fluorite

Apatite

Orthoclase

Quartz

Topaz

Corundum

Diamond

BOOK OF LISTS

HOW HOT?

In 1912, Wilbur Scoville developed the Scoville test to measure the heat levels in chillies:

0 to 5000 . . . . .Mild

5000 to 20,000 . . . . .Medium

20,000 to 70,000 . . . . .Hot

70,000 to 300,000 . . . . . . .Extreme

SOME CHILLIES AND THEIR RATINGS

Anaheim . . . . .1000 to 1400

Jalapeno . . . . .3500 to 4500

Cayenne 35,000

Tabasco . . . . .30,000 to 50,000

Red Amazon 75,000

Habernero . . . . . . .200,000 to 300,000

SCIENCE

BIRTH FLOWERS

January	Carnation
February	Primrose
March	Violet
April	Daisy
May	Lily of the valley
June	Rose
July	Water lily
August	Poppy
September	Aster
October	Marigold
November	Chrysanthemum
December	Narcissus

BIRTHSTONES

January	Garnet
February	Amethyst
March	Aquamarine
April	Diamond
May	Emerald
June	Pearl
July	Ruby
August	Peridot
September	Sapphire
October	Opal
November	Topaz
December	Turquoise

PEOPLE OF THE PAST WITH FATHERLY NICKNAMES

The Father of Antiseptics . . . . Joseph Lister

The Father of the Atomic Bomb . . . . . Robert Oppenheimer

The Fathers of Aviation . . . . The Wright Brothers

The Father of Bacteriology . . . . Louis Pasteur

The Father of Frozen Food . . . . Clarence Birdseye

The Father of the Helicopter . . . . Igor Sikorsky

The Father of the Hydrogen Bomb . . Edward Teller

The Father of Immunology . . . . Edward Jenner

The Father of Medicine . . . . Hippocrates

The Father of Modern Chemistry . . . Antoine Lavoisier

The Father of Modern Philosophy . . . René Descartes

The Father of Numbers . . . . Pythagoras

The Father of Penicillin . . . . Alexander Fleming

The Father of Plastic . . . . Leo Baekeland

The Father of Pottery . . . . Josiah Wedgwood

The Father of Printing . . . . William Caxton

The Father of Psychoanalysis . . . . . . Sigmund Freud

The Father of the Railway . . . . George Stephenson

The Father of the Telephone . . . . Alexander Graham Bell

The Father of Television . . . . John Logie Baird

Wright brothers

SCIENCE

ALLOY, ALLOY, ALLOY

ALLOY	CONSTITUENTS
Brass	Copper, zinc
Bronze	Copper, tin
Cupronickel	Copper, nickel
Duraluminium	Aluminium, copper, manganese, magnesium
Electrum	Gold, silver, copper
Solder	Tin, lead
Stainless steel	Iron, chromium, nickel
Stellite	Cobalt, chromium, tungsten, carbon
Sterling silver	Silver, copper

THE CHEMICAL FORMULAE OF EVERDAY ITEMS

Alcohol	C_2H_5OH
Butane	C_4H_{10}
Caffeine	$C_8H_{10}N_4O_2$
Chalk	$CaCO_3$
Glucose	$C_6H_{12}O_6$
Methane	CH_4
Nicotine	$C_{10}H_{14}N_2$
Salt	$NaCl$
Vinegar	CH_3COOH
Vitamin C	$C_6H_8O_6$

Caffeine

BOOK OF LISTS

FAMOUS PEOPLE AND THEIR CATS

Warren Beatty . . . . Cake

Winston Churchill . . . . Blackie

Bill Clinton . . . . Socks

James Dean . . . . Marcus

Charles Dickens. . . . . Williamina

Linda Evans. . . . . She

F Scott Fitzgerald . . . . Chopin

Anne Frank. . . . . Moortje

Ernest Hemingway. . . . . Dillinger

Cyndi Lauper . . . . Weasel

Marilyn Monroe. . . . . Mitsou

Florence Nightingale. . . . . . Bismarck

Edgar Allen Poe . . . . Catarina

Ronald Reagan. . . . . Sara

Theodore Roosevelt . . . . Slippers

Sir Walter Scott. . . . . Hinse

OJ Simpson. . . . . Sheena

Harriet Beecher Stowe. . . . . Calvin

Andy Warhol . . . . Hester

Tennessee Williams. . . . . Topaz

SCIENCE

THE RAT PACK

A group of rats is called a mischief

Rats have no tonsils and no gall bladder

Rats are actually allergic to cheese

A male rat is called a buck

The rat is the first symbol in the Chinese zodiac

The gestation period of a rat is 21 days

Rats can last longer without water than a camel

Research at the University of Wisconsin in 1998 showed that rats were mentally stimulated by classical music

Rats are the first to desert a sinking ship. When sailing vessels were made of wood, rats nested in the hold and were the first to know if a leak had developed

20 SPECIES OF RAT

- Brown rat
- Rice rat
- Field rat
- Black Rat
- Norwegian rat
- Kangaroo rat
- Polynesian rat
- Indian mole rat
- Bamboo rat
- Yellow-nosed cotton rat
- Hairless rat
- Cape mole rat
- Bushy-tailed wood rat
- River rat
- White-throated wood rat
- Naked mole rat
- Gambian giant pouched rat
- Fancy rat
- Dusky-footed wood rat
- Tawny-bellied cotton rat

Naked mole rat

BOOK OF LISTS

PRODUCTS OF PLANTS

PRODUCT	PLANT OBTAINED FROM
Amber	Pine tree resin
Chewing gum	Sapodilla tree
Cocoa	Cacao plant
Cork	Cork oak tree
Copra	Coconut
Digitalis	Foxglove
Gin	Flavoured from juniper berries
Hessian	Jute
Kirsch	Cherries
Linen	Flax
Linseed oil	Flax
Opium	Opium poppy
Quinine	Cinchona bark
Rum	Distilled from the molasses of sugar beet
Saffron	Crocus
Sake	Rice
Sarsaparilla	Smilax plant
Tapioca	Cassava plant
Tequila	Agave
Turmeric	Curcuma plant

Cacao plant

SCIENCE

GEMS

ORGANIC	PRECIOUS	SEMI-PRECIOUS
Coral	Diamond	Amethyst
Jet	Emerald	Garnet
Pearl	Ruby	Moonstone
Amber	Sapphire	Quartz

Ruby

10 FAMOUS GEMS

Cullinan diamond . . . . Set in the imperial sceptre of the British crown jewels

Cullinan II diamond . . . Set in the imperial state crown of British monarchs

Delong Star Ruby . . . . . Currently resides at the Natural History Museum in New York

Hixon Ruby Crystal . . . On display at the Natural History Museum, Los Angeles

Hope Diamond . . . . The largest blue diamond in the world, on display in Washington, DC

Koh-i-Noor . . . . 108-carat diamond at the centre of the crown of the British royal family

Midnight Star Ruby . . . On display at the Natural History Museum, New York

Star of Asia . . . . 329.7 carat sapphire on display at the Smithsonian Institute

Star of Bombay . . . . . . Sapphire, once given to Mary Pickford by her husband Douglas Fairbanks Snr, later bequeathed to the Smithsonian Institute

Star of India . . . . 563.5 carats, the world's largest sapphire

State crown and Koh-i-Noor diamond

ASTRONOMY GLOSSARY

Aurora	Spectacular show of light in the night sky, caused by the particles of the Sun striking the Earth's atmosphere
Baily's Beads	Small beads of sunlight that appear before a solar eclipse
Blue Dwarf	Star of a high temperature
Cassini's Division	Gap between the rings of Saturn
Magnitude	The measured brightness of stars
Nebula	Cloud caused by a cluster of stars
Nova	A star that brightens suddenly, giving the impression that a new star has been created
Supernova	Explosion that destroys a star
Red Dwarf	A fainter star
White Dwarf	A dying star

Aurora

190

SCIENCE

15 ASTRONOMERS ROYAL

- John Flamsteed
- Edmund Halley
- James Bradley
- Nathaniel Bliss
- Nevil Maskelyne
- John Pond
- Sir George Airy
- Sir William Christie
- Sir Frank Dyson
- Sir Harold Jones
- Sir Richard Woolley
- Sir Martin Ryle
- Sir Francis Graham-Smith
- Sir Arnold Wolfendale
- Sir Martin Rees

HALLEY'S COMET

Appeared in 1066 and is depicted on the Bayeux Tapestry

Its orbit was first computed by Edmund Halley and it returns every 76 years

The comet last appeared in 1986 and will reappear in 2062

Mark Twain was born and died in the years of the comet's appearances of 1835 and 1910

Bayeux Tapestry

ORIGINS OF DOG BREED NAMES

BREED	NAMED AFTER
Airedale terrier	Aire Valley in Yorkshire
Alsatian	The region of Alsace Lorraine
Basenji	The Swahili word meaning 'bush thing'
Basset hound	From the French word for 'low or dwarf'
Bloodhound	Named as its blood lines were kept pure for breeding purposes
Borzoi	From the Russian for 'swift'
Boxer	Derived from the German word for 'biter'
Chihuahua	The Mexican region of Chihuahua
Dalmatian	Adriatic coastal region of Dalmatia
Dandy Dinmont	Character in the 1814 Walter Scott novel, *Guy Mannering*
Daschund	German for 'badger dog', initially bred for hunting small game
Doberman	German tax collector Louis Dobermann, who developed the breed
Gordon Setter	Duke of Gordon in Scotland
Jack Russell	Reverend John Russell, whose terriers accompanied him on fox-hunting trips
King Charles Spaniel	King Charles II
Lhasa Apso	Lhasa, the capital of Tibet, originally bred as a guard dog for Tibetan monasteries
Newfoundland	Canadian island of Newfoundland
Pekinese	Peking, former name of Beijing
Pomeranian	Historical region of Pomerania, on the Baltic shores
Samoyed	A Siberian nomadic tribe

SCIENCE

IMPERIAL MEASURES

WEIGHT

16 drams in 1 ounce

16 ounces in 1 pound

14 pounds in 1 stone

2 stones in 1 quarter

4 quarters in 1 hundredweight

20 hundredweights in 1 ton

AREA

1 furlong x 1 pole = 1 rood

4 roods in 1 acre

4840 sq yards in 1 acre

640 acres in 1 sq mile

LENGTH

12 inches in 1 foot

4 inches in 1 hand

9 inches in 1 span

3 feet in 1 yard

22 yards in 1 chain

10 chains in 1 furlong

8 furlongs in 1 mile

1760 yards in 1 mile

LIQUID

5 fluid ounces in 1 gill

4 gills in 1 pint

2 pints in 1 quart

8 pints in 1 gallon

2 gallons in 1 peck

4 pecks in 1 bushel

Scales

BOOK OF LISTS

MYTHICAL BEASTS

Argus . . . . 100-eyed giant from Greek mythology

Banshee . . . . Spirit whose wailing foretold a death

Brownie . . . . Scottish goblin

Bunyip . . . . Flesh-eating beast that lived by billabongs and rivers in Aboriginal folklore

Centaur . . . . Half man, half horse

Cerberus . . . . Three-headed dog, guarding the entrance to Hades

Cyclops . . . . One-eyed cannibalistic giant

Faun . . . . Half man, half goat

Gorgon . . . . Bronze hands, golden wings and living snakes for hair

Griffin . . . . Head of a lion, wings and talons of an eagle

Harpy . . . . Half woman, half vulture

Hippocampus . . Half horse, half fish

Hydra . . . . Nine-headed serpent monster

Incubus . . . . Male demon that seeks sexual intercourse with sleeping women

Manticour . . . . . Lion's body, human head, scorpion's tail

Minotaur . . . . . . Half man, half bull

Niddhog . . . . Evil serpent from Norse mythology

Phoenix . . . . Bird reincarnated from its own ashes

Sphinx . . . . Body of a lion, head of a man

Succubus . . . . . . Female counterpart of an incubus

Unicorn . . . . Fabled equine creature possessing a single horn in the middle of its forehead

Cerberus

SCIENCE

NATIVE AMERICAN ANIMAL SYMBOLS

ANIMAL	SYMBOLIZES
Alligator	Aggression, adaptability and stealth
Ant	Teamwork and perseverance
Badger	Aggression and passion
Bear	Physical strength and leadership
Coyote	Bad luck omen
Crane	Independence
Deer	Gentleness and sensitivity
Dolphin	Kindness
Eagle	Divine spirit and protector from evil
Elk	Power and nobility
Fox	Cunning and intelligence
Moose	Integrity
Otter	Laughter and curiosity
Owl	Wisdom and truth
Porcupine	Innocence and trust
Salmon	Instinct and determination
Shark	Hunting prowess and survival
Swan	Innocence and grace
Turtle	Fertility
Wolf	Loyalty and success

Eagle

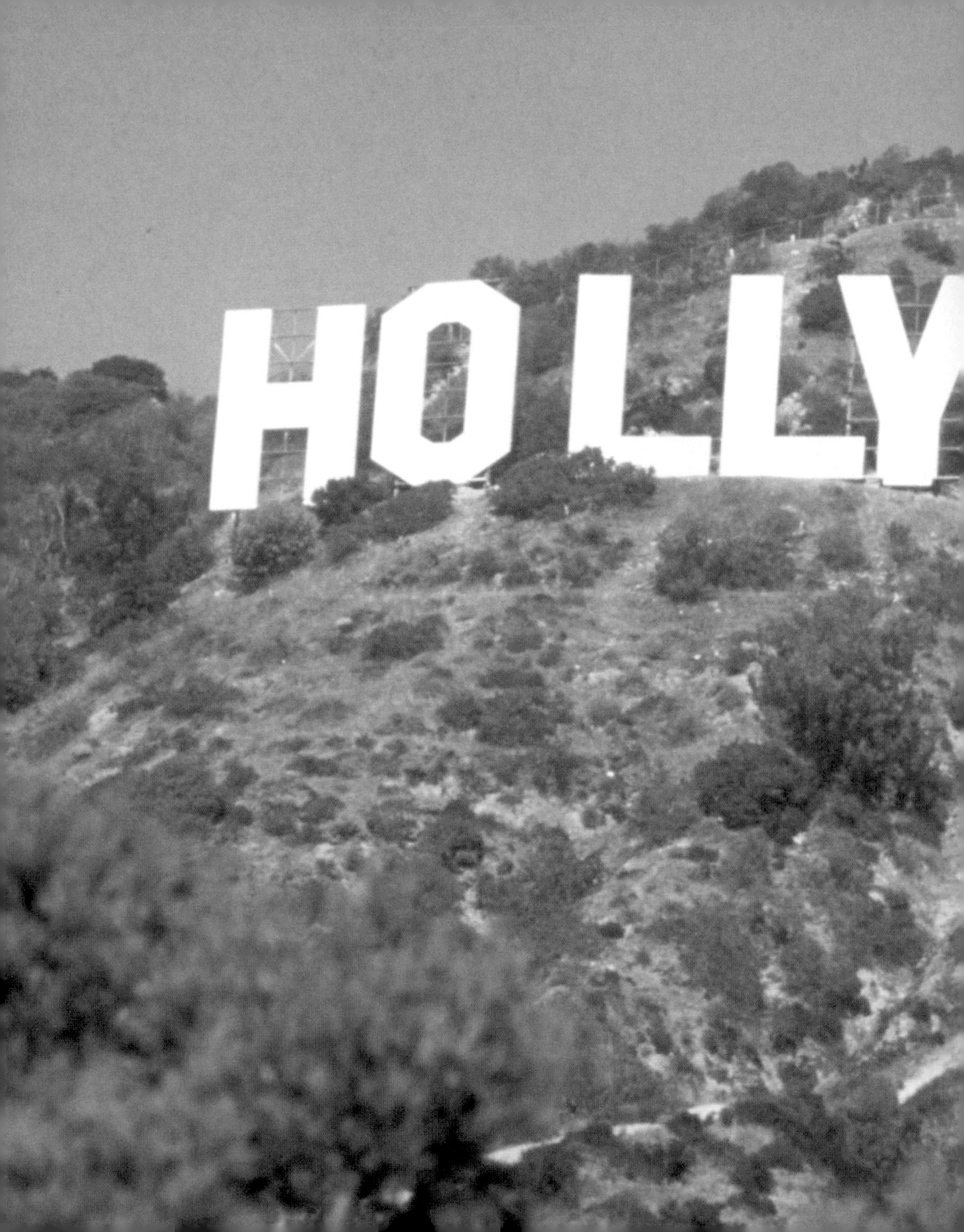
HOLLY

TV & FILM

Your knowledge of TV and film trivia will grow to King Kong proportions after a short time spent on the following 'lot'. You'll discover the names that Walt Disney *rejected* for his seven dwarfs, the Jedi code of honour, the names of all the Bond girls, the taglines for some highly promoted movies, famous holders of 'Razzie' awards, the surprising real names of the stars, the last words spoken from some notable films and even the full addresses of everything from the Addams Family to The Simpsons. And this is just a rehearsal!

FILM FIRSTS

1927	'Talkie'	*The Jazz Singer*
1928	Best Film Oscar	*Wings*
1937	Feature-length Walt Disney animation	*Snow White and the Seven Dwarfs*
1939	Colour film to win Best Film Oscar	*Gone with the Wind*
1939	African American to win an Oscar	Hattie McDaniel (Best Supporting Actress) for *Gone with the Wind*
1940	Film in stereosound	*Fantasia*
1942	Twins to win an Oscar	Julius and Philip Epstein (Best Screenplay) for *Casablanca*
1948	British film to win Best Film Oscar	*Hamlet*
1953	Film to be released in Cinemascope	*The Robe*
1963	African American to win a Best Actor Oscar	Sidney Poitier for *Lilies of the Field*
1964	Bond movie to win an Oscar	*Goldfinger* for Best Effects & Sound Effects
1969	X rated film to win Best Film Oscar	*Midnight Cowboy*
1970	Actor to refuse a Best Actor Oscar	George C Scott for Patton
1974	Sequel to win Best Film Oscar	*The Godfather Part II*
1975	Film released in Sensurround	*Earthquake*
1976	Woman to be nominated for Best Director Oscar	Linda Wertmuller for *Seven Beauties*

TV & FILM

FILM FIRSTS

1976 Posthumous winner of Best Actor Oscar . . . . Peter Finch for *Network*

1991 Animated film to be nominated for
Best Film Oscar . . . . *Beauty and the Beast*

1995 Wholly computer-generated film . . . . *Toy Story*

2001 African American woman to win
Best Actress Oscar . . . . Halle Berry for *Monster's Ball*

Gone with the Wind

THE MAGNIFICENT SEVEN
The 7 actors who played the original
Magnificent Seven characters

- Yul Brynner as Chris
- Steve McQueen as Vin
- Horst Buchholz as Chico
- Charles Bronson as Bernardo
- Robert Vaughn as Lee
- James Coburn as Brit
- Brad Dexter as Harry

The Magnificent Seven

THE 7 DESTINATIONS OF THE 'ROAD' FILMS STARRING BOB HOPE, BING CROSBY AND DOROTHY LAMOUR

- Bali
- Hong Kong
- Morocco
- Rio
- Singapore
- Utopia
- Zanzibar

THE FIRST 7 *CARRY ON* FILMS

- *Carry on Sergeant*
- *Carry on Nurse*
- *Carry on Teacher*
- *Carry on Constable*
- *Carry on Regardless*
- *Carry on Cruising*
- *Carry on Cabby*

THE 7 DEADLY SINS DEPICTED IN THE 1995 FILM *SEVEN* STARRING BRAD PITT AND MORGAN FREEMAN

- Envy
- Gluttony
- Greed
- Lust
- Pride
- Sloth
- Wrath

SNOW WHITE'S 7 DWARFS

- Bashful
- Doc
- Dopey
- Grumpy
- Happy
- Sleepy
- Sneezy

7 NAMES THAT WERE REJECTED BY WALT DISNEY FOR THE 7 DWARFS

- Blabby
- Crabby
- Dizzy
- Gloomy
- Jaunty
- Lazy
- Shifty

Dopey

TV & FILM

7 WOMEN WHO HAVE KISSED HARRISON FORD ON SCREEN

- Karen Allen
- Kate Capshaw
- Carrie Fisher
- Melanie Griffith
- Anne Heche
- Kelly McGillis
- Greta Scacchi

7 WOMEN WHO HAVE KISSED CLARK GABLE ON SCREEN

- Claudette Colbert
- Joan Crawford
- Jean Harlow
- Vivien Leigh
- Myrna Loy
- Marilyn Monroe
- Rosalind Russell

7 WOMEN WHO HAVE KISSED JACK NICHOLSON ON SCREEN

- Kathy Bates
- Helen Hunt
- Diane Keaton
- Jessica Lange
- Shirley Maclaine
- Susan Sarandon
- Meryl Streep

MOVIE STAR NICKNAMES
The nicknames of 30 film stars

FILM STAR	NICKNAME
Gene Autry	The Singing Cowboy
Lucille Ball	Queen of the B Movies
Brigitte Bardot	The Pout
John Barrymore	The Great Profile
Clara Bow	The It Girl
Richard Burton	The Voice
Charlie Chaplin	The Little Tramp
Lon Chaney Snr.	The Man of a Thousand Faces
Joan Crawford	Cranberry
Bette Davis	The Fifth Warner Brother
Doris Day	The Professional Virgin
Diana Dors	The English Marilyn Monroe
Errol Flynn	The Baron
Clark Gable	The King of Hollywood
Betty Grable	The Girl with the Million Dollar Legs
Oliver Hardy	Babe
Jean Harlow	The Platinum Blonde
Rita Hayworth	The Love Goddess
Rock Hudson	The Baron of Beefcake
Buster Keaton	The Great Stone Face
Carole Lombard	The Profane Angel

MOVIE STAR NICKNAMES
The nicknames of 30 film stars

FILM STAR	NICKNAME
Mary Pickford	The World's Sweetheart
Roy Rogers	King of the Cowboys
Arnold Schwarzenegger	The Austrian Oak
Sylvester Stallone	The Italian Stallion
Lana Turner	The Sweater Girl
Jean Claude Van Damme	The Muscles from Brussels
John Wayne	Duke
Esther Williams	Hollywood's Mermaid
Fay Wray	The Queen of Scream

Charlie Chaplin

BOOK OF LISTS

MAY THE FORCE BE WITH YOU
The 'Star Wars' episodes

Episode I . . . .*The Phantom Menace*

Episode II . . . .*Attack of the Clones*

Episode III . . . .*Revenge of the Sith*

Episode IV . . . .*A New Hope* (originally released as *Star Wars*)

Episode V . . . .*The Empire Strikes Back*

Episode VI . . . .*The Return of the Jedi*

R2D2 and C3PO

TV & FILM

STAR WARS: THE TRIVIA

Princess Leia's surname is Organa

The 'Star Wars' films were based on the books of Terry Brooks

Endor is the name of the home planet of the Ewoks

Three different actors portrayed Darth Vader. David Prowse provided the body. James Earl Jones provided the voice of Vader and Sebastian Shaw provided the face, when Vader was unmasked

Vader means, 'father' in the Dutch language

Luke Skywalker's home planet is called Tatooine

The Return of the Jedi was originally entitled *The Revenge Of The Jedi,* but this title was changed as the emotion of revenge was not deemed worthy of a Jedi

Kashyyyk is the name of the home planet of Chewbacca

ET, the movie creation of Steven Spielberg, makes a background appearance in *The Phantom Menace*

On the 2001 UK census, Jedi was listed as a religion

THE JEDI CODE OF HONOUR

- There is no emotion, there is peace
- There is no ignorance, there is knowledge
- There is no passion, there is serenity
- There is no death, there is the force

BOOK OF LISTS

10 TV PROGRAMMES LATER MADE INTO FILMS

- *The Avengers*
- *Charlie's Angels*
- *The Flintstones*
- *The Fugitive*
- *I Spy*
- *Mission Impossible*
- *Scooby Doo*
- *Starsky and Hutch*
- *SWAT*
- *The Untouchables*

10 FILMS LATER MADE INTO TV PROGRAMMES

- *Alien Nation*
- *Buffy The Vampire Slayer*
- *Fame*
- *Logan's Run*
- *MASH*
- *9 to 5*
- *Peyton Place*
- *Planet of the Apes*
- *Private Benjamin*
- *Working Girl*

10 FILMS ADAPTED FROM SHAKESPEARE'S PLAYS

FILM	PLAY
The Boys from Syracuse	The Comedy of Errors
Chimes at Midnight	Henry V
The Forbidden Planet	The Tempest
An Honourable Murder	Julius Caesar
Kiss Me Kate	Taming of the Shrew
Let the Devil Wear Black	Hamlet
My Own Private Idaho	Henry IV Part I
Ran	King Lear
Throne of Blood	Macbeth
West Side Story	Romeo and Juliet

10 STEPHEN KING STORIES ADAPTED INTO FILMS

NOVEL / FILM	STARRING
Apt Pupil	Ian McKellen as Kurt Dussander
The Body (film title Stand By Me)	River Phoenix as Chris Chambers
Carrie	Sissy Spacek as Carrie
The Dead Zone	Christopher Walken as Johnny Smith
Dolores Claiborne	Kathy Bates as Dolores Claiborne
The Green Mile	Tom Hanks as Paul Edgecomb
Misery	James Caan as Paul Sheldon
Salem's Lot	David Soul as Ben Mears
The Shawshank Redemption	Tim Robbins as Andy Dufrense
The Shining	Jack Nicholson as Jack Torrance

BOOK OF LISTS

AN INNUENDO-LADEN LIST OF 'CARRY ON' CHARACTERS

FILM	CHARACTER	PLAYED BY
Carry on Sergeant	Corporal Copping	Bill Owen
Carry on Constable	WPC Gloria Passworthy	Joan Sims
Carry on Regardless	Penny Panting	Fenella Fielding
Carry on Jack	Albert Poop-Decker	Bernard Cribbins
Carry on Spying	James Bind	Charles Hawtrey
Carry on Spying	Daphne Honeybutt	Barbara Windsor
Carry on Cowboy	The Rumpo Kid	Sid James
Carry on Screaming	Detective Sergeant Bung	Harry H Corbett
Don't Lose Your Head	Citizen Bidet	Peter Butterworth
Follow That Camel	Sergeant Knocker	Phil Silvers
Carry on up The Khyber	The Khasi Of Kalabar	Kenneth Williams
Carry on up The Khyber	Sir Sidney Ruff Diamond	Sid James
Carry on up The Khyber	Bungit Din	Bernard Bresslaw
Carry on Again Doctor	Dr James Nookey	Jim Dale
Carry on at Your Convenience	WC Boggs	Kenneth Williams
Carry on Girls	Augusta Prodworthy	June Whitfield
Carry on Dick	Sergeant Jock Strapp	Jack Douglas
Carry on England	Sergeant S Melly	Kenneth Connor
Carry on Emmanuelle	Harold Hump	Henry McGee

THE BOND GIRLS

FILM	BOND GIRL	PLAYED BY
Dr No	Honey Rider	Ursula Andress
From Russia With Love	Tatiana Romanova	Daniela Bianchi
Goldfinger	Pussy Galore	Honor Blackman
Thunderball	Domino	Claudine Auger
You Only Live Twice	Kissy	Mie Hama
Casino Royale	Miss Goodthighs	Jacqueline Bisset
On Her Majesty's Secret Service	Teresa Di Vicenzo	Diana Rigg
Diamonds Are Forever	Tiffany Case	Jill St John
Live And Let Die	Solitaire	Jane Seymour
The Man With The Golden Gun	Mary Goodnight	Britt Ekland
The Spy Who Loved Me	Anya Amasova	Barbara Bach
Moonraker	Holly Goodhead	Lois Chiles
For Your Eyes Only	Melina Havelock	Carole Bouquet
Octopussy	Octopussy	Maud Adams
Never Say Never Again	Domino	Kim Basinger
A View To A Kill	May Day	Grace Jones
The Living Daylights	Kara Milovy	Maryam d'Abo
Licence To Kill	Pam Bouvier	Carey Lowell
Goldeneye	Natalya Simonova	Izabella Scorupco
Tomorrow Never Dies	Paris Carver	Teri Hatcher
The World Is Not Enough	Elektra King	Sophie Marceau
Die Another Day	Jinx	Halle Berry

10 ACTORS WHO HAVE PLAYED SHERLOCK HOLMES

- John Barrymore
- Jeremy Brett
- Michael Caine
- Peter Cook
- Peter Cushing
- Frank Langella
- Christopher Lee
- Roger Moore
- Christopher Plummer
- Basil Rathbone

Sherlock Holmes

10 ACTORS WHO HAVE PLAYED DR WATSON

- Nigel Bruce
- Donald Houston
- Ben Kingsley
- Patrick Macnee
- James Mason
- Dudley Moore
- Reginald Owen
- Nigel Stock
- Thorley Walters
- Richard Woods

TV & FILM

THE THREE MUSKETEERS:
6 ACTORS WHO HAVE PLAYED ARAMIS

- Richard Chamberlain
- Jeremy Irons
- John King
- Eugene Pallette
- Charlie Sheen
- Gary Watson

6 ACTORS WHO HAVE PLAYED ATHOS

- Leon Barry
- Douglas Dumbrille
- John Malkovich
- Oliver Reed
- Kiefer Sutherland
- Jeremy Young

6 ACTORS WHO HAVE PLAYED PORTHOS

- Brian Blessed
- Gerard Depardieu
- Frank Finlay
- Russell Hicks
- Oliver Platt
- George Siegmann

6 ACTORS WHO HAVE PLAYED D'ARTAGNAN

- Don Ameche
- Gabriel Byrne
- Douglas Fairbanks Snr
- Jeremy Brett
- Chris O'Donnell
- Michael York

10 ACTORS WHO HAVE PLAYED ROBIN HOOD

- Patrick Bergin
- Jason Connery
- Sean Connery
- Kevin Costner
- Cary Elwes
- Douglas Fairbanks Snr
- Errol Flynn
- Richard Greene
- Michael Praed
- Patrick Troughton

Kevin Costner

10 ACTORS WHO HAVE PLAYED TARZAN

- Lex Barker
- Buster Crabbe
- Ron Ely
- Travis Fimmel
- Mike Henry
- Christopher Lambert
- Wolf Larson
- Elmo Lincoln
- Miles O'Keeffe
- Johnny Weissmuller

10 ACTORS WHO HAVE PLAYED COUNT DRACULA

- John Carradine
- Denholm Elliott
- George Hamilton
- Frank Langella
- Christopher Lee
- Bela Lugosi
- Leslie Nielsen
- Gary Oldman
- Jack Palance
- Richard Roxburgh

Count Dracula

10 ACTORS WHO HAVE PLAYED DRACULA'S NEMESIS, VAN HELSING

- Bernard Archard
- Richard Benjamin
- Mel Brooks
- Peter Cushing
- Nigel Davenport
- Anthony Hopkins
- Hugh Jackman
- Laurence Olivier
- Christopher Plummer
- Edward Van Sloan

BOOK OF LISTS

TIME FOR THE TAGLINES

FILM	TAGLINE
Alien	In space no one can hear you scream
Arachnophobia	Eight legs, two fangs and an attitude
Armageddon	The Earth's darkest day will be man's finest
A Beautiful Mind	He saw the world in a way no one could have imagined
Black Hawk Down	Leave no man behind
Bonnie And Clyde	They're young…they're in love…and they kill people
Carrie	If only they knew she had the power
Chicago	In a city where everyone loves a legend, there's only room for one
Cleopatra	The love affair that shook the world
Cliffhanger	Hang on
Dial M for Murder	If a woman rings…hang on for dear life
Edward Scissorhands	His story will touch you, even though he can't
Erin Brockovich	She brought a small town to its feet and a huge corporation to its knees
ET	He is afraid, he is totally alone, he is three million light years from home
Face Off	In order to catch him, he must become him
The Full Monty	The year's most revealing comedy
Gandhi	His triumph changed the world forever
Gladiator	What we do in life echoes in eternity
Good Morning Vietnam	The wrong man. In the wrong place. At the right time
Highlander	There can be only one

TIME FOR THE TAGLINES

FILM	TAGLINE
Hook	What if Peter Pan grew up?
Ice Age	The coolest event in 16,000 years
Jaws II	Just when you thought it was safe to go back in the water
Jurassic Park	An adventure 65 million years in the making
Love Story	Love means never having to say you're sorry
Mars Attacks	Nice planet, we'll take it
The Matrix	The fight for the future begins
Men in Black II	Same scum, new planet
Ocean's Eleven	They're having so much fun, its illegal
Pearl Harbor	Experience the event that changed the world
Poltergeist	They're here
Psycho	Don't give away the ending, it's the only one we've got
Rocky	His whole life was a million to one shot
The Sixth Sense	Not every gift is a blessing
Spy Kids	Real spies... only smaller
Star Wars	A long time ago in a galaxy far far away
Superman	You'll really believe a man can fly
Terminator	Your future is in his hands
Three Men and a Baby	They changed her diapers. She changed their lives
Titanic	Nothing on Earth could come between them
Total Recall	They stole his mind. Now he wants it back
The Usual Suspects	Five criminals. One line up. No coincidence

10 FAMOUS NAMES FROM THE WORLD OF FILMS WHO DIED IN 2000

- Douglas Fairbanks Jnr
- Sir John Gielgud
- Charles Gray
- Sir Alec Guinness
- Hedy Lamarr
- Walter Matthau
- Jane Peters

- Jason Robards
- Roger Vadim
- Loretta Young

10 FAMOUS NAMES FROM THE WORLD OF FILMS WHO DIED IN 2001

Anthony Quinn

- Dale Evans
- Nigel Hawthorne
- Stanley Kramer
- Jack Lemmon
- Peggy Mount
- Nyree Dawn Porter
- Anthony Quinn
- Harry Secombe
- Joan Sims
- Michael Williams

10 FAMOUS NAMES FROM THE WORLD OF FILMS WHO DIED IN 2002

- James Coburn
- Richard Harris
- Stratford Johns
- Chuck Jones
- Spike Milligan
- Dudley Moore
- Rod Steiger

- John Thaw
- Robert Urich
- Billy Wilder

10 FAMOUS NAMES FROM THE WORLD OF FILMS WHO DIED IN 2003

Katharine Hepburn

- Sir Alan Bates
- Charles Bronson
- Richard Crenna
- Buddy Ebsen
- David Hemmings
- Katharine Hepburn
- Gregory Hines
- Bob Hope
- Gregory Peck
- John Ritter

30 ACTORS WHO HAVE RECEIVED A KNIGHTHOOD

- Sir Richard Attenborough
- Sir Stanley Baker
- Sir Alan Bates
- Sir Dirk Bogarde
- Sir Michael Caine
- Sir Charlie Chaplin
- Sir Sean Connery
- Sir Tom Courtenay
- Sir Noel Coward
- Sir Michael Gambon
- Sir John Gielgud
- Sir Alec Guinness
- Sir Richard Harris (knighted in Denmark)
- Sir Rex Harrison
- Sir Nigel Hawthorne
- Sir Alfred Hitchcock
- Sir Ian Holm
- Sir Anthony Hopkins
- Sir Michael Hordern
- Sir Derek Jacobi
- Sir Ben Kingsley
- Sir Alexander Korda
- Sir David Lean
- Sir Ian McKellen
- Sir John Mills
- Sir Roger Moore
- Sir Laurence Olivier
- Sir Michael Redgrave
- Sir Ralph Richardson
- Sir Peter Ustinov

10 ACTRESSES WHO HAVE BEEN CREATED A DAME

- Dame Julie Andrews
- Dame Judi Dench
- Dame Edna Everage (self proclaimed)
- Dame Thora Hird
- Dame Helen Mirren
- Dame Diana Rigg
- Dame Margaret Rutherford
- Dame Maggie Smith
- Dame Sybil Thorndike
- Dame Elizabeth Taylor

THE GOLDEN RASPBERRIES
These films have been awarded the worst film 'Razzie':

- *Battlefield Earth*
- *Bolero*
- *Can't Stop The Music*
- *Cocktail*
- *Color Of Night*
- *Freddie Got Fingered*
- *Gigli*
- *Howard The Duck*
- *Hudson Hawk*
- *Inchon*
- *Indecent Proposal*
- *Mommie Dearest*
- *The Postman*
- *Rambo: First Blood Part II*
- *Shining Through*
- *Showgirls*
- *Star Trek V: The Final Frontier*
- *Striptease*
- *Swept Away*
- *Wild Wild West*

Rambo

BOOK OF LISTS

10 NOTABLE ACTORS WHO WON THE WORST ACTOR 'RAZZIE'

ACTOR	FILM
Ben Affleck	*Gigli*
Robert Benigni	*Pinocchio*
Kevin Costner	*Robin Hood Prince Of Thieves*
Neil Diamond	*The Jazz Singer*
Laurence Olivier	*Inchon*
Burt Reynolds	*Cop And A Half*
Adam Sandler	*Big Daddy*
Sylvester Stallone	*Rhinestone*
John Travolta	*Battlefield Earth*
Bruce Willis	*Armageddon*

Armageddon

TV & FILM

10 NOTABLE ACTRESSES WHO WON WORST ACTRESS 'RAZZIE'

Mariah Carey

ACTRESS	FILM
Mariah Carey	Glitter
Bo Derek	Tarzan the Ape Man
Heather Donahue	The Blair Witch Project
Jennifer Lopez	Gigli
Madonna	Shanghai Surprise
Liza Minnelli	Arthur 2: On The Rocks
Demi Moore	GI Jane
Brooke Shields	The Blue Lagoon
Britney Spears	Crossroads
Sharon Stone	The Specialist

30 FAMOUS FILM STARS WHO NEVER WON AN OSCAR

- Lauren Bacall
- Dirk Bogarde
- Richard Burton
- James Dean
- Douglas Fairbanks Jnr
- Douglas Fairbanks Snr
- WC Fields
- Albert Finney
- Errol Flynn
- Greta Garbo
- Ava Gardner
- Jean Harlow
- Richard Harris
- Rita Hayworth
- Trevor Howard
- Rock Hudson
- Boris Karloff
- Buster Keaton
- Janet Leigh
- Carole Lombard
- Groucho Marx
- Steve McQueen
- Robert Mitchum
- Marilyn Monroe
- Maureen O'Hara
- Edward G Robinson
- Peter Sellers
- Gloria Swanson
- Lana Turner
- Natalie Wood

TV & FILM

30 CLASSIC MOVIES THAT FAILED TO WIN AN OSCAR

- Angels with Dirty Faces
- Bad Day at Black Rock
- The Birds
- Brief Encounter
- Cat on a Hot Tin Roof
- The Color Purple
- Deliverance
- Dr Strangelove
- Easy Rider
- The Elephant Man
- Full Metal Jacket
- Gangs of New York
- The Great Escape
- High Society
- It's a Wonderful Life
- King Kong
- The Magnificent Seven
- The Maltese Falcon
- Marathon Man
- Papillon
- Psycho
- Rear Window
- Rebel without a Cause
- The Shawshank Redemption
- The Shining
- Singin' in the Rain
- Snow White and the Seven Dwarfs
- Taxi Driver
- 12 Angry Men
- Vertigo

FILMS THAT HAVE WON 11 OSCARS

- *Ben Hur*
- *Titanic*
- *The Lord of the Rings: The Return of the King*

FILMS THAT HAVE WON 10 OSCARS

- *West Side Story*

FILMS THAT HAVE WON 9 OSCARS

- *Gigi*
- *The Last Emperor*
- *The English Patient*

The English Patient

FILMS THAT HAVE WON 8 OSCARS

- *Gone with the Wind*
- *From here to Eternity*
- *On the Waterfront*
- *My Fair Lady*
- *Cabaret*
- *Gandhi*
- *Amadeus*

FILMS THAT HAVE WON 7 OSCARS

- *Going My Way*
- *The Best Years of our Lives*
- *The Bridge on the River Kwai*
- *Lawrence of Arabia*
- *Patton*
- *The Sting*
- *Out of Africa*
- *Dances with Wolves*
- *Schindler's List*
- *Shakespeare in Love*

My Fair Lady

BOOK OF LISTS

WHAT'S IN A NAME?
The real names of 30 male movie stars

FILM STAR	REAL NAME
Woody Allen	Allan Stewart Konisberg
Fred Astaire	Frederick Austerlitz
Tom Berenger	Thomas Michael Moore
Yul Brynner	Taidje Khan
Michael Caine	Maurice Micklewhite
Tom Cruise	Thomas Mapother IV
Tony Curtis	Bernard Schwartz
Kirk Douglas	Issur Danielovitch Demsky
WC Fields	William Claude Dukenfield
Peter Finch	William Mitchell
George Formby	George Booth
Cary Grant	Archibald Alexander Leech
Charlton Heston	John Charlton Carter
William Holden	William Beedle
Rock Hudson	Roy Harold Scherer Jnr
Al Jolson	Asa Yoelson
Boris Karloff	William Henry Pratt
Michael Keaton	Michael John Douglas
Howard Keel	Howard Leek
Ben Kingsley	Krishna Bhanji
Stan Laurel	Arthur Stanley Jefferson

WHAT'S IN A NAME?
The real names of 30 male movie stars

FILM STAR	REAL NAME
Jerry Lewis	Joseph Levitch
Jack Palance	Vladimir Palanuik
Edward G Robinson	Emmanuel Goldenberg
Roy Rogers	Leonard Slye
Mickey Rooney	Joe Yule Jnr
Christian Slater	Christian Hawkins
Kevin Spacey	Kevin Matthew Fowler
John Wayne	Marion Michael Morrison
Gene Wilder	Jerome Silberman

Charlton Heston

BOOK OF LISTS

WHAT'S IN A NAME?
The real names of 30 female movie stars

FILM STAR	REAL NAME
Julie Andrews	Julia Wells
Lauren Bacall	Betty Joan Perske
Brigitte Bardot	Camille Javal
Joan Crawford	Lucille Fay le Sueur
Doris Day	Doris Mary Ann von Kappelhoff
Bo Derek	Mary Cathleen Collins
Angie Dickinson	Angeline Brown
Diana Dors	Diana Fluck
Greta Garbo	Greta Lovisa Gustafsson
Judy Garland	Frances Ethel Gumm
Paulette Goddard	Marion Lev
Whoopi Goldberg	Caryn Elaine Johnson
Rita Hayworth	Margarita Carmen Cansino
Diane Keaton	Diane Hall
Piper Laurie	Rosetta Jacobs
Janet Leigh	Jeanette Morrison
Carole Lombard	Jane Peters
Jayne Mansfield	Vera Jane Palmer
Helen Mirren	Ilynea Lydia Mironoff
Marilyn Monroe	Norma Jean Baker
Demi Moore	Demetria Gene Guynes

WHAT'S IN A NAME?
The real names of 30 female movie stars

Brigitte Bardot

FILM STAR	REAL NAME
Julianne Moore	Julie Anne Smith
Mary Pickford	Gladys Smith
Ginger Rogers	Virginia McMath
Meg Ryan	Margaret Hyra
Winona Ryder	Winona Horowitz
Susan Sarandon	Susan Abigail Tomaling
Barbara Stanwyck	Ruby Stevens
Shelley Winters	Shirley Schrift
Natalie Wood	Natasha Gurdin

BOOK OF LISTS

10 ACTORS WHO HAVE DRESSED AS WOMEN ON FILM

- Tony Curtis in *Some Like it Hot*
- Michael J Fox in *Back to the Future*
- Alec Guinness in *Kind Hearts and Coronets*
- Dustin Hoffman in *Tootsie*
- Jack Lemmon in *Some Like it Hot*
- Eddie Murphy in *The Nutty Professor*
- Anthony Perkins in *Psycho*
- Alistair Sim in the 'St Trinian's' movies
- Patrick Swayze in *To Wong Foo, Thanks For Everything! Julie Newmar*
- Robin Williams in *Mrs Doubtfire*

10 ACTORS WHO HAVE APPEARED IN FULL-FRONTAL NUDE SCENES ON FILM

Trainspotting

- Kevin Bacon in *Wild Things*
- Alan Bates in *Women in Love*
- Simon Callow in *A Room with a View*
- Richard Gere in *Yanks*
- Harvey Keitel in *The Piano*
- Malcolm McDowell in *Caligula*
- Ewan McGregor in *Trainspotting*
- Oliver Reed in *Women in Love*
- Geoffrey Rush in *Quills*
- Bruce Willis in *Color of Night*

TV & FILM

FOLLOW MY LEADER
20 famous leaders who have been played on film

LEADER	PLAYED BY	FILM
John Quincy Adams	Anthony Hopkins	*Amistad*
King Arthur	Richard Harris	*Camelot*
Napoleon Bonaparte	Marlon Brando	*Desiree*
Julius Caesar	Rex Harrison	*Cleopatra*
Duke of Wellington	Christopher Plummer	*Waterloo*
Edward I	Patrick McGoohan	*Braveheart*
Elizabeth I	Judi Dench	*Shakespeare in Love*
George III	Nigel Hawthorne	*The Madness of King George*
Henry II	Peter O'Toole	*The Lion in Winter/ Becket*
Henry VIII	Richard Burton	*Anne of a Thousand Days*
Andrew Jackson	Charlton Heston	*The President's Lady*
Genghis Khan	John Wayne	*The Conqueror*
Abraham Lincoln	Henry Fonda	*Young Mr Lincoln*
David Lloyd George	Anthony Hopkins	*Young Winston*
Nelson Mandela	Morgan Freeman	*Long Walk to Freedom*
Richard the Lionheart	Sean Connery	*Robin Hood Prince of Thieves*
Franklin D Roosevelt	Jon Voight	*Pearl Harbor*
Margaret Thatcher	Janet Brown	*For Your Eyes Only*
Queen Victoria	Judi Dench	*Mrs Brown*
Zeus	Laurence Olivier	*Clash of the Titans*

40 FAMOUS PEOPLE OF THE PAST PLAYED ON FILM

PERSON	PLAYED BY	FILM
Joy Adamson	Virginia McKenna	*Born Free*
Marc Antony	Richard Burton	*Cleopatra*
Gladys Aylward	Ingrid Bergman	*The Inn of the Sixth Happiness*
Douglas Bader	Kenneth More	*Reach for the Sky*
JM Barrie	Johnny Depp	*Finding Neverland*
Ludwig van Beethoven	Gary Oldman	*Immortal Beloved*
Steve Biko	Denzel Washington	*Cry Freedom*
Billy the Kid	Emilio Estevez	*Young Guns*
Al Capone	Robert DeNiro	*The Untouchables*
Geoffrey Chaucer	Paul Bettany	*A Knight's Tale*
Chopin	Hugh Grant	*Impromptu*
John Christie	Richard Attenborough	*10 Rillington Place*
Cleopatra	Amanda Barrie	*Carry on Cleo*
Thomas Cromwell	Leo McKern	*A Man for all Seasons*
General George Custer	Errol Flynn	*They Died With their Boots on*
Thomas Alva Edison	Mickey Rooney	*Young Tom Edison*
Paul Gauguin	Anthony Quinn	*Lust for Life*
General Charles Gordon	Charlton Heston	*Khartoum*
Guinevere	Keira Knightley	*King Arthur*
Doc Holliday	Val Kilmer	*Tombstone*
Howard Hughes	Leonardo DiCaprio	*The Aviator*
Judas Iscariot	Harvey Keitel	*The Last Temptation of Christ*

TV & FILM

40 FAMOUS PEOPLE OF THE PAST PLAYED ON FILM

PERSON	PLAYED BY	FILM
James Joyce	Ewan McGregor	*Nora*
Rudyard Kipling	Christopher Plummer	*The Man Who Would Be King*
TE Lawrence	Peter O'Toole	*Lawrence of Arabia*
Franz Liszt	Dirk Bogarde	*Song Without End*
Marquis de Sade	Geoffrey Rush	*Quills*
Michelangelo	Charlton Heston	*The Agony and the Ecstasy*
Sir Thomas More	Paul Schofield	*A Man for all Seasons*
Moses	Charlton Heston	*The Ten Commandments*
Mozart	Tom Hulce	*Amadeus*
Nero	Peter Ustinov	*Quo Vadis*
Lee Harvey Oswald	Gary Oldman	*JFK*
Pontius Pilate	David Bowie	*The Last Temptation of Christ*
William Shakespeare	Joseph Fiennes	*Shakespeare in Love*
Toulouse-Lautrec	John Leguizamo	*Moulin Rouge*
Vincent Van Gogh	Kirk Douglas	*Lust for Life*
William Wallace	Mel Gibson	*Braveheart*
Barnes Wallis	Michael Redgrave	*The Dambusters*
Virginia Woolf	Nicole Kidman	*The Hours*

40 FILM STARS AND 40 CITIES

FILM STAR	BORN IN
Dan Aykroyd	Ottawa
Ursula Andress	Bern
Brigitte Bardot	Paris
Drew Barrymore	Los Angeles
Ingrid Bergman	Stockholm
Kenneth Branagh	Belfast
John Candy	Toronto
Charlie Chaplin	London
Chevy Chase	New York
Sean Connery	Edinburgh
Russell Crowe	Wellington
Doris Day	Cincinnati
Judi Dench	York
Olivia de Havilland	Tokyo
Marlene Dietrich	Berlin
Errol Flynn	Hobart
Michael J Fox	Edmonton
Cary Grant	Bristol
Audrey Hepburn	Brussels
Samuel L Jackson	Washington DC
Klaus Kinski	Danzig
Hedy Lamarr	Vienna

Samuel L Jackson

TV & FILM

40 FILM STARS AND 40 CITIES

FILM STAR	BORN IN
Gene Kelly	Pittsburgh
Grace Kelly	Philadelphia
Nicole Kidman	Honolulu
Vivien Leigh	Darjeeling
Jack Lemmon	Boston
Sophia Loren	Rome
Leo McKern	Sydney
Sidney Poitier	Miami
Basil Rathbone	Johannesburg
Keanu Reeves	Beirut
Edward G Robinson	Bucharest
Arnold Schwarzenegger	Graz
Omar Sharif	Alexandria
William Shatner	Montreal
Patrick Swayze	Houston
Spencer Tracey	Milwaukee
Johnny Weissmuller	Friedorf
Natalie Wood	San Francisco

10 ACTORS WHO STARRED IN THE FILM
THE GREAT ESCAPE

- Richard Attenborough as Big X
- Charles Bronson as the Tunnel King
- James Coburn as the Manufacturer
- James Garner as the Scrounger
- Gordon Jackson as Head of Intelligence
- John Leyton as the Tunneller
- David McCallum as Dispersal
- Steve McQueen as the Cooler King
- Donald Pleasence as the Forger
- Nigel Stock as the Surveyor

The Great Escape

TV & FILM

THE LAST WORDS SPOKEN IN 20 FAMOUS FILMS

Arsenic and Old Lace . . . . "I'm not a cab driver. I'm a coffee pot."

Beverly Hills Cop . . . . "I know the perfect place, you guys will love it. Trust me."

Butch Cassidy and the Sundance Kid . . "Good, for a moment there I thought we were in trouble."

Casablanca . . . . "Louis, I think this is the beginning of a beautiful friendship."

Citizen Kane . . . . "Rosebud."

Dead Poets' Society . . . . "Thank you boys. Thank you."

Four Weddings And A Funeral . . . . "I do."

Gone with the Wind . . . . "After all tomorrow is another day."

How to Marry a Millionaire . . . . "Gentlemen, to our wives."

It's a Wonderful Life . . . . "That's right. That's right. Attaboy Clarence."

Jaws . . . . "I used to hate the water. I can't imagine why."

King Kong . . . . "It wasn't the planes, it was beauty killed the beast."

Little Caesar . . . . "Mother of mercy. Is this the end of Rico?"

Seven Brides for Seven Brothers . . . . . . "I now pronounce you men and wives."

Some Like it Hot . . . . "Well nobody's perfect."

Sunset Boulevard . . . . "All right Mr DeMille, I'm ready for my close up."

True Grit . . . . "Well come see a fat old man sometime."

Whatever Happened to Baby Jane? . . . . "You mean all this time we could've been friends?"

White Heat . . . . "Made it Ma! Top of the world."

The Wizard of Oz . . . . "Oh, Auntie Em, there's no place like home."

BOND TRIVIA

Casino Royale was the first Bond novel penned by Ian Fleming

Avengers stars Diana Rigg, Joanna Lumley and Honor Blackman have all played Bond girls

The author Roald Dahl wrote the screenplay for *You Only Live Twice*

Christopher Lee, who played the Bond villain Scaramanga, is the cousin of Ian Fleming

The full title of Q is Major Boothroyd

The singing voice of Ursula Andress, in the famous beach scene in *Dr No*, was dubbed by Diana Coupland, the actress who played the wife of Sid James in the sitcom *Bless This House*

James Bond

BOND TRIVIA

In the Bond novels, 007's favoured weapon is a Walther PPK

The first name of Miss Moneypenny is Penny

The face of the Bond villain Ernst Blofeld was first revealed in *You Only Live Twice*, portrayed by Donald Pleasence

The terrorist organization Spectre stands for Special Executor For Counter Intelligence Terrorism

The epitaph on the headstone of Bond's wife Tracy Draco reads, 'We have all the time in the world'

The family motto of James Bond is, 'Non Sufficit Orbis', which translates as 'The World Is Not Enough'

The Bond villain Auric Goldfinger was named after Erno Goldfinger, an Hungarian architect who enraged Ian Fleming by building modernist homes in Hampstead

Desmond Llewelyn has appeared in a record number of Bond movies, 17 in total, in his role as Q

James Bond was named by Ian Fleming after an author who penned a book entitled *Birds of the West Indies*

In the original Bond novels, 007 drove a Bentley car

The first film Pierce Brosnan ever saw at the cinema was *Goldfinger*

Pierce Brosnan bought a typewriter once owned by Ian Fleming for £52,800

Bob Holness, the host of the TV game show *Blockbusters*, and the actor Rex Harrison have both voiced the character of Bond in radio serials

Christopher Walken was the first Oscar-winning actor to play a Bond villain, when he portrayed Max Zorin in *A View to a Kill*

BOOK OF LISTS

10 FILM STARS WHO FOLLOWED IN A PARENT'S FOOTSTEPS

- Drew Barrymore, daughter of John Barrymore Jnr
- Jeff Bridges, son of Lloyd Bridges
- David Carradine, son of John Carradine
- Michael Douglas, son of Kirk Douglas
- Kate Hudson, daughter of Goldie Hawn
- Angelina Jolie, daughter of Jon Voight
- Liza Minnelli, daughter of Judy Garland
- Amanda Plummer, daughter of Christopher Plummer
- Vanessa Redgrave, daughter of Michael Redgrave
- Joely Richardson, daughter of Vanessa Redgrave

10 PAIRS OF SILVER SCREEN SIBLINGS

- Patricia and Rosanna Arquette
- Warren Beatty and Shirley Maclaine
- James and John Belushi
- Peter and Jane Fonda
- Joan Fontaine and Olivia de Havilland
- Dennis and Randy Quaid
- Julia and Eric Roberts
- Charlie Sheen and Emilio Estevez
- Ben and Amy Stiller
- Luke and Owen Wilson

THE AMERICAN FILM INSTITUTE'S TOP 10 MALE SCREEN LEGENDS

1	Humphrey Bogart
2	Cary Grant
3	James Stewart
4	Marlon Brando
5	Fred Astaire
6	Henry Fonda
7	Clark Gable
8	James Cagney
9	Spencer Tracy
10	Charlie Chaplin

THE AMERICAN FILM INSTITUTE'S TOP 10 FEMALE SCREEN LEGENDS

1	Katharine Hepburn
2	Bette Davis
3	Audrey Hepburn
4	Ingrid Bergman
5	Greta Garbo
6	Marilyn Monroe
7	Elizabeth Taylor
8	Judy Garland
9	Marlene Dietrich
10	Joan Crawford

THE AMERICAN FILM INSTITUTE'S TOP 100 FILMS OF THE 20TH CENTURY

1	*Citizen Kane*	26	*Dr Strangelove*
2	*Casablanca*	27	*Bonnie and Clyde*
3	*The Godfather*	28	*Apocalypse Now*
4	*Gone with the Wind*	29	*Mr Smith Goes to Washington*
5	*Lawrence of Arabia*	30	*The Treasure of the Sierra Madre*
6	*The Wizard of Oz*	31	*Annie Hall*
7	*The Graduate*	32	*The Godfather Part II*
8	*On the Waterfront*	33	*High Noon*
9	*Schindler's List*	34	*To Kill a Mockingbird*
10	*Singin' in the Rain*	35	*It Happened One Night*
11	*It's a Wonderful Life*	36	*Midnight Cowboy*
12	*Sunset Boulevard*	37	*The Best Years of our Lives*
13	*The Bridge on the River Kwai*	38	*Double Indemnity*
14	*Some Like It Hot*	39	*Dr Zhivago*
15	*Star Wars*	40	*North by North West*
16	*All About Eve*	41	*West Side Story*
17	*The African Queen*	42	*Rear Window*
18	*Psycho*	43	*King Kong*
19	*Chinatown*	44	*The Birth of a Nation*
20	*One Flew over the Cuckoo's Nest*	45	*A Streetcar Named Desire*
21	*The Grapes of Wrath*	46	*A Clockwork Orange*
22	*2001: A Space Odyssey*	47	*Taxi Driver*
23	*The Maltese Falcon*	48	*Jaws*
24	*Raging Bull*	49	*Snow White and the Seven Dwarfs*
25	*ET*	50	*Butch Cassidy and the Sundance Kid*

TV & FILM

THE AMERICAN FILM INSTITUTE'S TOP 100 FILMS OF THE 20TH CENTURY

51	*The Philadelphia Story*	76	*City Lights*
52	*From here to Eternity*	77	*American Graffiti*
53	*Amadeus*	78	*Rocky*
54	*All Quiet on the Western Front*	79	*The Deer Hunter*
55	*The Sound Of Music*	80	*The Wild Bunch*
56	*MASH*	81	*Modern Times*
57	*The Third Man*	82	*Giant*
58	*Fantasia*	83	*Platoon*
59	*Rebel without a Cause*	84	*Fargo*
60	*Raiders of the Lost Ark*	85	*Duck Soup*
61	*Vertigo*	86	*Mutiny on the Bounty*
62	*Tootsie*	87	*Frankenstein*
63	*Stagecoach*	88	*Easy Rider*
64	*Close Encounters of the Third Kind*	89	*Patton*
65	*The Silence of the Lambs*	90	*The Jazz Singer*
66	*Network*	91	*My Fair Lady*
67	*The Manchurian Candidate*	92	*A Place in the Sun*
68	*An American in Paris*	93	*The Apartment*
69	*Shane*	94	*Goodfellas*
70	*The French Connection*	95	*Pulp Fiction*
71	*Forrest Gump*	96	*The Searchers*
72	*Ben Hur*	97	*Bringing up Baby*
73	*Wuthering Heights*	98	*Unforgiven*
74	*The Gold Rush*	99	*Guess Who's Coming to Dinner*
75	*Dances with Wolves*	100	*Yankee Doodle Dandy*

BOOK OF LISTS

TV FIRSTS

- Cost of the first TV licence £2
- First product to be advertised on British TV . . . . . . Gibbs SR toothpaste
- The first *Blue Peter* presenters . . . . Leila Williams and Christopher Trace
- The first victim on *This Is Your Life* . . . . Eamon Andrews
- The first US sitcom to be shown in Britain . . . . *I Love Lucy*
- The first words spoken on *Coronation Street* . . . . . "Now the next thing you've got to do is get a sign writer in" (Elsie Lappin to Florrie Lindley)
- The first character to die in *Coronation Street* . . . . May Hardman
- The first character to die in *Eastenders* . . . . Reg Cox
- The first actor to play Dr Who . . . . William Hartnell
- The first twice-weekly British soap opera . . . . *Emergency Ward 10*
- The first two teams to feature on *Match of the Day* . . . . Arsenal v Liverpool in 1964
- The first programme to be screened on BBC 2 . . . . *Play School*
- The first film to be screened on BBC 2 . . . . *Kiss Me Kate*
- The first programme to be screened on Channel 4 . . . . *Countdown*
- The first winners of *University Challenge* . . . . Leicester University
- The first product to be advertised on Channel 5 . . . Chanel No. 5
- Britain's first national female newsreader . . . . Angela Rippon
- The first woman to present *Grandstand* . . . . Helen Rollason
- The first person to win £1 million on *Who Wants to Be a Millionaire* . . . . Judith Keppel

TV & FILM

TV ADDRESSES

TV SHOW / RESIDENTS	FAMILY ADDRESS
The Addams Family	Cemetery Lane, Cemetery Ridge
Bless This House / The Abbots	Birch Avenue, Putney
The Beverly Hillbillies / The Clampetts	518 Crestview Drive, Beverly Hills
Bonanza / The Cartwrights	Ponderosa Ranch, Virginia City, Nevada
Bread / The Boswells	30 Kelsall Street, Liverpool
The Cosby Show / The Huxtables	10 Stigwood Avenue, New York
Forever Green / The Boults	Meadows Green Farm, Gloucestershire
George & Mildred / The Ropers	46 Peacock Crescent, Hampton Wick
Hancock's Half Hour / Tony Hancock	23 Railway Cuttings, East Cheam
Happy Days / The Cunninghams	565 North Clinton Drive, Milwaukee
The Jetsons	Skypad Apartments, Orbit City
The Liver Birds / Beryl & Sandra	Huckisson Road, Liverpool
Mr Benn	52 Festive Road, London
The Munsters	1313 Mockingbird Lane, Mockingbird Heights
The Partridge Family	698 Sycamore Road, San Pueblo
Roseanne / The Connors	714 Delaware St, Lanford, Illinois
Shelley	Pangloss Road, London
The Simpsons	742 Evergreen Terrace, Springfield
Steptoe & Son	24 Oil Drum Lane, London
Upstairs Downstairs / The Bellamys	165 Eaton Place, London

BOOK OF LISTS

10 TV SITCOMS SET IN NEW YORK

- *Becker*
- *Diff'rent Strokes*
- *Friends*
- *I Love Lucy*
- *The Odd Couple*
- *Seinfeld*
- *Spin City*
- *Taxi*
- *Veronica's Closet*
- *Will And Grace*

Friends

10 TV SITCOMS SET IN LONDON

- *Absolutely Fabulous*
- *Are You Being Served?*
- *Drop the Dead Donkey*
- *Gimme Gimme Gimme*
- *Men Behaving Badly*
- *Only Fools and Horses*
- *Some Mothers Do 'ave 'em*
- *The Thin Blue Line*
- *Yes Prime Minister*
- *The Young Ones*

TV & FILM

THE THEMES AND THE SINGERS

TV THEME	SINGERS
Absolutely Fabulous	Julie Tippet and Adrian Edmondson
Auf Wiedersehen Pet	Joe Fagin
Brush Strokes	Dexy's Midnight Runners
Cheers	Gary Portnoy
Dad's Army	Bud Flanagan
The Dukes Of Hazzard	Waylon Jennings
Friends	The Rembrandts
Hearbeat	Nick Berry
The Likely Lads	Manfred Mann
The Liver Birds	The Scaffold
The Love Boat	Jack Jones
Minder	Dennis Waterman
Moonlighting	Al Jarreau
One Foot In The Grave	Eric Idle
Only Fools And Horses	John Sullivan
Prisoner Cell Block H	Lynne Hamilton
Rawhide	Frankie Laine
The Royle Family	Oasis
The Sopranos	Alabama 3
Supergran	Billy Connolly
The Wonder Years	Joe Cocker

MUSIC

However obscure or detailed your knowledge of music might be, you are certain to discover something new in this section. Let's put this to the test. See how many of the following facts you already knew: Ricky Gervais performed in a band called Seona Dancing; Freddy Mercury's real name was Faroukh Bulsara; Abba's former name was The Engaged Couples; *The Mikado* is also known as The Town of Titipu; and the final resting place of Jim Morrison is in Paris. And ask yourself this: what was the first duo to top the UK charts and when? Now turn the page.

BOOK OF LISTS

MUSIC FIRSTS

1942	Act to receive a gold disc	Glenn Miller for 'Chattanooga Choo Choo'
1952	Number one hit	'Here in my Heart' by Al Martino
1953	Group to top the UK charts	The Stargazers with 'Broken Wings'
1956	Teenager to top the UK charts	Frankie Lymon with 'Why do Fools Fall in Love?'
1956	Country to win the Eurovision Song Contest	Switzerland
1958	Female teenager to top the UK charts	Connie Francis with 'Who's Sorry now?'
1958	Duo to top the UK charts	Everly Brothers with All I Have to do Is Dream'

Everly Brothers

MUSIC

MUSIC FIRSTS

1962	British act to top the US charts	The Tornados with 'Telstar'
1965	Australian act to top the UK charts	The Seekers with 'I'll Never Find Another You'
1974	French act to top the UK charts	Charles Aznavour with 'She'
1974	Swedish act to top the UK charts	Abba with 'Waterloo'
1976	Dutch act to top the UK charts	Pussycat with 'Mississippi'
1977	Spanish act to top the UK charts	Baccara with 'Yes Sir I Can Boogie'
1981	Video to feature on MTV	'Video Killed the Radio Star' by Buggles
1981	German act to top the UK charts	Kraftwerk with 'The Model'
1985	Norwegian act to top the UK charts	A-Ha with 'The Sun Always Shines on TV'
1986	Austrian act to top the UK charts	Falco with 'Rock Me Amadeus'
1987	Group to be inducted into the Rock And Roll Hall of Fame	The Coasters
1987	Woman to be inducted into the Rock And Roll Hall of Fame	Aretha Franklin
2003	Russian act to top the UK charts	Tatu with 'All the Things She Said'

BOOK OF LISTS

FAMOUS PEOPLE WHO HAVE PERFORMED IN BANDS AND POP GROUPS

Woody Allen	Eddy Davis New Orleans Jazz Band
Michael Barrymore	Fine China
Tony Blair	The Ugly Rumours
Pat Cash and John McEnroe	The Full Metal Rackets
Chevy Chase	Leather Canary
Michelle Collins	Mari Wilson And The Wilsations
Billy Connolly	The Humblebums
Russell Crowe	30 Odd Foot Of Grunts
Angus Deayton	The Hee Bee Gee Bees
Johnny Depp	The Kids
Richard Gere	Syracuse Symphony Orchestra
Ricky Gervais	Seona Dancing
Jeff Goldblum	The Mildred Snitzer Orchestra
Robson Green	The Workie Tickets
Jeremy Irons	The Four Pillars Of Wisdom
Ewan McGregor	Scarlet Pride
Jimmy Nail	The Crabs
Jamie Oliver	Scarlet Division
Joe Pesci	Joey Dee And The Starliters
Keanu Reeves	Dogstar

MUSIC

THE FAB FOUR
THE BEATLES' UK NO.1 HIT SINGLES

1963	'From Me To You'	1966	'Yellow Submarine/ Eleanor Rigby'
1963	'She Loves You'	1967	'All You Need Is Love'
1963	'I Want To Hold Your Hand'	1967	'Hello Goodbye'
1964	'Can't Buy Me Love'	1968	'Lady Madonna'
1964	'A Hard Day's Night'	1968	'Hey Jude'
1964	'I Feel Fine'	1969	'Get Back'
1965	'Ticket To Ride'	1969	'The Ballad Of John And Yoko'
1965	'Help'		
1965	'Day Tripper/ We Can Work It Out'		
1966	'Paperback Writer'		

8 BEATLES SONGS THAT WERE NO.1 IN THE USA BUT NOT IN THE UK

- 'Love Me Do'
- 'Yesterday'
- 'Penny Lane'
- 'Eight Days A Week'
- 'Come Together'
- 'Let It Be'
- 'The Long And Winding Road'
- 'Something'

30 FAMOUS FACES ON THE ALBUM COVER OF 'SERGEANT PEPPER'S LONELY HEARTS CLUB BAND'

- Stan Laurel
- Oliver Hardy
- Fred Astaire
- HG Wells
- Tony Curtis
- Lewis Carroll
- Bob Dylan
- Tom Mix
- Marlon Brando
- Max Miller
- Sir Robert Peel
- Edgar Allan Poe
- Mae West
- TE Lawrence
- WC Fields
- Dr David Livingstone
- Dylan Thomas
- Tyrone Power
- Aldous Huxley
- Marilyn Monroe
- William Burroughs
- Karl Marx

- Diana Dors
- Marlene Dietrich
- Tommy Handley
- Oscar Wilde
- Sonny Liston
- Lenny Bruce
- George Bernard Shaw
- Stuart Sutcliffe

Dr David Livingstone

MUSIC

LENNON & McCARTNEY COMPOSITIONS THAT WERE NO. 1 HITS FOR OTHER ACTS

- 'Bad To Me' for Billy J Kramer and The Dakotas
- 'A World Without Love' for Peter And Gordon
- 'With a Little Help from My Friends' for Joe Cocker
- 'Ob-La-Di-Ob-La-Da' for Marmalade
- 'With A Little Help From My Friends' for Wet Wet Wet
- 'She's Leaving Home' for Billy Bragg and Cara Tivey
- 'The Long and Winding Road' for Will Young and Gareth Gates
- 'With a Little Help from My Friends' for Sam and Mark

OTHER SONGS GIVEN AWAY BY THE BEATLES

- 'I'll Keep You Satisfied' recorded by Billy J Kramer and the Dakotas
- 'Hello Little Girl' recorded by the Fourmost
- 'Nobody I Know' recorded by Peter and Gordon
- 'Step Inside Love' recorded by Cilla Black
- 'That Means a Lot' recorded by PJ Proby
- 'Come and Get it' recorded by Badfinger
- 'Like Dreamers Do' recorded by the Applejacks
- 'Goodbye' recorded by Mary Hopkin

BOOK OF LISTS

10 ROCK AND ROLL SUICIDES

1973	Paul Williams of the Temptations, shot himself
1975	Peter Ham of Badfinger, hanging
1979	Donny Hathaway, threw himself from the 15th floor of a New York hotel
1980	Ian Curtis of Joy Division, hanging
1983	Danny Rapp of Danny and the Juniors, shot himself
1990	Del Shannon, shot himself
1994	Kurt Cobain, shot himself
1996	Faron Young, shot himself
1997	Michael Hutchence, hanging
1999	Screaming Lord Sutch, hanging

10 POP STARS WHO WERE SHOT DEAD

1964	Sam Cooke
1971	Bobby Bloom
1975	Al Jackson of Booker T and the MGs
1980	John Lennon
1984	Marvin Gaye
1987	Peter Tosh of the Wailers
1996	Tupac Shakur
1997	Notorious B.I.G.
2002	Jam Master Jay
2004	John Whitehead of McFadden and Whitehead

MUSIC

THE FIRST 10 INDUCTEES IN THE US ROCK AND ROLL HALL OF FAME

- Chuck Berry
- James Brown
- Ray Charles
- Sam Cooke
- Fats Domino
- The Everly Brothers
- Buddy Holly
- Jerry Lee Lewis
- Little Richard
- Elvis Presley

THE FIRST 10 BRITISH GROUPS TO BE INDUCTED INTO THE US ROCK AND ROLL HALL OF FAME

- The Beatles
- The Rolling Stones
- The Who
- The Kinks
- The Yardbirds
- Cream
- The Animals
- Led Zeppelin
- The Police
- The Clash

The Rolling Stones

BOOK OF LISTS

DERIVATIONS OF POP GROUP NAMES

GROUP	NAMED AFTER
Abba	The initials letters of the first names of the group members
All Saints	All Saints Road in London
Aswad	The Arabic for 'black'
Bad Company	The title of a 1972 film, starring Jeff Bridges
Bauhaus	A German art movement
The Beatles	A play on the group name of the Crickets
Buffalo Springfield	A model of steamroller
Clannad	Gaelic for 'family'
The Communards	A historical group of Parisian revolutionaries
Depeche Mode	From a French magazine name, meaning, 'Fashion News'
Dexy's Midnight Runners	The stimulant Dexedrine
Doobie Brothers	A slang term for a marijuana joint
Duran Duran	The villain in the 1976 sci-fi movie *Barbarella*
Erasure	The cult movie Erasurehead
Everything But The Girl	A second-hand furniture store in Hull
The Fugees	A shortened form of the word refugees
Heaven 17	A fictitious band in the film *A Clockwork Orange*
Iron Maiden	A medieval torture instrument
Jethro Tull	The inventor of the seed drill
Kraftwerk	German for 'power plant'
Led Zeppelin	A Keith Moon comment, "They would go down like a lead balloon"

MUSIC

DERIVATIONS OF POP GROUP NAMES

GROUP	NAMED AFTER
Level 42	Answer to the meaning of life in *The Hitchhiker's Guide To The Galaxy*
Lynyrd Skynyrd	A cantankerous gym teacher called Leonard Skinner
Marillion	JRR Tolkien novel *The Silmarillion*
Ned's Atomic Dustbin	An episode of *The Goon Show*
Nirvana	The state of enlightenment in Buddhism
Oasis	A Swindon sports centre
Pink Floyd	The blues musicians Pink Anderson and Floyd Council
The Pretenders	The song 'The Great Pretender'
REO Speedwagon	A model of a fire engine
The Rolling Stones	Muddy Waters song
The Searchers	The John Wayne film of the same name
Sigue Sigue Sputnik	A Russian street gang
Sisters Of Mercy	A Dublin religious group founded by Catherine McAuley in 1831
Steppenwolf	A novel by Herman Hesse
Styx	The mythological river across which souls were ferried to the underworld
Supertramp	WH Davies book *Autobiography of a Supertramp*
The Thompson Twins	Cartoon characters in Hergé's *Adventures of Tin Tin*
T'Pau	A Vulcan priestess in *Star Trek*
UB40	Unemployment benefit form
Uriah Heep	Character in the Dickens novel *David Copperfield*

REAL NAMES OF 50 MALE POP STARS

SINGER	REAL NAME
Adam Ant	Stuart Goddard
Badly Drawn Boy	Damon Gough
Dave Berry	Dave Grundy
Buster Bloodvessel	Douglas Trendle
Michael Bolton	Michael Bolotin
David Bowie	David Jones
Boy George	George O'Dowd
Captain Sensible	Ray Burns
Chubby Checker	Ernest Evans
Eric Clapton	Eric Clapp
Coolio	Artis Ivey Jnr
Alice Cooper	Vincent Furnier
Elvis Costello	Declan McManus
Bobby Darin	Walden Robert Cassotto
John Denver	Henry John Deutschendorf
Neil Diamond	Noah Kaminsky
Bob Dylan	Robert Zimmerman
David Essex	David Cook
Adam Faith	Terence Nelhams
Georgie Fame	Clive Powell
Wayne Fontana	Glynn Ellis
Billy Fury	Ronald Wycherley
Gary Glitter	Paul Gadd
Steve Harley	Steve Nice
Michael Holliday	Norman Milne

Stevie Wonder

MUSIC

REAL NAMES OF 50 MALE POP STARS

SINGER	REAL NAME
Engelbert Humperdinck	Arnold Dorsey
Billy Idol	William Broad
Elton John	Reginald Dwight
Tom Jones	Thomas Woodward
Ben E King	Benjamin Nelson
Frankie Laine	Frankie Lovecchio
Barry Manilow	Barry Pincus
Dean Martin	Dino Crocetti
Meat Loaf	Marvin Lee Aday
Freddie Mercury	Faroukh Bulsara
George Michael	Georgios Panayiotou
Matt Monro	Terence Perkins
Van Morrison	George Ivan
Gary Numan	Gary Webb
Marti Pellow	Mark McLoughlin
Cliff Richard	Harry Webb
Axl Rose	William Bailey
Del Shannon	Charles Westover
Alvin Stardust	Bernard Jewry
Shakin' Stevens	Michael Barratt
Sting	Gordon Sumner
Dickie Valentine	Richard Brice
Frankie Vaughan	Frank Abelson
Bobby Vee	Robert Vellino
Stevie Wonder	Steveland Judkins

BOOK OF LISTS

REAL NAMES OF 30 FEMALE POP STARS

SINGER	REAL NAME
Aneka	Mary Sandeman
Cheryl Baker	Rita Crudgington
Pat Benatar	Patricia Andrzejewski
Cilla Black	Priscilla White
Elkie Brooks	Elaine Bookbinder
Mel C	Melanie Chisholm
Patsy Cline	Virginia Hensley
Taylor Dayne	Leslie Wunderman
Kiki Dee	Pauline Matthews
Gloria Estefan	Gloria Fajardo
Connie Francis	Concetta Franconero
Macy Gray	Natalie McIntyre
Chaka Khan	Yvette Marie Stevens
Beverley Knight	Beverley Smith
Brenda Lee	Brenda Tarpley
Dee C Lee	Diane Sealey
Little Eva	Eva Boyd
Julie London	Julie Peck
Vera Lynn	Vera Welsh
Mica Paris	Michelle Wallen
Queen Latifah	Dana Owens
Sabrina	Sabrina Salerno

MUSIC

REAL NAMES OF 30 FEMALE POP STARS

SINGER	REAL NAME
Sandie Shaw	Sandra Goodrich
Anne Shelton	Patricia Sibley
Sonia	Sonia Evans
Dusty Springfield	Mary O'Brien
Donna Summer	LaDonna Gaines
Tina Turner	Annie Mae Bullock
Holly Valance	Holly Vukadinovic
Kim Wilde	Kim Smith

Chaka Khan

BOOK OF LISTS

FORMER NAMES OF 40 POP GROUPS

GROUP	FORMER NAME
Abba	The Engaged Couples
The Bangles	The Supersonic Bangs
The Beach Boys	Carl and the Passions
The Beatles	The Quarrymen
Black Sabbath	Earth
Blondie	Angel and the Snakes
Blur	Seymour
Boomtown Rats	The Nightlife Thugs
Chicago	Chicago Transit Authority
Commodores	The Mighty Mystics
Culture Club	In Praise of Lemmings
The Cure	The Easy Cure
Depeche Mode	Composition of Sound
Dire Straits	The Café Racers
Dr. Hook	The Chocolate Papers
The Four Tops	The Four Aims
Frankie Goes to Hollywood	Hollycaust
Genesis	Garden Wall
Gerry and the Pacemakers	The Mars Bars
The Hollies	The Deltas
INXS	The Farriss Brothers
The Kinks	The Ravens

MUSIC

FORMER NAMES OF 40 POP GROUPS

GROUP	FORMER NAME
Led Zeppelin	The New Yardbirds
Madness	The Invaders
The Mamas and the Papas	The Mugwumps
New Kids on the Block	NYNUK
The Pogues	Pogue Mahone
The Righteous Brothers	The Paramours
The Rolling Stones	Satan's Jesters
The Shadows	The Drifters
Slade	The N'Betweens
Simply Red	The Frantic Elevators
The Spice Girls	Touch
Status Quo	The Spectres
The Stranglers	The Guildford Stranglers
The Supremes	The Primettes
Sweet	Wainwright's Gentlemen
Talking Heads	The Vague Dots
T Rex	Tyrannosaurus Rex
The Who	The High Numbers

BOOK OF LISTS

10 POP HITS BY FOOTBALL CLUBS

CLUB	SONG	CHART POSITION	YEAR
Arsenal	'Hot Stuff'	No. 9	1998
Chelsea	'Blue Is The Colour'	No. 5	1972
Coventry City	'Go For It'	No. 42	1987
Everton	'Here We Go'	No. 14	1985
Leeds United	'Leeds United'	No. 10	1972
Liverpool	'Anfield Rap'	No. 3	1988
Manchester United	'Come On You Reds'	No. 1	1994
Middlesbrough	'Let's Dance'	No. 44	1997
Nottingham Forest	'We've Got The Whole World In Our Hands'	No. 24	1978
Tottenham Hotspur	'Ossie's Dream'	No. 5	1981

MUSIC

10 POP HITS BY CHILDREN'S CHARACTERS

CHARACTER	SONG	CHART POSITION	YEAR
The Archies	'Sugar Sugar'	No. 1	1969
Bob the Builder	'Can We Fix It?'	No. 1	1993
Grange Hill Cast	'Just Say No'	No. 5	1986
Mr Blobby	'Mr Blobby'	No. 1	1993
The Muppets	'Halfway Down the Stairs'	No. 7	1977
The Simpsons	'Do the Bartman'	No. 1	1991
The Smurfs	'The Smurf Song'	No. 2	1978
Teletubbies	'Say Eh-Ho'	No. 1	1997
The Tweenies	'Number 1'	No. 5	2000
The Wombles	'The Wombling Song'	No. 4	1974

Mr Blobby

BOOK OF LISTS

20 ACTORS WHO HAVE HAD CHART HITS

ACTOR	SONG	CHART POSITION	YEAR
Nick Berry	'Every Loser Wins'	No. 1	1986
Dora Bryan	'All I Want for Christmas is a Beatle'	No. 20	1963
Richard Chamberlain	'Three Stars Will Shine Tonight'	No. 12	1962
Jim Dale	'Be My Girl'	No. 2	1957
Anita Dobson	'Anyone Can Fall in Love'	No. 4	1986
Clive Dunn	'Grandad'	No. 1	1970
Windsor Davies & Don Estelle	'Whispering Grass'	No. 1	1975
Judy Garland	'The Man that Got Away'	No. 18	1955
Benny Hill	'Ernie (The Fastest Milkman in the West)'	No. 1	1971
Don Johnson	'Till I Loved You'	No. 16	1988
Danny Kaye	'Wonderful Copenhagen'	No. 5	1953
Lee Marvin	'Wand'rin' Star'	No. 1	1970
Jimmy Nail	'Ain't No Doubt'	No. 1	1992
Telly Savalas	'If'	No. 1	1975
David Soul	'Don't Give up on us Baby'	No. 1	1976
Bill Tarmey	'One Voice'	No. 16	1993
Dennis Waterman	'I Could be so Good for You'	No. 3	1980
Bruce Willis	'Under The Boardwalk'	No. 2	1987
Kate Winslet	'What if?'	No. 6	2001
Edward Woodward	'The Way You Look Tonight'	No. 42	1971

MUSIC

30 FAMOUS PEOPLE MENTIONED IN THE LYRICS OF THE BILLY JOEL HIT 'WE DIDN'T START THE FIRE'

- Brigitte Bardot
- Marlon Brando
- Fidel Castro
- Chubby Checker
- Davy Crockett
- Doris Day
- James Dean
- Charles De Gaulle
- Joe Di Maggio
- Bob Dylan
- Albert Einstein
- Dwight Eisenhower
- Ernest Hemingway
- Buddy Holly
- Lawrence of Arabia
- Liberace
- Rocky Marciano
- Joe McCarthy
- Ho Chi Minh
- Marilyn Monroe
- Richard Nixon
- Boris Pasternak
- Juan Peron
- Elvis Presley
- Johnny Ray
- Ronald Reagan
- Sally Ride
- Josef Stalin
- Harry Truman
- Malcolm X

Joseph Stalin

BOOK OF LISTS

TRIBUTE TUNES

SONG	SINGER	TRIBUTE TO
'American Pie'	Don McLean	Buddy Holly
'Abraham, Martin and John'	Marvin Gaye	Abraham Lincoln, Martin Luther King & John F Kennedy
'Angel of Harlem'	U2	Billie Holliday
'Angie'	The Rolling Stones	Angie Bowie
'Black Superman'	Johnny Wakelin	Muhammed Ali
'Candle in the Wind'	Elton John	Marilyn Monroe
'Geno'	Dexy's Midnight Runners	Geno Washington
'Happy Birthday'	Stevie Wonder	Martin Luther King
'Killing Me Softly with his Song'	Roberta Flack	Don McLean
'Layla'	Derek & The Dominoes	Patti Boyd
'Now I Know What Made Otis Blue'	Paul Young	Otis Redding
'Oh Carol'	Neil Sedaka	Carole King
'Pearl's a Singer'	Elkie Brooks	Janis Joplin
'Philadelphia Freedom'	Elton John	Billie Jean King
'Shine on you Crazy Diamond'	Pink Floyd	Syd Barrett
'Sir Duke'	Stevie Wonder	Duke Ellington
'Vincent'	Don McLean	Vincent Van Gogh
'When Smokey Sings'	ABC	Smokey Robinson
'Where do You go to My Lovely'	Peter Sarstedt	Sophia Loren

MUSIC

10 RECORDS THAT WERE BANNED BY THE BBC

ARTIST	SONG
Wings	'Give Ireland back to the Irish'
The Sex Pistols	'God Save The Queen'
The Troggs	'I Can't Control Myself'
George Michael	'I Want Your Sex'
Jane Birkin & Serge Gainsbourg	'Je t'Aime…Mois Non Plus'
The Rolling Stones	'Let's Spend the Night Together'
Donna Summer	'Love to Love You Baby'
The Stranglers	'Peaches'
Frankie Goes To Hollywood	'Relax'
Ricky Valance	'Tell Laura I Love Her'

The Sex Pistols

BOOK OF LISTS

UK NO.1 HITS AT CHRISTMAS

1959	Emile Ford & The Checkmates	'What Do You Want to Make those Eyes at Me for'
1960	Cliff Richard	'I Love You'
1961	Danny Williams	'Moon River'
1962	Elvis Presley	'Return to Sender'
1963	The Beatles	'I Want to Hold your Hand'
1964	The Beatles	'I Feel Fine'
1965	The Beatles	'Day Tripper/ We Can Work it Out'
1966	Tom Jones	'Green Green Grass of Home'
1967	The Beatles	'Hello Goodbye'
1968	The Scaffold	'Lily the Pink'
1969	Rolf Harris	'Two Little Boys'
1970	Dave Edmunds	'I Hear You Knocking'
1971	Benny Hill	'Ernie (The Fastest Milk Man in the West)'
1972	Little Jimmy Osmond	'Long Haired Lover from Liverpool'
1973	Slade	'Merry Xmas Everybody'
1974	Mud	'Lonely this Christmas'
1975	Queen	'Bohemian Rhapsody'
1976	Johnny Mathis	'When a Child Is Born'
1977	Wings	'Mull of Kintyre/ Girls' School'
1978	Boney M	'Mary's Boy Child'
1979	Pink Floyd	'Another Brick in the Wall'
1980	St Winifred's School Choir	'There's No One Quite Like Grandma'
1981	Human League	'Don't You Want Me?'

MUSIC

UK NO.1 HITS AT CHRISTMAS

1982	Renee & Renato	'Save Your Love'
1983	The Flying Pickets	'Only You'
1984	Band Aid	'Do They Know it's Christmas?'
1985	Shakin' Stevens	'Merry Christmas Everyone'
1986	Jackie Wilson	'Reet Petite'
1987	Pet Shop Boys	'Always on my Mind'
1988	Cliff Richard	'Mistletoe and Wine'
1989	Band Aid II	'Do They Know it's Christmas?'
1990	Cliff Richard	'Saviour's Day'
1991	Queen	'Bohemian Rhapsody'
1992	Whitney Houston	'I Will Always Love You'
1993	Mr Blobby	'Mr Blobby'
1994	East 17	'Stay Another Day'
1995	Michael Jackson	'Earth Song'
1996	Spice Girls	'2 Become 1'
1997	Spice Girls	'Too Much'
1998	Spice Girls	'Goodbye'
1999	Westlife	'I Have a Dream/ Seasons in the Sun'
2000	Bob the Builder	'Can We Fix It?'
2001	Robbie Williams & Nicole Kidman	'Somethin' Stupid'
2002	Girls Aloud	'Sound of the Underground'
2003	Michael Andrews & Gary Jules	'Mad World'
2004	Band Aid 20	'Do They Know it's Christmas?'
2005	Shayne Ward	'That's My Goal'

BOOK OF LISTS

ROCKING ALL OVER THE WORLD
Pop groups named after places

GROUP	BIGGEST HIT
America	'A Horse with no Name'
Atlantic Starr	'Always'
Babylon Zoo	'Spaceman'
Berlin	'Take my Breath Away'
Boston	'More than a Feeling'
Chicago	'If You Leave Me Now'
Detroit Emeralds	'Feel the Need in Me'
Detroit Spinners	'Working my Way back to You'
Europe	'The Final Countdown'
Hollywood Beyond	'What's the Colour of Money?'
Japan	'Ghosts'
Manhattan Transfer	'Chanson D'Amour'
Merseybeats	'I Think of You'
Nashville Teens	'Tobacco Road'
Nazareth	'Broken Down Angel'
New York City	'I'm Doin' Fine Now'
Ohio Express	'Yummy Yummy Yummy'
Salford Jets	'Who You Looking at?'
Texas	'Say What You Want'

MUSIC

22 NO. 2 HITS

NO. 2 SONG/ARTIST	KEPT OFF NO. 1 BY...
'American Pie'/ Don McLean	'Son of My Father'/ Chicory Tip
'Black Night'/ Deep Purple	'The Wonder of You'/ Elvis Presley
'Common People'/ Pulp	'Unchained Melody'/ Robson & Jerome
'Flowers In The Rain'/ The Move	'The Last Waltz'/ Engelbert Humperdinck
'Heal The World'/ Michael Jackson	'I Will always Love You'/ Whitney Houston
'In The Air Tonight'/ Phil Collins	'Imagine'/ John Lennon
'Jean Genie'/ David Bowie	'Long Haired Lover from Liverpool'/ Jimmy Osmond
'Last Christmas'/ Wham	'Do They Know it's Christmas?'/ Band Aid
'Lola'/ The Kinks	'In the Summertime'/ Mungo Jerry
'Manic Monday'/ The Bangles	'When the Going Gets Tough'/ Billy Ocean
'My Generation'/ The Who	'The Carnival is over'/ The Seekers
'Oliver's Army'/ Elvis Costello	'Heart of Glass'/ Blondie
'Penny Lane'/ The Beatles	'Release Me'/ Engelbert Humperdinck
'Ride A White Swan'/ T Rex	'Grandad'/ Clive Dunn
'Save The Last Dance For Me'/ The Drifters	'It's now or never'/ Elvis Presley
'Sir Duke'/ Stevie Wonder	'Knowing Me Knowing You'/ Abba
'Sit Down'/ James	'The One and Only'/ Chesney Hawkes
'Sunshine Superman'/ Donovan	'Green Green Grass of Home'/ Tom Jones
'Suspicious Minds'/ Elvis Presley	'Two Little Boys'/ Rolf Harris
'Tubthumping'/ Chumbawumba	'Men in Black'/ Will Smith
'Vienna'/ Ultravox	'Shaddup You Face'/ Joe Dolce
'Wonderwall'/ Oasis	'I Believe'/ Robson & Jerome

BOOK OF LISTS

10 SINGERS WHO TOPPED THE CHARTS AS A TEENAGER

SINGER	AGE	SONG
Helen Shapiro	14	'You Don't Know'
Donny Osmond	14	'Puppy Love'
Billie Piper	15	'Because We Want to'
Paul Anka	16	'Diana'
Tiffany	16	'I Think We're Alone now'
Britney Spears	17	'Baby One More Time'
Gareth Gates	17	'Unchained Melody'
Craig David	18	'Fill Me in'
Cliff Richard	18	'Living Doll'
Kylie Minogue	19	'I Should Be so Lucky'

Craig David

MUSIC

10 SINGERS WHO TOPPED THE CHARTS PAST THEIR 50TH BIRTHDAY

SINGER	SONG
50-year-old Charles Aznavour	'She'
50-year-old Clive Dunn	'Grandad'
51-year-old Telly Savalas	'If'
51-year-old Frank Sinatra	'Somethin' Stupid' (duet with Nancy Sinatra)
52-year-old Cher	'Believe'
55-year-old Elton John	'Sorry Seems to be the Hardest Word' (with Blue)
57-year-old Gene Pitney	'Something's Gotten Hold of my Heart' (with Marc Almond)
58-year-old George Harrison	'My Sweet Lord' (2 months after his death aged 58)
59-year-old Cliff Richard	'Millennium Prayer'
66-year-old Louis Armstrong	'What a Wonderful World'

Frank Sinatra

BOOK OF LISTS

NO. 1 HITS THAT ASKED A QUESTION

1953	'How Much is that Doggie in the Window?'	Lita Roza
1956	'Why do Fools Fall in Love?'	Frankie Lymon
1958	'Who's Sorry now?'	Connie Francis
1959	'What do You Want?'	Adam Faith
1959	'What do You Want to Make Those Eyes at Me for?'	Emile Ford
1960	'Why?'	Anthony Newley
1961	'Are You Lonesome Tonight?'	Elvis Presley
1963	'How do You Do it?'	Gerry & The Pacemakers
1964	'Have I the Right?'	The Honeycombs
1965	'Where Are You now my Love?'	Jackie Trent
1969	'Where do You Go to my Lovely?'	Peter Sarstedt
1972	'How Can I Be Sure?'	David Cassidy
1974	'When Will I See You again?'	The Three Degrees
1979	'Are Friends Electric?'	Tubeway Army
1980	'What's Another Year?'	Johnny Logan
1981	'Don't You Want Me?'	Human League
1982	'Do You Really Want to Hurt Me?'	Culture Club
1983	'Is There Something I Should Know?'	Duran Duran
1984	'Do They Know it's Christmas?'	Band Aid
1987	'Who's that Girl?'	Madonna
1996	'How Deep Is Your Love?'	Take That
1997	'Who Do You Think You Are?'	Spice Girls
2000	'Can We Fix it?'	Bob the Builder

MUSIC

SONGS THAT WON A 'BEST SONG' OSCAR

SONG	FILM
'Baby it's Cold Outside'	*Neptune's Daughter*
'Born Free'	*Born Free*
'Can You Feel the Love Tonight?'	*The Lion King*
'Chim Chim Cheree'	*Mary Poppins*
'Fame'	*Fame*
'High Hopes'	*A Hole in the Head*
'I Just Called to Say I Love You'	*The Woman in Red*
'Moon River'	*Breakfast at Tiffany's*
'My Heart Will Go on'	*Titanic*
'Over the Rainbow'	*The Wizard of Oz*
'Raindrops Keep Falling on my Head'	*Butch Cassidy & the Sundance Kid*
'Secret Love'	*Calamity Jane*
'Streets of Philadelphia'	*Philadelphia*
'Take my Breath away'	*Top Gun*
'Talk to the Animals'	*Dr Doolittle*
'Time of my Life'	*Dirty Dancing*
'Up Where We Belong'	*An Officer and a Gentleman*
'Whatever Will Be Will Be'	*The Man who Knew too Much*
'When You Wish upon a Star'	*Pinocchio*
'White Christmas'	*Holiday Inn*

BOOK OF LISTS

10 SINGERS BORN IN WALES

- Shirley Bassey
- Charlotte Church
- Dave Edmunds
- Mary Hopkin
- Tom Jones
- Cerys Matthews
- Harry Secombe
- Shakin' Stevens
- Bonnie Tyler
- Malcolm Vaughan

10 SINGERS BORN IN SCOTLAND

- Karl Denver
- Lonnie Donegan
- Donovan
- Sheena Easton
- Jim Kerr
- Mark Knopfler
- Annie Lennox
- Lulu
- Marti Pellow
- Lena Zavaroni

MUSIC

10 SINGERS BORN IN IRELAND

- Sinead O'Connor
- Val Doonican
- Enya
- Bob Geldof
- Ronan Keating
- Van Morrison
- Samantha Mumba
- Ruby Murray
- Feargal Sharkey
- Gilbert O'Sullivan

10 SINGERS BORN IN LONDON

- David Bowie
- Phil Collins
- Ray Davies
- Adam Faith
- Elton John
- George Michael
- Helen Shapiro
- Dusty Springfield
- Alvin Stardust
- Rod Stewart

BOOK OF LISTS

IT TAKES TWO

DUO	MEMBERS
Alisha's Attic	Shellie & Karen Poole
Appleton	Natalie & Nicole Appleton
Baccara	Maria Mendiola & Mayte Mateos
Bellamy Brothers	David & Howard Bellamy
Black Lace	Alan Barton & Colin Routh
Bob & Earl	Bobby Relf & Earl Nelson
Bob & Marcia	Bob Andy & Marcia Griffiths
Brian & Michael	Kevin Parrott & Michael Coleman
Buggles	Trevor Horn & Geoff Downes
The Carpenters	Karen & Richard Carpenter
Charles & Eddie	Charles Pettigrew & Eddie Chacon
Chas & Dave	Charles Hodges & David Peacock
The Cheeky Girls	Gabriella & Monica Irimia
The Chemical Brothers	Tom Rowlands & Ed Symons
Erasure	Vince Clarke & Andy Bell
Eurythmics	Annie Lennox & Dave Stewart
The Everly Brothers	Don & Phil Everly
Everything But The Girl	Tracy Thorn & Ben Watt
Glenn & Chris	Glenn Hoddle & Chris Waddle
Go West	Peter Cox & Richard Drummie
Hall & Oates	Daryl Hall & John Oates
Hue & Cry	Greg & Pat Kane

MUSIC

IT TAKES TWO

DUO	MEMBERS
Jan & Dean	Jan Berry & Dean Torrence
Kalin Twins	Al & Herb Kalin
Kris Kross	Chris Kelly & Chris Smith
Orbital	Paul & Phil Hartnoll
Peaches & Herb	Linda Green & Herbert Feemter
Pepsi & Shirlie	Helen DeMacque & Shirlie Holliman
Peter & Gordon	Peter Asher & Gordon Waller
Pet Shop Boys	Neil Tennant & Chris Lowe
Proclaimers	Charles & Craig Reid
Righteous Brothers	Bill Medley & Bobby Hatfield
Robson & Jerome	Robson Green & Jerome Flynn
Roxette	Marie Fredriksson & Per Gessle
Salt N Pepa	Cheryl "Salt" James & Sandra "Pepa" Denton
Sam & Dave	Sam Moore & Dave Prater
Savage Garden	Darren Hayes & Daniel Jones
Shakespear's Sister	Marcella Detroit & Siobhan Fahey
Soft Cell	Marc Almond & Dave Ball
Sonny & Cher	Salvator Bono & Cherilyn LaPierre
2 Unlimited	Anita Dels & Ray Slijngaard
Utah Saints	Tim Garbutt & Jez Willis
Was Not Was	Don Fagenson & David Weiss
White Stripes	Jack & Meg White

BOOK OF LISTS

THREE'S A CROWD

TRIO NAME	MEMBERS
A-Ha	Morten Harket, Paul Waaktaar-Savoy, Magn Furuholmen
The Bachelors	John Stokes, Con Cluskey, Declan Cluskey
The Beastie Boys	Adam Horowitz, Michael Diamond, Adam Yauch
Bee Gees	Barry, Maurice and Robin Gibb
Busted	James Bourne, Matt Jay, Charlie Simpson
Cream	Eric Clapton, Ginger Baker, Jack Bruce
Destiny's Child	Beyonce Knowles, Michelle Williams, Kelly Rowland
Fine Young Cannibals	Roland Gift, Andy Cox, David Steele
Fun Boy Three	Terry Hall, Lynval Golding, Neville Staples
The Jam	Paul Weller, Bruce Foxton, Rick Buckler
Nirvana	Kurt Cobain, David Grohl, Chris Novoselic
The Police	Sting, Andy Summers, Stewart Copeland
Right Said Fred	Richard Fairbrass, Fred Fairbrass, Rob Manzoli
The Ronettes	Estelle Bennett, Ronnie Bennett, Nedra Talley
Scaffold	Mike McGear, Roger McGough, John Gorman
Shalamar	Jody Watley, Howard Hewett, Jeffrey Daniel
Supergrass	Gaz Coombes, Micky Quinn, Danny Goffey
The Thompson Twins	Tom Bailey, Alannah Currie, Joe Leeway
The Three Degrees	Sheila Ferguson, Fayette Pinkney, Valerie Holiday
TLC	Tionne 'T-Boz' Watkins, Lisa 'Left-eye' Lopez, Rozonda 'Chilli' Thomas

MUSIC

MUSICAL INSTRUCTIONS

INSTRUCTION	MEANING
Accelerando	Becoming faster
Adagio	Slow tempo
Adagissimo	Very slow tempo
Addolorato	Sorrowfully
Allegretto	Medium quickly
Allegro	Quickly
Ancora	Repeat
Brio	With vigour
Calcando	Quicken gradually
Crescendo	Becoming louder
Da capo	From the beginning
Diminuendo	Becoming quieter
Forte	Loudly
Fortissimo	Very loudly
Largo	Slow tempo
Lento	Slow
Pizzicato	Plucking the strings
Presto	Fast
Rallentando	Becoming gradually slower
Subito	Suddenly
Tacet	Stop playing

BOOK OF LISTS

A NIGHT AT THE OPERA

OPERA	COMPOSER
Aida	Giuseppe Verdi
The Barber of Seville	Antonio Rossini
The Bartered Bride	Bedrich Smetana
The Beggars Opera	Christoph Pepusch
Billy Budd	Benjamin Britten
La Bohème	Giacomo Puccini
Boris Godunov	Modeste Mussorgsky
Candide	Leonard Bernstein
Carmen	Georges Bizet
Cosi fan tutte	Wolfgang Amadeus Mozart
Don Giovanni	Wolfgang Amadeus Mozart
Elektra	Richard Strauss
The Fall of the House of Usher	Claude Debussy
Falstaff	Giuseppe Verdi
Fidelio	Ludwig van Beethoven
Die Fledermaus	Johann Strauss II
The Flying Dutchman	Richard Wagner
Hansel and Gretel	Engelbert Humperdinck
King Priam	Michael Tippett
Madame Butterfly	Giacomo Puccini
The Magic Flute	Wolfgang Amadeus Mozart
The Marriage of Figaro	Wolfgang Amadeus Mozart

MUSIC

A NIGHT AT THE OPERA

OPERA	COMPOSER
The Merry Widow	Franz Lehar
Orpheus in the Underworld	Jacques Offenbach
Parsifal	Richard Wagner
The Pearl Fishers	Georges Bizet
Peter Grimes	Benjamin Britten
The Pilgrim's Progress	Ralph Vaughan Williams
Porgy and Bess	George Gershwin
Prince Igor	Alexander Borodin
The Rake's Progress	Igor Stravinsky
Rigoletto	Giuseppe Verdi
The Snow Maiden	Rimsky Nicolai Korsakov
The Thieving Magpie	Antonio Rossini
The Threepenny Opera	Kurt Weill
Tosca	Giacomo Puccini
La Traviata	Giuseppe Verdi
Turandot	Giacomo Puccini

Madame Butterfly

THE ALTERNATIVE TITLES OF
10 GILBERT & SULLIVAN OPERETTAS

TITLE	ALSO KNOWN AS
The Gondoliers	The King of Barataria
The Grand Duke	The Statutory Duel
HMS Pinafore	The Lass that Loved a Sailor
Iolanthe	The Peer and the Peri
The Mikado	The Town of Titipu
Patience	Bunthorne's Bride
The Pirates of Penzance	The Slave of Duty
Princess Ida	Castle Adamant
Ruddigore	The Witch's Curse
The Yeoman of the Guard	The Merryman and his Maid

Gilbert & Sullivan

MUSIC

THE ALTERNATIVE NAMES OF 10 SYMPHONIES

Beethoven

SYMPHONY	ALSO KNOWN AS
Beethoven's Symphony No. 3 in E flat minor	The Eroica
Beethoven's Symphony No. 9 in D minor	The Choral
Dvorak's Symphony No. 9 in E minor	The New World
Haydn's Symphony No. 94 in G major	The Surprise
Haydn's Symphony No. 101 in D	The Clock
Mendelssohn's Symphony No. 5 in D minor	The Reformation
Mozart's Symphony No. 31 in D	The Paris
Mozart's Symphony No. 41 in C major	The Jupiter
Schubert's Symphony No. 8 in B minor	The Unfinished
Tchaikovsky's Symphony No. 6 in B minor	The Pathétique

BOOK OF LISTS

BACKING BANDS

ARTIST	and the...
Cliff Bennett	Rebel Rousers
Acker Bilk	Paramount Jazz Band
James Brown	Famous Flames
Joe Brown	Bruvvers
Nick Cave	Bad Seeds
Elvis Costello	Attractions
Kid Creole	Coconuts
Desmond Dekker	Aces
Dion	Belmonts
Disco Tex	Sex-O-Lettes
Ian Dury	Blockheads
Adam Faith	Roulettes
Georgie Fame	Blue Flames
Wayne Fontana	Mindbenders
Emile Ford	Checkmates
Bill Haley	Comets
Jimmy James	Vagabonds
Tommy James	Shondells
Joan Jett	Blackhearts
Johnny Kidd	Pirates
Gladys Knight	Pips
Billy J Kramer	Dakotas

Gladys Knight and the Pips

MUSIC

BACKING BANDS

ARTIST	and the...
Huey Lewis	News
Frankie Lymon	Teenagers
Rob Marley	Wailers
Ziggy Marley	Melody Makers
Harold Melvin	Bluenotes
Graham Parker	Rumour
Iggy Pop	Stooges
Elvis Presley	Jordanaires
Prince	Revolution
Otis Redding	Bar Kays
Martha Reeves	Vandellas
Smokey Robinson	Miracles
Bob Seger	Silver Bullet Band
Bruce Springsteen	E Street Band
Tommy Steele	Steelmen
Gene Vincent	Blue Caps
Junior Walker	All Stars
Yazz	Plastic Population

BOOK OF LISTS

RECORD LABELS

LABEL	FOUNDED BY
A & M	Herb Alpert and Jerry Moss
Brother Records	The Beach Boys
Dark Horse	George Harrison
Edison	Thomas Alva Edison (first ever record label, founded in 1877)
Factory Records	Tony Wilson
Island Records	Chris Blackwell
Maverick	Madonna
Motown	Berry Gordy Jnr
RAK	Mickie Most
Virgin	Richard Branson

LABEL	INITIALS STAND FOR
BMG	Bertelsmann Music Group
CBS	Columbia Broadcasting System
EMI	Electric and Musical Industries
HMV	His Master's Voice
IRS	International Record Syndicate
MCA	Music Corporation of America
PWL	Pete Waterman Ltd
RCA	Radio Corporation of America
RSO	Robert Stigwood Organization
UK Records	United King (founded by Jonathan King)

MUSIC

THE 9 UK NO. 1 HITS OF ABBA

1974 'Waterloo'
1975 'Mamma Mia'
1976 'Fernando'
1976 'Dancing Queen'
1977 'Knowing Me, Knowing You'
1977 'The Name Of The Game'
1978 'Take A Chance On Me'
1980 'The Winner Takes It All'
1980 'Super Trouper'

Abba

THE 8 UK NO. 1 HITS OF THE ROLLING STONES

1964 'It's All Over Now'
1964 'Little Red Rooster'
1965 'The Last Time'
1965 'I Can't Get no Satisfaction'
1965 'Get off My Cloud'
1966 'Paint it Black'
1968 'Jumpin' Jack Flash'
1969 'Honky Tonk Woman'

BOOK OF LISTS

THE 7 UK NO. 1 HITS OF MICHAEL JACKSON

1981	'One Day in your Life'
1983	'Billie Jean'
1987	'I just Can't Stop Loving You'
1991	'Black or White'
1995	'You are not Alone'
1995	'Earth Song'
1997	'Blood on the Dancefloor'

THE 8 UK NO. 1 HITS OF TAKE THAT

1993	'Pray'
1993	'Relight My Fire'
1993	'Babe'
1994	'Everything Changes'
1994	'Sure'
1995	'Back for Good'
1995	'Never Forget'
1996	'How Deep Is Your Love'

Take That

MUSIC

THE 9 UK NO. 1 HITS OF THE SPICE GIRLS

1996	'Wannabe'
1996	'Say You'll Be There'
1996	'2 Become 1'
1997	'Mama / Who Do You Think You Are?'
1997	'Spice up Your Life'
1997	'Too Much'
1998	'Viva Forever'
1998	'Goodbye'
2000	'Holler / Let Love Lead the Way'

THE 7 UK NO. 1 HITS OF GEORGE MICHAEL

1984	'Careless Whisper'
1986	'A Different Corner'
1987	'I Knew You Were Waiting' (duet with Aretha Franklin)
1991	'Don't Let the Sun Go Down on Me' (duet with Elton John)
1993	'Five Live'
1996	'Jesus to a Child'
1996	'Fastlove'

George Michael

BOOK OF LISTS

THE MUSICALS OF ANDREW LLOYD WEBBER

SHOW TITLE	COLLABORATED WITH
Aspects of Love	Don Black & Charles Hart
The Beautiful Game	Ben Elton
Bombay Dreams	Shekhar Kapur & AR Rahman
By Jeeves	Alan Ayckbourn
Cats	Trevor Nunn
Evita	Tim Rice
Jesus Christ Superstar	Tim Rice
Joseph and the Technicolour Dreamcoat	Tim Rice
Phantom of the Opera	Charles Hart & Richard Stilgoe
Song and Dance	Don Black
Starlight Express	Richard Stilgoe
Sunset Boulevard	Don Black
Tell Me on a Sunday	Don Black
Whistle down the Wind	Jim Steinman
The Woman in White	David Zippel

Starlight Express

MUSIC

THE FINAL RESTING PLACES OF POP STARS

STAR	RESTING PLACE
Louis Armstrong	Flushing Cemetery, New York
Marc Bolan	Golders Green Crematorium, London
Bing Crosby	Holy Cross Cemetery, Culver City, California
Billy Fury	Paddington Cemetery, London
Jimi Hendrix	Greenwood Memorial Park, Washington
Buddy Holly	City of Lubbock Cemetery, Texas
Brian Jones	Prior Road Cemetery, Gloucestershire
Phil Lynott	St Fintan's Cemetery, Sutton, Ireland
Bob Marley	Bob Marley Mausoleum, Nine Mile, Jamaica
Dean Martin	Westwood Memorial Park, Los Angeles
Jim Morrison	Cimetière du Père Lachaise, Paris
Roy Orbison	Westwood Memorial Park, Los Angeles
Robert Palmer	Lugano Cemetery, Switzerland
Elvis Presley	Graceland Mansion Estates, Memphis
Johnnie Ray	Hopewell Cemetery, Oregon
Dusty Springfield	St Mary the Virgin Church, Henley-on-Thames
Edwin Starr	Wilford Hill Cemetery, Nottingham
Jackie Wilson	Westlawn Cemetery, Wayne, Michigan
Tammy Wynette	Woodlawn Memorial Park, Nashville

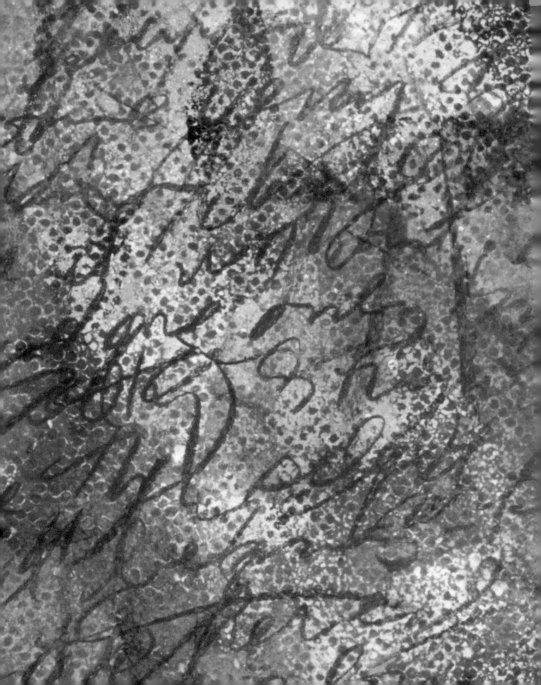

ART & LITERATURE

Painting, sculpture, drama, both adult and children's fiction – as well as many of the talented people who have created works in these areas – are all featured in this section. These are just some of the artists, writers and characters about whom you will discover something: John Constable, Pablo Picasso, Edward Lutyens, Jacob Epstein, Charles Dickens, Kelsey Grammer, Jerry Cruncher, Paul Sweedlepipe, William Shakespeare, Alicia Silverstone, Tabaqui, Chippy Hackee, Samuel Langhorne Clemens, The Prisoner of Zenda... and countless others.

PROFILE OF VINCENT VAN GOGH

Born: March 30, 1853

Birthplace: Groot Zundert, Netherlands

Parents: Theodorus Van Gogh and Anna Cornelia Carbentus

Paintings sold: One during his lifetime, *The Red Vineyard*

Died: July 29, 1890

DID YOU KNOW?

In the 1870s Van Gogh worked as a teacher at the Reverend William P Stokes School in Ramsgate

On December 23, 1888, in a fit of madness, Van Gogh severed the lower portion of his left ear before wrapping it in a cloth and delivering it to a local brothel

In the 1870s Van Gogh worked as a mission preacher in Wasruses

In 1889, Van Gogh was confined to the St Paul de Mausole asylum under the supervision of Dr Théophile Zacharie

On June 2, 1973 the Vincent Van Gogh Museum was opened to the public in Amsterdam

10 PAINTINGS BY VINCENT VAN GOGH

- *Sunflowers*
- *Irises*
- *Portrait of Dr Gachet*
- *Portrait of Père Tangui*
- *The Potato Eaters*
- *Starry Night*
- *Wheat Field with Cypresses*
- *Thistles*
- *Haystacks in Provence*
- *Basket of Apples*

ART & LITERATURE

PROFILE OF REMBRANDT

Born: July 15, 1606

Birthplace: Leiden, Netherlands

Apprentice to: Pieter Lastman

Wife: Saskia van Uylenburgh, the cousin of a successful art dealer

Died: October 4, 1669

DID YOU KNOW?

Rembrandt's full name is Rembrandt Harmenszoon van Rijn

Rembrandt's wife Saskia died in 1642. Later his housekeeper Hendrickje Stoffels became his common-law wife and the model for many of his paintings

Rembrandt and Saskia bore four children, however only their last born son Titus survived into adulthood

It is estimated that Rembrandt painted up to 100 self-portraits, many of which were lost

Rembrandt died in poverty in 1669 and was buried in an unmarked grave in the Dutch town of Westerkerk

10 PAINTINGS BY REMBRANDT

- *The Night Watch*
- *The Jewish Bride*
- *Portrait of Nicolaes Ruts*
- *Anatomy Lesson of Dr Tulp*
- *Bathsheba*
- *The Blinding of Samson*
- *The Return of the Prodigal Son*
- *The Music Party*
- *Adoration of the Shepherds*
- *The Syndics of the Cloth Guild*

BOOK OF LISTS

PROFILE OF PABLO PICASSO

Born: October 25, 1881

Birthplace: Malaga, Spain

Parents: Don Jose Ruiz Blasco and Dona Maria Picasso y Lopez

Women in his life: Wife Jacqueline Roque and a string of lovers including Dora Mar and Francoise Gilot

Died: April 8, 1973

DID YOU KNOW?

Picasso signed his early works with the name of Ruiz Blasco, and from 1901 onwards used his mother's name of Picasso

Picasso began his Blue Period in 1901 after the death of his friend, an artist by the name of Casagemas, who committed suicide after being rejected by a woman

Picasso was an ardent pacifist and remained neutral in the Spanish Civil War, World War I and World War II

Picasso's full name is Pablo Diego Jose Santiago Francisco de Paula Juan Nepomuceno Crispin Crispiniano de los Remedios Cipriano de la Santisima Trinidad Ruiz Blasco y Picasso

10 PAINTINGS BY PICASSO

- *Guernica*
- *Weeping Woman*
- *Charnel House*
- *The First Communion*
- *Boy with a Pipe*
- *Science and Charity*
- *Death of Casagemas*
- *Le Moulin de la Galette*
- *The Pipes of Pan*
- *The Lovers*

ART & LITERATURE

PROFILE OF L S LOWRY

Born: November 1, 1887

Birthplace: Rusholme, Manchester

Full name: Laurence Stephen Lowry

Parents: Father Robert an estate agent and mother Elizabeth a piano teacher

Died: February 23, 1976

DID YOU KNOW?

In 1910 Lowry worked as a rent collector for the Manchester property firm Pall Mall Company. It was this job, walking through the working-class areas of Manchester, that inspired his later works

Lowry's painting *Going to the Match*, was purchased by the Professional Footballers Association for £1.9 million

In 1964, the Prime Minister Harold Wilson used a picture of a Lowry painting, *The Pond*, as his official Christmas card

Lowry had no wife or family when he died and left his entire estate to Carol Lowry. They were unrelated and first met in 1957 after she wrote to her namesake for advice on how to become an artist.

10 PAINTINGS BY LOWRY

- *Going to the Match*
- *The Fever Van*
- *The Two Brothers*
- *The Beach*
- *Industrial Town*
- *Great Ancoats Street*
- *Burford Church*
- *The Tall Tower*
- *The Cart*
- *Outside the Mill*

BOOK OF LISTS

PROFILE OF JOHN CONSTABLE

Born: June 11, 1776

Birthplace: East Burgholt, Suffolk

Parents: Golding, a prosperous businessman who owned Flatford Mill and mother Ann

Wife: Maria Bicknell

Died: March 31, 1837

DID YOU KNOW?

Constable was a fellow student of JMW Turner at the Royal Academy School, but failed to match the success of Turner in Britain, selling only 20 paintings in his lifetime

Constable's talent was more appreciated in France, where he was awarded the prestigious Gold Medal for his works

The area surrounding the river Stour on the Essex/Suffolk border, which includes Dedham, East Bergholt and Flatford Mill, is today known as Constable Country as it provided the inspiration for many of his landscapes

Quote by John Constable, "The sound of water escaping from mill dams, willows, old rotten planks, slimy posts and brickwork, I love such things. These scenes made me a painter."

10 PAINTINGS BY JOHN CONSTABLE

- *The Haywain*
- *Flatford Mill*
- *Brighton Beach*
- *The White Horse*
- *The Lock at Dedham*
- *Tree Trunks*
- *Valley of the Stour*
- *Cornfield*
- *Willy Lott's Cottage*
- *Hampstead Heath*

ART & LITERATURE

ART FOR ART'S SAKE
20 famous paintings and 20 famous painters

PAINTING	ARTIST
A Bar at the Folies-Bergère	Edouard Manet
At the Moulin Rouge	Henri de Toulouse-Lautrec
The Birth of Venus	Sandro Botticelli
The Blue Boy	Thomas Gainsborough
Campbell's Soup Cans	Andy Warhol
The Colossus	Francisco de Goya
The Descent from the Cross	Peter Paul Rubens
The Fighting Temeraire	Joseph Mallord William Turner
The Laughing Cavalier	Franz Hals
The Man with a Straw Hat	Paul Cézanne
The Massacre of the Innocents	Pieter Brueghel the Elder
Monarch of the Glen	Edwin Landseer
Nude Descending a Staircase	Marcel Duchamp
The Rake's Progress	William Hogarth
The Rokeby Venus	Diego Velázquez
Samson and Delilah	Anthony Van Dyck
The Scream	Edvard Munch
Spring Trees by a Lake	Claude Monet
Portrait of the Artist's Mother	James Whistler
The Yellow Christ	Paul Gauguin

BOOK OF LISTS

STATUESQUE
20 statues and sculptures

STATUE/SCULPTURE	SCULPTOR
Abraham Lincoln	Daniel Chester French
Angel of the North	Antony Gormley
Awakening	Paul Philippe
The Cenotaph	Edward Lutyens
Christ the Redeemer	Paul Landowski
The Feast of Herod	Donatello
The Kiss	Auguste Rodin

The Little Mermaid

ART & LITERATURE

STATUESQUE
20 statues and sculptures

STATUE/SCULPTURE	SCULPTOR
La Fuega d'Attila	Alessandro Algardi
Lions at the base of Nelson's Column	Edwin Landseer
The Little Mermaid	Edvard Eriksen
Madonna and Child	Henry Moore
Mannekin Pis	Based on a sculpture by Francois Duquesnoy
Mount Rushmore, President's heads	John Gutzon Borglum
Night and Day	Jacob Epstein
Oscar statuette	Designed by Cedric Gibbons
Pieta for St Peter's Basilica	Michelangelo Buonarroti
David	Michelangelo Buonarroti
Statue of Liberty	Frederic Auguste Bartholdi
St Michael and the Devil	Jacob Epstein
The Thinker	Auguste Rodin

BOOK OF LISTS

OPENING LINES OF FAMOUS NOVELS

■ *Alice's Adventures In Wonderland*

'Alice was beginning to get very tired of sitting by her sister on the bank.'

■ *Black Beauty*

'The first place that I can well remember, was a large pleasant meadow with a pond of clear water in it.'

■ *The Children of the New Forest*

'The circumstances which I am about to relate to my juvenile readers took place in the year 1647.'

■ *A Christmas Carol*

'Marley was dead to begin with.'

■ *Gulliver's Travels*

'My father had a small estate in Nottinghamshire; I was the third of five sons.'

■ *Harry Potter and the Philosopher's Stone*

'Mr and Mrs Dursley, of number four Privet Drive, were proud to say that they were perfectly normal.'

■ *The Hobbit*

'In a hole in the ground there lived a Hobbit.'

■ *James and the Giant Peach*

'Until he was four years old, James Henry Trotter had a happy life.'

■ *The Lion, The Witch and the Wardrobe*

'Once there were four children whose names were Peter, Susan, Edmund and Lucy.'

■ *Little Women*

'"Christmas won't be Christmas without any presents", grumbled Jo, lying on the rug.'

ART & LITERATURE

OPENING LINES OF FAMOUS NOVELS

■ *Mary Poppins*

'If you want to find Cherry Tree Lane all you have to do is ask a policeman at the crossroads.'

■ *Peter Pan*

'All children, except one, grow up.'

■ *Rebecca*

'Last night I dreamt I went to Manderley again.'

■ *The Secret Garden*

'When Mary Lennox was sent to Misselthwaite Manor to live with her Uncle, everybody said she was the most disagreeable looking child ever seen.'

■ *Pride and Prejudice*

'It is a truth universally acknowledged, that a single man in possession of a good fortune, must be in want of a wife.'

■ *The Water Babies*

'Once upon a time, there was a little chimney-sweep and his name was Tom.'

■ *White Fang*

'Dark spruce forest frowned on either side of the frozen waterway.'

■ *The Wind in the Willows*

'The Mole had been working hard all the morning spring cleaning his little home.'

■ *The Wonderful Wizard of Oz*

'Dorothy lived in the midst of the great Kansas prairies with Uncle Henry, who was a farmer, and Aunt Em, who was the farmer's wife.'

BOOK OF LISTS

WHAT THE DICKENS
A Charles Dickens timeline

1812	Born in Portsmouth on February 7, to parents John and Elizabeth
1821	Attends William Giles's School
1824	Begins work at Warren's Blacking Factory
1827	Takes up a clerical post at Ellis and Blackmore, a firm of solicitors
1831	Begins work as a parliamentary reporter
1834	Becomes a reporter for the *Morning Chronicle* newspaper
1836	Marries Catherine Hogarth
1836	Publication of *The Pickwick Papers*
1837	Publication of *Oliver Twist*
1838	Publication of *Nicholas Nickleby*
1840	Publication of *The Old Curiosity Shop*
1841	Publication of *Barnaby Rudge*
1843	Publication of *Martin Chuzzlewit* and *A Christmas Carol*
1846	Publication of *Dombey And Son*
1849	Publication of *David Copperfield*
1852	Publication of *Bleak House*
1854	Publication of *Hard Times*
1855	Publication of *Little Dorrit*
1859	Publication of *A Tale Of Two Cities*
1860	Publication of *Great Expectations*
1864	Publication of *Our Mutual Friend*
1870	Dies on June 9, leaving *The Mystery of Edwin Drood* unfinished

ART & LITERATURE

10 ACTORS WHO HAVE PORTRAYED EBENEZER SCROOGE

Albert Finney

- Michael Caine
- George C Scott
- Albert Finney
- Simon Callow
- Seymour Hicks
- Noel Leslie
- Reginald Owen
- Kelsey Grammer
- Michael Hordern
- John Carradine

10 ACTORS WHO HAVE PORTRAYED FAGIN

- Alec Guinness
- Ben Kingsley
- Ron Moody
- George C Scott
- Eric Porter
- Lon Chaney
- Gary Farmer
- Richard Dreyfuss
- Robert Lindsay
- Max Adrian

Alec Guinness

BOOK OF LISTS

A DICKENSIAN JOB CENTRE

CHARACTER	NOVEL	OCCUPATION
Bayham Badger	*Bleak House*	Doctor
Mrs Bangham	*Little Dorrit*	Prison charlady
Stephen Blackpool	*Hard Times*	Mill worker
Noddy Boffin	*Our Mutual Friend*	Servant
Sampson Brass	*The Old Curiosity Shop*	Attorney
Jefferson Brick	*Martin Chuzzlewit*	Journalist
Serjeant Buzfuz	*The Pickwick Papers*	Lawyer
Sydney Carton	*A Tale of Two Cities*	Lawyer
Bob Cratchit	*A Christmas Carol*	Clerk
David Crimple	*Martin Chuzzlewit*	Pawnbroker
Jerry Cruncher	*A Tale of Two Cities*	Grave robber
Ernest Defarge	*A Tale of Two Cities*	Keeper of a wine shop
Sir John Fielding	*Barnaby Rudge*	Magistrate
Joe Gargery	*Great Expectations*	Blacksmith
Arthur Gride	*Nicholas Nickleby*	Moneylender
William Guppy	*Bleak House*	Clerk
Bradley Headstone	*Our Mutual Friend*	School teacher
Uriah Heep	*David Copperfield*	Clerk
Madame Mantalini	*Nicholas Nickleby*	Dressmaker
Nancy	*Oliver Twist*	Prostitute
Susan Nipper	*Nicholas Nickleby*	Maid
Seth Pecksniff	*Martin Chuzzlewit*	Surveyor

ART & LITERATURE

A DICKENSIAN JOB CENTRE

CHARACTER	NOVEL	OCCUPATION
Daniel Peggotty	*David Copperfield*	Fisherman
Henrietta Petowker	*Nicholas Nickleby*	Actress
Thomas Sapsea	*The Mystery of Edwin Drood*	Auctioneer
Paul Sweedlepipe	*Martin Chuzzlewit*	Barber
Gabriel Varden	*Barnaby Rudge*	Locksmith
Silas Wegg	*Our Mutual Friend*	Street vendor
Allan Woodcourt	*Bleak House*	Surgeon

Clerk

BOOK OF LISTS

TO BE OR NOT TO BE
A profile of William Shakespeare

Born: April 23, 1564

Birthplace: Stratford-upon-Avon

Parents: John and Mary

Children: Susanna and twins Judith and Hamnet

Wife: Anne Hathaway. William was 18 when he married 26-year-old Anne

First play: *Henry VI*

Last play: *The Two Noble Kinsmen*

Plays written: 37

Sonnets written: 154

Longest play: *Hamlet*

Shortest play: *The Comedy of Errors*

William Shakespeare

Only Shakespeare play with an animal in the title: *The Taming of The Shrew*

Only Shakespeare play with a British place name in the title: *The Merry Wives of Windsor*

Only Shakespeare play with a capital city in the title: *Timon of Athens*

Died: April 23, 1616

Buried: Holy Trinity Church, Stratford-upon-Avon

ART & LITERATURE

40 WORDS INVENTED BY WILLIAM SHAKESPEARE

- Arouse
- Assassination
- Amazement
- Blanket
- Blushing
- Champion
- Compromise
- Courtship
- Countless
- Disheartened
- Dwindle
- Equivocal
- Fashionable
- Flawed
- Frugal
- Generous
- Gossip
- Hobnob
- Impede
- Jaded
- Laughable
- Lonely
- Luggage
- Majestic
- Mimic
- Moonbeam
- Mountaineer
- Obscene
- Outbreak
- Puking
- Radiance
- Remorseless
- Scuffle
- Submerge
- Summit
- Swagger
- Torture
- Tranquil
- Worthless
- Zany

BOOK OF LISTS

KENNETH BRANAGH MEETS WILLIAM SHAKESPEARE

Henry V

CHARACTER	PLAYED BY
Henry V	Kenneth Branagh
Duke of Exeter	Brian Blessed
Duke of Gloucester	Simon Shepherd
Captain Fluellen	Ian Holm
Chorus	Derek Jacobi

Othello

CHARACTER	PLAYED BY
Iago	Kenneth Branagh
Othello	Laurence Fishburne
Desdemona	Irene Jacob

Kenneth Branagh

Love's Labour's Lost

CHARACTER	PLAYED BY
Berowne	Kenneth Branagh
Nathaniel	Richard Briers
Don Armado	Timothy Spall
The Princess of France	Alicia Silverstone

ART & LITERATURE

Much Ado About Nothing

CHARACTER	PLAYED BY
Signior Benedick	Kenneth Branagh
Beatrice	Emma Thompson
Signior Leonato	Richard Briers
Don John	Keanu Reaves
Don Pedro	Denzel Washington
Hero	Kate Beckinsale
Signior Antonio	Brian Blessed

Hamlet

CHARACTER	PLAYED BY
Hamlet	Kenneth Branagh
Ophelia	Kate Winslet
Yorick	Ken Dodd
Polonius	Richard Briers
Guildestern	Reece Dinsdale
Reynaldo	Gérard Depardieu
Gertrude	Julie Christie
Hecuba	Judi Dench
Gravedigger	Billy Crystal

'JUNGLE BOOK' ANIMALS

NAME	ANIMAL
Akela	Wolf
Bagheera	Panther
Baloo	Bear
Darzee	Tailorbird
Hathi	Elephant
Ikki	Porcupine
Kaa	Python
Kotick	Seal
Mang	Bat
Mowgli	Man cub
Nagaina	Cobra
Rann	Kite
Rikki Tikki Tavi	Mongoose
Shere Khan	Tiger
Tabaqui	Jackal

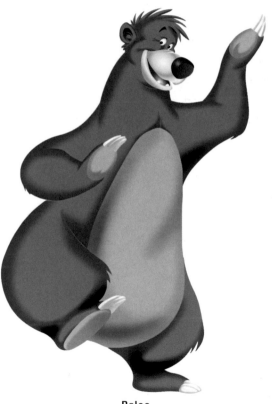

Baloo

ART & LITERATURE

ANIMALS OF BEATRIX POTTER

Badger	Tommy Brock
Cats	Tom Kitten, Squintina, Tabitha Twitchit, Simpkin
Chicken	Sally Henny Penny
Chipmunk	Chippy Hackee
Dogs	Gypsy, Tipkins, Pirate, Pickles, Stumpy
Duck	Jemima Puddle-Duck
Ferret	John Stoat Ferret
Fox	Vixen Tod
Frog	Jeremy Fisher
Goat	Nanny Nennigoat
Hedgehog	Mrs Tiggy-Winkle
Mole	Diggory Delvet
Mice	Tom Titmouse, Tom Thumb, Timmy Willie
Newt	Sir Isaac Newton
Owl	Old Mrs Brown
Pigs	Aunt Pettitoes, Miss Dorcas, Spot
Porcupine	Mr Pricklepin
Rabbits	Benjamin Bunny, Mr Benjamin Bouncer, Peter Rabbit, Flopsy, Mopsy, Cottontail
Rats	Anna Maria, Samuel Whiskers
Sheep	Simon Ram
Squirrels	Squirrel Nutkin, Timmy Tiptoes, Twinkleberry

Mrs Tiggy-Winkle

BOOK OF LISTS

A HARRY POTTER GLOSSARY

Animagus . . . . .A wizard or witch that can transform into an animal

Azkaban . . . . .Dreaded prison where wizards are incarcerated

Beater . . . . .Defensive position in the game of Quidditch

Blast-ended skrewt . . . . . . .Vicious crablike beast bred by Hagrid

Bludger . . . . .A ball in Quidditch that attempts to knock players from their broomsticks

Boggart . . . . .An evil beast that transforms into a person's worst fears

Chaser . . . . .Attacking position in the game of Quidditch

Daily Prophet . . . . .Wizard newspaper, complete with moving photographs

Death Eaters . . . . .Followers of the evil Lord Voldemort

Dementors . . . . .Guardians of Azkaban that can suck out a person's soul with a kiss

Forbidden Forest . . . . .Forest surrounding Hogwarts School

Firebolt . . . . .Super-fast broomstick

Flourish & Blotts . . . . .Bookstore in Diagon Alley

Galleons, Sickles & Knuts . .Wizard money. 29 Knuts in a Sickle, 17 Sickles in a Galleon 1 Galleon is equivalent to £5

Gillyweed . . . . .Plant that when eaten enables wizards to breathe underwater

Golden Snitch . . . . .The most important ball in Quidditch. Catching the snitch wins a team 150 points and usually wins the game

Gringotts . . . . .The wizard bank

Gryffindor . . . . .House at Hogwarts, to which Harry, Ron and Hermione belong

ART & LITERATURE

A HARRY POTTER GLOSSARY

Hogsmeade . . . . .Village near Hogwarts, where pupils can visit Zonko's Joke Shop and Honeyduke's Sweet Shop

Hogwart's Express . . . . .Train leaving Platform $9^3/_4$ at Kings Cross Station

Howler . . . . .Screaming letter delivered to wizards

Houses . . . . .Rival houses to Gryffindor are Hufflepuff, Slytherin and Ravenclaw

Knight Bus . . . . .Magical bus that appears out of nowhere to rescue stranded wizards

The Leaky Cauldron . . . . . . .Public house in Diagon Alley

Mudblood . . . . .Derogatory term given to a person born to non-magical parents

Muggle . . . . .Name given by wizards to non-magical people

O.W.Ls . . . . .School examinations, standing for Ordinary Wizarding Levels

Parselmouth . . . . .Person with the ability to talk to snakes

Patronus . . . . .Image conjured to guard against evil forces. Harry Potter's patronus to guard against the Dementors comes in the form of a stag

Pensieve . . . . .Magical bowl that holds a wizard's memories

Quaffle . . . . .The ball that scores a goal in Quidditch

Seeker . . . . .Harry Potter's position in Quidditch. His job is to catch the Golden Snitch

Sorting Hat . . . . .Talking hat that sorts pupils at Hogwarts into their respective houses

Whomping Willow . . . . .Giant tree at Hogwarts that launches fierce attacks with its branches

BOOK OF LISTS

THE GOOD BOOK
The 10 most-mentioned animals in the Bible

1	Sheep	6	Horse
2	Lamb	7	Bullock
3	Lion	8	Ass
4	Ox	9	Goat
5	Ram	10	Camel

BIBLE FACTS

- The first book in the Old Testament . . . . Genesis
- The last book in the Old Testament . . . . Malachi
- The first book in the New Testament . . . . The Gospel According to St Matthew
- The last book in the New Testament . . . . Revelation
- Number of books in the Bible 66
- Number of books in the New Testament 27
- Number of chapters in the Old Testament 929
- Number of chapters in the New Testament 260
- Shortest verse in the Bible . . . . Jesus wept (John 11:35)
- The two books of the Bible named after women . . . Ruth and Esther
- The oldest person in the Bible . . . . Methuselah, 969 years old
- Only nuts mentioned in the Bible . . . . Almonds and pistachios
- Only miracle performed by Jesus mentioned in all four Gospels . . . . Feeding of the 5000

ART & LITERATURE

NOMS DE PLUME

PEN NAME	REAL NAME
Richard Bachman	Stephen King
RM Ballantyne	Robert Michael Ballantyne Comus
Lewis Carroll	Reverend Charles Lutwidge Dodgson
Leslie Charteris	Leslie Charles Bowyer
Susan Coolidge	Sarah Chauncy Woolsey
Daniel Defoe	Daniel Foe
Dr Seuss	Theodore Seuss Geisel
George Eliot	Mary Ann Evans
Maxim Gorky	Max Peshkov
James Herriot	Alfred Wight
PD James	Phyllis White
John Le Carré	David Cornwell
Jack London	John Griffith
George Orwell	Eric Arthur Blair
Harold Robbins	Francis Kane
Sax Rohmer	Arthur Sarsfield Ward
Saki	Hector Hugh Munro
George Sand	Amandine Dupin
Tom Stoppard	Tom Straussler
Mark Twain	Samuel Langhorne Clemens
Voltaire	Francois Marie Arouet

BOOK OF LISTS

10 AUTHORS THAT HAVE BEEN DEPICTED ON UK STAMPS

- Charlotte Brontë
- Robert Burns
- Thomas Gray
- William Shakespeare
- Thomas Hardy
- Emily Brontë
- Walter Scott
- Edward Lear
- George Eliot
- John Keats

John Keats

10 AUTHORS THAT HAVE BEEN DEPICTED ON US STAMPS

Edgar Allan Poe

- TS Eliot
- Louisa May Alcott
- Jack London
- Nathaniel Hawthorne
- Eugene O'Neill
- Herman Melville
- F Scott Fitzgerald
- Washington Irving
- James Fenimore Cooper
- Edgar Allan Poe

ART & LITERATURE

WATCHING THE DETECTIVES

DETECTIVE	CREATED BY
Sexton Blake	Harry Blyth
Father Brown	GK Chesterton
Brother Cadfael	Ellis Peters
Albert Campion	Margery Allingham
Charlie Chan	Earl Biggers
Jonathan Creek	David Renwick
Dalziel & Pascoe	Reginald Hill
Mike Hammer	Mickey Spillane
Sherlock Holmes	Arthur Conan Doyle
Inspector Maigret	Georges Simenon
Philip Marlowe	Raymond Chandler
Inspector Morse	Colin Dexter
Hercule Poirot	Agatha Christie
Inspector Rebus	Ian Rankin
Sam Spade	Dashiel Hammett
Simon Templar	Leslie Charteris
Dick Tracy	Chester Gould
Inspector Wexford	Ruth Rendell
Lord Peter Wimsey	Dorothy L Sayers
Nero Wolfe	Rex Stout

David Suchet as Hercule Poirot

BOOK OF LISTS

NOVEL-TITLE CHARACTERS

NOVEL	TITLE CHARACTER
Anne of Green Gables	Anne Shirley
Billy Liar	William Fisher
The Borrowers	Arrietty, Homily and Pod
Charlie and the Chocolate Factory	Charlie Bucket
Cider with Rosie	Rosie Burdock
The Count of Monte Cristo	Edmond Dante
Emma	Emma Woodhouse
The English Patient	Count Laszlo de Almasy
The Exorcist	Father Lankester Merrin
The Famous Five	Julian, George, Dick, Anne and Timmy the dog
The French Lieutenant's Woman	Sarah Woodruff
Goodbye Mr Chips	Arthur Chipping
Harry Potter and the Prisoner of Azkaban	Sirius Black (the prisoner)
The Hobbit	Bilbo Baggins
Lady Chatterley's Lover	Oliver Mellors
Little Dorrit	Amy Dorrit
Little Lord Fauntleroy	Cedric Erroll
The Mayor of Casterbridge	Michael Henchard
Our Mutual Friend	John Harmon
Papillon	Henri Charrière

ART & LITERATURE

NOVEL-TITLE CHARACTERS

NOVEL	TITLE CHARACTER
The Prince and the Pauper	Edward (the prince) and Tom Canty (the pauper)
The Prisoner of Zenda	King Rudolf V
The Saint	Simon Templar
The Secret Seven	Peter, Janet, Jack, Barbara, George, Colin, Pam
The Witches of Eastwick	Jane Spofford, Alexandra Medford, Sukie Ridgemont

Charlie and the Chocolate Factory

BOOK OF LISTS

NURSERY RHYME ORIGINS

■ **Baa Baa Black Sheep**

A lament against high taxes. In the Middle Ages one third of the taxes went to the king (the master), one third went to the nobility (the dame), and one third was kept for yourself (little boy down the lane)

■ **Dr Foster**

King Edward I when travelling to Gloucester fell off his horse into a large puddle

■ **The Grand Old Duke of York**

Inspired by the defeat of Richard III in the Wars of the Roses

■ **Jack and Jill**

The French King, Louis XVI represented Jack, who 'lost his crown', with his wife Marie Antoinette representing Jill who 'came tumbling after'

■ **Jack be Nimble**

A notorious 16th-century pirate who managed to evade capture

■ **Jack Sprat**

Inspired by Charles I who became 'lean' as a result of Parliament's refusal to finance a war against Spain

■ **Humpty Dumpty**

The nickname given to a large cannon in the English Civil War that was placed on a wall

■ **Little Tommy Tucker**

In the Middle Ages orphans begged for food by singing

■ **London Bridge is Falling Down**

Early versions of the bridge were made of wood and were destroyed by Viking raiders and later in the 13th century fell down after catching fire

ART & LITERATURE

NURSERY RHYME ORIGINS

■ **London Bridge is Broken Down**

Chronicles the rise and fall of Anne Boleyn

■ **Mary Mary Quite Contrary**

Mary Tudor or Bloody Mary. The 'silver bells and cockleshells' are symbols of instruments of torture and 'the pretty maids all in a row' are death row prisoners awaiting execution

■ **Old King Cole**

Tells of an ancient ruler of England in the 3rd century responsible for founding the city of Colchester

■ **Oranges and Lemons**

Title from a medieval dance

■ **Ride a Cock Horse**

The 'fine lady' in the rhyme refers to Elizabeth I, who rode to Banbury to view a new large cross that had been built

■ **Ring a Ring of Roses**

A rhyme written to commemorate the bubonic plague

■ **There Was an Old Woman Who Lived in a Shoe**

The woman in question refers to Queen Caroline II, who bore King George II eight children

■ **Three Blind Mice**

The trio consists of the Protestant clergymen Thomas Cranmer, Hugh Latimer and Nicholas Ridley, whose death warrants were signed by Mary Queen of Scots

■ **Who Killed Cock Robin?**

Refers to the death of the legendary Robin Hood

CLOSING LINES OF FAMOUS NOVELS

- *Agnes Grey*

  'And now I think I have said sufficient.'

- *Animal Farm*

  'The creatures outside looked from pig to man, and from man to pig, and from pig to man again; but already it was impossible to say which was which.'

- *Catch 22*

  'The knife came down missing him by inches and he took off.'

- *A Christmas Carol*

  'And so as Tiny Tim observed "God Bless Us, Every One!"'

- *Frankenstein*

  'He was soon borne away by the waves and lost in darkness and distance.'

- *The Great Gatsby*

  'So we beat on, boats against the current, borne back ceaselessly into the past.'

- *Harry Potter and the Philosopher's Stone*

  'They don't know we're not allowed to use magic at home. I'm going to have a lot of fun with Dudley this summer…'

- *The Hound of the Baskervilles*

  'We can stop at Mancini's for a little dinner on the way.'

- *The Last of the Mohicans*

  'And yet, before the night has come, have I lived to see the last warrior of the wise race of the Mohicans.'

- *The Lion, the Witch and the Wardrobe*

  'But if the Professor was right it was only the beginning of the adventures of Narnia.'

ART & LITERATURE

CLOSING LINES OF FAMOUS NOVELS

■ **Little Women**

"'Oh, my girls, however long you may live, I never can wish you a greater happiness than this!'"

■ **The Pit and the Pendulum**

'The Inquisition was in the hands of its enemies. The French army had entered Toledo.'

■ **The Prisoner of Zenda**

'I will live as becomes the man whom she loves and, for the other side, I must pray a dreamless sleep.'

■ **Silas Marner**

"'O Father", said Eppie, "what a pretty home ours is. I think nobody could be happier than we are.'"

■ **Swiss Family Robinson**

'Like thee, may New Switzerland flourish and prosper…good, happy and free!'

■ **Tarzan of the Apes**

"'I was born there", said Tarzan quietly, "My mother was an ape, and of course she couldn't tell me much about it. I never knew who my father was.'"

■ **To Kill a Mockingbird**

'He would be there all night, and he would be there when Jem woke up in the morning.'

■ **Treasure Island**

"'Pieces of eight! Pieces of eight!'"

■ **War of the Worlds**

'And strangest of all is to hold my wife's hand again, and to think that I have counted her, and that she has counted me, among the dead.'

SPORT

The subject of sport is alive with snippets of specialist and little-known facts. The fact that Errol Flynn competed in the Olympics as a boxer. That Julio Iglesias kept goal for Real Madrid reserves. That St Adjutor is the patron saint of swimmers. That a score of 57 in darts is called a Heinz. That Manchester United was once called Newton Heath. That the first athlete to run 100m in under 10 seconds was Armin Harry. And that the first hole at Augusta is called Asian Tea Olive.

BOOK OF LISTS

SPORTING FIRSTS

- The first cricket Test Match . . . . Australia vs England (1876)
- The first winner of the Grand National . . . . The Duke
- The first winner of the Epsom Derby . . . . Diomed
- The first modern Olympics . . . . Athens (1896)
- The first winter Olympics . . . . Chamonix, France (1924)
- The first Commonwealth Games . . . . Hamilton, Canada (1930)
- The first winners of football's World Cup . . . . Uruguay (1930)
- The first winners of baseball's World Series . . . . Boston Red Sox
- The first winners of the Superbowl . . . . Green Bay Packers
- The first sub-four minute mile . . . . Roger Bannister in a time of
  3mins 59.4secs
- The first athlete to run 100m in under 10 seconds . . . Armin Hary
- The first BBC 'Sports Personality of the Year' . . . . Christopher Chataway
- The first Formula One World Champion . . . . Giuseppe Farina
- The first jockey to receive a knighthood . . . . Sir Gordon Richards
- The first footballer to receive a knighthood . . . . Sir Stanley Matthews
- The first boxer to defeat Mohammed Ali . . . . Joe Frazier
- The first darts world champion . . . . Leighton Rees
- The first black footballer to be capped for England . . Viv Anderson
- The first player to score a goal in
  England's Premiership . . . . Brian Deane for Sheffield United
- The first foreign player to score a hat trick
  in the Premiership . . . . Eric Cantona

SPORT

10 TROPHIES NAMED AFTER PEOPLE

TROPHY	SPORT	NAMED AFTER
Curtis Cup	Golf	Golfing sisters, Harriot & Margaret Curtis
Eisenhower Trophy	Golf	President Dwight Eisenhower
Frank Worrell Trophy	Cricket	West Indian cricket star, Frank Worrell
Gordon Bennett Trophy	Motor racing	American publisher, James Gordon Bennett
Jules Rimet Trophy	Football	The founder of the first World Cup tournament
Lonsdale Belt	Boxing	Hugh Cecil Lowther, the 5th Earl of Lonsdale
Ryder Cup	Golf	Entrepreneur, Samuel Ryder
Thomas Cup	Badminton	Sir George Alan Thomas
Vince Lombardi Trophy	American football	Former coach of the Green Bay Packers
Wightman Cup	Tennis	US tennis star, Hazel Hotchkiss Wightman

Boxing

BOOK OF LISTS

AUTOBIOGRAPHICAL
The autobiographies of 30 sports stars

SPORTS STAR	AUTOBIOGRAPHY
Tony Adams	*Addicted*
Lance Armstrong	*It's not about the Bike*
Mike Atherton	*Opening Up*
Roger Bannister	*The First Four Minutes*
David Beckham	*My Side*
Boris Becker	*The Player*
George Best	*Scoring at Half Time*
Roger Black	*How Long's the Course*
Frank Bruno	*From Hero To Zero*
Linford Christie	*To be Honest with You*
Alex Ferguson	*Managing my Life*
George Foreman	*By George*
John Francome	*Born Lucky*
Graham Gooch	*Testing Times*
Darren Gough	*Dazzler*
Denise Lewis	*Personal Best*
Diego Maradona	*El Diego*
John McEnroe	*Serious: The Autobiography*
Paul Merson	*Rock Bottom*
Colin Montgomerie	*The Real Monty*
Jack Nicklaus	*The Greatest Game of All*

SPORT

AUTOBIOGRAPHICAL
The autobiographies of 30 sports stars

SPORTS STAR	AUTOBIOGRAPHY
Stuart Pearce	*Psycho*
Pele	*My Life and the Beautiful Game*
Jenny Pitman	*Glorious Uncertainty*
Steve Redgrave	*A Golden Age*
Viv Richards	*Hitting Across the Line*
Harvey Smith	*V is for Victory*
Alec Stewart	*Playing for Keeps*
Virginia Wade	*Courting Triumph*
Clive Woodward	*Winning*

Boris Becker

30 FAMOUS PEOPLE AND THE FOOTBALL TEAMS THEY SUPPORT

Clive Anderson . . . . Arsenal

David Baddiel . . . . Chelsea

Cilla Black . . . . Liverpool

Tony Blair . . . . Newcastle United

Jasper Carrott . . . . Birmingham City

Steve Cram . . . . Sunderland

Phil Collins . . . . Tottenham Hotspur

Jim Davidson . . . . Charlton Athletic

Angus Deayton . . . . Manchester United

Noel Edmonds . . . . West Ham United

David Frost . . . . Southampton

Liam Gallagher . . . . Manchester City

Nick Hornby . . . . Arsenal

Mick Hucknall . . . . Manchester United

Peter Kay . . . . Bolton Wanderers

Nigel Kennedy . . . . Aston Villa

Richard Littlejohn . . . . Tottenham Hotspur

Rory McGrath . . . . Arsenal

Jimmy Nail . . . . Newcastle United

James Nesbitt . . . . Manchester United

Ozzy Osbourne . . . . Aston Villa

John Parrott . . . . Everton

SPORT

30 FAMOUS PEOPLE AND THE FOOTBALL TEAMS THEY SUPPORT

Jeremy Paxman . . . . Leeds United

Chris Rea . . . . Middlesbrough

Steve Redgrave . . . . Chelsea

Frank Skinner . . . . West Bromwich Albion

Claire Sweeney . . . . Everton

Jimmy Tarbuck . . . . Liverpool

June Whitfield . . . . Wimbledon

Robbie Williams . . . . Port Vale

9 FOREIGN FOOTBALLERS WHO HAVE BEEN VOTED 'FOOTBALLER OF THE YEAR' IN ENGLAND

- Thierry Henry
- Robert Pires
- David Ginola
- Dennis Bergkamp
- Gianfranco Zola
- Eric Cantona
- Jurgen Klinsmann
- Frans Thijssen
- Bert Trautmann

MAGNIFICENT SEVENS
7 Famous Olympians

- Buster Crabbe competed in the Olympics as a swimmer
- Geena Davis competed in the Olympics as an archer
- Errol Flynn competed in the Olympics as a boxer
- Princess Anne competed in the Olympics as a show jumper
- George Patton competed in the Olympics in the modern pentathlon
- Benjamin Spock competed in the Olympics in rowing events
- Johnny Weissmuller competed in the Olympics in swimming and water polo

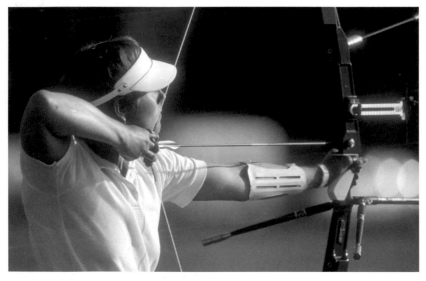

Archery

SPORT

7 EVENTS IN THE HIGHLAND GAMES

- Tossing the caber
- Solo bagpipe
- Scottish sword dancing
- Sheaf toss
- Herding dog trials
- Tug of war
- Mountain marathon

7 FAMOUS PEOPLE WHO COULD HAVE BEEN FOOTBALLERS

- Nicky Byrne of Westlife was released by Leeds Utd when he was 18 years old
- Ronnie Corbett was turned down by Hearts as he was too small
- Angus Deayton had trials for Crystal Palace
- Julio Iglesias was a goalkeeper for Real Madrid reserves
- Pope John Paul II was a highly rated amateur goalkeeper in his native Poland
- Gordon Ramsey was on the books of Rangers FC
- Rod Stewart was on the books of Brentford Rovers

Julio Iglesias

BOOK OF LISTS

SHIRT SPONSORS OF PREMIERSHIP FOOTBALL TEAMS 2004 – 5

TEAM	SPONSOR
Arsenal	02
Aston Villa	DWS
Birmingham City	flybe
Blackburn Rovers	HSA simply health
Bolton Wanderers	Reebok
Charlton Athletic	Allsports
Chelsea	Fly Emirates
Crystal Palace	Churchill
Everton	Chang Beer
Fulham	dabs.com
Liverpool	Carlsberg
Manchester City	Thomas Cook
Manchester United	Vodafone
Middlesbrough	888.com
Newcastle United	Northern Rock
Norwich City	Lotus Cars
Portsmouth	ty
Southampton	Friends Provident
Tottenham Hotspur	Thomson
West Bromwich Albion	T Mobile

SPORT

GAMES AND SPORTS AND THEIR INVENTORS

GAME/SPORT	INVENTED BY
Baseball	Abner Doubleday (rules first codified by Alexander J Cartwright)
Basketball	James Naismith
Cluedo	Anthony Pratt
Jigsaw puzzle	George Spilsbury
Monopoly	Charles Darrow
Rugby	William Webb Ellis
Scrabble	Alfred Butts (sold the rights to James Brunot)
Softball	George Hancock
Trivial Pursuit	Chris Haney and Scott Abbott
Volleyball	William G Morgan

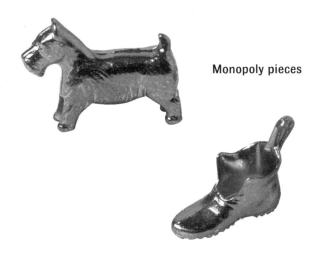

Monopoly pieces

BOOK OF LISTS

THE BBC 'SPORTS PERSONALITY OF THE YEAR'

1954	Christopher Chataway	1980	Robin Cousins
1955	Gordon Pirie	1981	Ian Botham
1956	Jim Laker	1982	Daley Thompson
1957	Dai Rees	1983	Steve Cram
1958	Ian Black	1984	Torvill & Dean
1959	John Surtees	1985	Barry McGuigan
1960	David Broome	1986	Nigel Mansell
1961	Stirling Moss	1987	Fatima Whitbread
1962	Anita Lonsbrough	1988	Steve Davis
1963	Dorothy Hyman	1989	Nick Faldo
1964	Mary Rand	1990	Paul Gascoigne
1965	Tommy Simpson	1991	Liz McColgan
1966	Bobby Moore	1992	Nigel Mansell
1967	Henry Cooper	1993	Linford Christie
1968	David Hemery	1994	Damon Hill
1969	Ann Jones	1995	Jonathan Edwards
1970	Henry Cooper	1996	Damon Hill
1971	Princess Anne	1997	Greg Rusedski
1972	Mary Peters	1998	Michael Owen
1973	Jackie Stewart	1999	Lennox Lewis
1974	Brendan Foster	2000	Steve Redgrave
1975	David Steele	2001	David Beckham
1976	John Curry	2002	Paula Radcliffe
1977	Virginia Wade	2003	Jonny Wilkinson
1978	Steve Ovett	2004	Kelly Holmes
1979	Sebastian Coe	2005	Andrew Flintoff

SPORT

PATRON SAINTS OF SPORT AND LEISURE

Patron saint of athletes . . . . St Sebastian

Patron saint of **Boy Scouts** . . . . St George

Patron saint of **chess** . . . . St Teresa of Avila

Patron saint of **cyclists** . . . . La Madonna di Ghisalo

Patron saint of **fencing** . . . . Michael the Archangel

Patron saint of **Girl Scouts** . . . . St Agnes of Rome

Patron saint of **hunters** . . . . St Eustachius

Patron saint of **horse-riders** . . . . St Martin of Tours

Patron saint of **ice-skaters** . . . . St Lydwina

Patron saint of **jockeys** . . . . St Eligius

Patron saint of **jugglers** . . . . Julian the Hospitaller

Patron saint of **motor cyclists** . . . . St Columbanus

Patron saint of **mountaineers** . . . . St Bernard of Montjoux

Patron saint of **numismatists** . . . . St Eligius

Patron saint of **potholers** . . . . St Benedict

Patron saint of **saddle-makers** . . . . St Crispin

Patron saint of **skiers** . . . . St Andronicus

Patron saint of **stamp collectors** . . . . . Gabriel the Archangel

Patron saint of **swimmers** . . . . St Adjutor

Patron saint of **toy-makers** . . . . Claude de la Columbière

BOOK OF LISTS

THE NICKNAMES OF SOME SCOTTISH FOOTBALL CLUBS

CLUB	NICKNAME
Aberdeen	The Dons
Airdrie United	The Diamonds
Albion Rovers	The Wee Rovers
Alloa Athletic	The Wasps
Arbroath	The Red Lichties
Ayr United	The Honest Men
Berwick Rangers	The Borderers
Celtic	The Bhoys
Clyde	The Bully Wee
Cowdenbeath	Blue Brazil
Dumbarton	The Sons
Dundee	The Dark Blues
Dundee United	The Terrors
Dunfermline Athletic	The Pars
Falkirk	The Bairns
Forfar Athletic	The Loons
Hamilton Academical	The Accies
Hearts	The Jam Tarts
Hibernian	The Hi-bees
Kilmarnock	Killie
Montrose	The Gable Endies
Motherwell	The Well

SPORT

THE NICKNAMES OF SOME SCOTTISH FOOTBALL CLUBS

CLUB	NICKNAME
Partick Thistle	The Jags
Queen of the South	The Doonhammers
Queen's Park	The Spiders
Rangers	The Gers
St Johnstone	The Saints
St Mirren	The Buddies
Stenhousemuir	The Warriors

The Spiders / Queen's Park

THE NICKNAMES OF 30 SPORTS STARS

STAR	NICKNAME
Mohammed Ali	The Louisville Lip
David Beckham	Goldenballs
Eric Bristow	The Crafty Cockney
Primo Carnera	The Ambling Alp
Jack Dempsey	The Manassa Mauler
Joe Di Maggio	The Yankee Clipper
Tom Finney	The Preston Plumber
Joel Garner	Big Bird
Wayne Gretzky	The Great One

**Joe Di Maggio with
Marilyn Monroe**

SPORT

THE NICKNAMES OF 30 SPORTS STARS

STAR	NICKNAME
Alex Higgins	Hurricane
Larry Holmes	The Eastern Assassin
Rod Laver	The Rockhampton Rocket
Joe Louis	The Brown Bomber
Rocky Marciano	The Brockton Blockbuster
Stanley Matthews	The Wizard of Dribble
John McEnroe	Superbrat
Barry McGuigan	The Clones Cyclone
Paavo Nurmi	The Flying Finn
Ronnic O'Sullivan	The Rocket
Pele	The Black Pearl
William Perry	The Refrigerator
Lester Piggott	The Longfellow
Gary Player	The Man in Black
Ferenc Puskas	The Galloping Major
Ken Rosewall	Muscles
Babe Ruth	The Sultan of Swat
Pete Sampras	Pistol Pete
Cliff Thorburn	The Grinder
Lee Trevino	Supermex
Jimmy White	Whirlwind

BEASTLY NICKNAMES OF SPORTING TEAMS
American Football

- Baltimore Ravens
- Chicago Bears
- Denver Broncos
- Miami Dolphins
- Philadelphia Eagles
- St Louis Rams

Baseball

- Chicago Cubs
- Detroit Tigers
- Toronto Blue Jays
- New Orleans Hornets

Basketball

- Chicago Bulls
- Memphis Grizzlies
- Minnesota Timberwolves

Cricket

- Derbyshire Scorpions
- Glamorgan Dragons
- Leicestershire Foxes
- Sussex Sharks
- Yorkshire Phoenix
- Essex Eagles
- Hampshire Hawks
- Surrey Lions
- Warwickshire Bears

Warwickshire Bears

SPORT

Ice Hockey

- Mighty Ducks of Anaheim
- Chicago Blackhawks
- Florida Panthers
- Pittsburgh Penguins

Rugby League

- Bradford Bulls
- Castleford Tigers
- Leeds Rhinos
- London Broncos
- USA The Eagles

Association Football

Bradford City	The Bantams	**Brentford**	The Bees
Brighton	The Seagulls	**Bristol City**	The Robins
Cardiff City	The Bluebirds	**Crystal Palace**	The Eagles
Derby County	The Rams	**Hull City**	The Tigers
Leicester City	The Foxes	**Mansfield Town**	The Stags
Millwall	The Lions	**Newcastle United**	The Magpies
Norwich City	The Canaries	**Notts County**	The Magpies
Sheffield Wednesday	The Owls	**Shrewsbury Town**	The Shrews
Sunderland	The Black Cats	**Swansea**	The Swans
Swindon Town	The Robins	**Torquay United**	The Gulls
Watford	The Hornets	**West Brom**	The Throstles
Wolverhampton Wanderers	The Wolves		

THE NICKNAMES OF 20 NON-LEAGUE FOOTBALL CLUBS 2004–2005

Accrington Stanley . . . . The Reds

Altrincham . . . . The Robins

Aylesbury United . . . . The Ducks

Barnet . . . . The Bees

Basingstoke United . . . . The Camrose Blues

Bath City . . . . The Romans

Burton Albion . . . . The Brewers

Canvey Island . . . . The Gulls

Crawley Town . . . . The Red Devils

Dagenham & Redbridge . . . . The Daggers

Evesham United . . . . The Robins

Hereford United . . . . The Bulls

Leigh RMI . . . . The Railwaymen

Margate . . . . The Gate

Morecambe . . . . The Shrimpers

Northwich Victoria . . . . The Vics

Scarborough . . . . The Seasiders

Tamworth . . . . The Lambs

Woking . . . . The Cards

York City . . . . The Minstermen

SPORT

HOWZAT?
A cricket glossary

Bunny . . . . Slang term for a poor batter

Deep cover . . . . . Fielding position close to the boundary

Dolly . . . . Term given to an easy catch

Dot ball. . . . . A delivery from which no runs are scored

Golden duck . . . . A score of zero by a batter who is dismissed on the first ball faced

Googly. . . . . Delivery by a spinner that turns the opposite way

Hat trick. . . . . . . When a bowler takes three wickets from three consecutive deliveries

Maiden over . . . . Over of six balls from which no runs are scored

Nelson . . . . Score of 111

Nightwatchman. . Batter sent into bat before his normal batting order usually at the end of a day's play. A tactic employed to protect the wicket of more proficient batters

Pie. . . . . Slang term for a poor bowling delivery

Runner . . . . Player who runs between the wickets for an injured batsman

Sheet anchor . . . Batter who employs defensive tactics during a long innings

Silly mid off. . . . . Fielding position close to the batsman

Sledging. . . . . Unsporting tactic of insulting opposition players to unsettle them

Slip . . . . Fielding position close to the wicket keeper, first slip being the closest

Tailender . . . . One of the last batsmen in the batting order, usually bowlers who are less proficient batters

Yorker . . . . Delivery that pitches at the feet of a batter

BOOK OF LISTS

THE 10 WAYS OF BEING GIVEN OUT AT CRICKET

- Caught
- Bowled
- LBW (leg before wicket)
- Run out
- Stumped
- Handling the ball
- Obstructing the field
- Hit the ball twice
- Hit wicket
- Timed out

WISDEN'S TOP 10 CRICKETERS OF THE 20TH CENTURY

1   Don Bradman
2   Garfield Sobers
3   Jack Hobb
4   Shane Warne
5   Viv Richards
6   Dennis Lillee
7   Frank Worrell
8   Wally Hammond
9   Dennis Compton
10 Richard Hadlee

SPORT

HORSES FOR COURSES
The venues for 20 famous horse races

RACE	HELD AT
Belmont Stakes	Belmont Park, Long Island
Cesarewitch	Newmarket
Ebor Handicap	York
English Derby	Epsom
French Derby	Chantilly
Grand National	Aintree
Irish Derby	The Curragh
Irish Grand National	Fairyhouse
Kentucky Derby	Churchill Downs, Louisville
Lincoln Handicap	Doncaster
Melbourne Cup	Flemington Racecourse
The Oaks	Epsom
1000 Guineas	Newmarket
Preakness Stakes	Pimlico Racecourse
Prix de l'Arc de Triomphe	Longchamps
Scottish Grand National	Ayr
St Leger	Doncaster
Triumph Hurdle	Cheltenham
2000 Guineas	Newmarket
Welsh Grand National	Chepstow

SPORTING ACRONYMS AND INITIALS

AAA . . . . .Amateur Athletic Association

ABA . . . . .American Basketball Association

AFC . . . . .American Football Conference

ASA . . . . .Amateur Swimming Association

BASE jumping . . . . . .Building, Antenna, Span, Earth

BBBC . . . . .British Boxing Board of Control

BMX . . . . .Bicycle Moto Cross

BSAD . . . . .British Sports Association for the Disabled

EWCB . . . . .England and Wales Cricket Board

FA . . . . .Football Association

FIFA . . . . .Fédération Internationale de Football Association

GAA . . . . .Gaelic Athletic Association

GMB . . . . .Grand Master Bowman

IAAF . . . . .International Association of Athletics Federation

IBF . . . . .International Boxing Federation

IBSF . . . . .International Billiards and Snooker Federation

IFN . . . . .International Federation of Netball

IOC . . . . .International Olympic Committee

ITF . . . . .International Tennis Federation

MCC . . . . .Marylebone Cricket Club

Basketball

SPORT

SPORTING ACRONYMS AND INITIALS

MLB . . . . .Major League Baseball

NASCAR . . . . .National Association for Stock Car Auto Racing

NBA . . . . .National Basketball Association

NHL . . . . .National Hockey League

NHU . . . . .National Homing Union (pigeon racing)

PFA . . . . .Professional Footballers Association

PGA . . . . .Professional Golfers Association

RFU . . . . .Rugby Football Union

TCCB . . . . .Test and County Cricket Board

UEFA . . . . .Union of European Football Associations

WBA . . . . .World Boxing Association

WBC . . . . .World Boxing Council

WBO . . . . .World Boxing Organisation

WBU . . . . .World Boxing Union

WPBSA . . . . .World Professional Billiards and Snooker Association

BOOK OF LISTS

THE 2005 FORMULA ONE SEASON

GRAND PRIX	COURSE	WINNER
Australian	Melbourne Grand Prix Circuit	Giancarlo Fisichella
Malaysian	Sepang International Circuit	Fernando Alonso
Bahrain	Bahrain International Circuit	Fernando Alonso
San Marino	Dino ferrari, Imola	Fernando Alonso
Spanish	Circuit du Cataluyna, Barcelona	Kimi Raikkonen
Monaco	Circuit de Monaco	Kimi Raikkonen
European	Nurburgring, Germany	Fernando Alonso
Canadian	Circuit Gilles Villeneuve, Montreal	Kimi Raikkonen
United States	Indianapolis	Michael Schumacher
French	Magny Cours	Fernando Alonso
British	Silverstone	Juan Pablo Montoya
German	Hockenheim Circuit	Fernando Alonso
Hungarian	Hungaroring	Kimi Raikkonen
Belgian	Spa-Francorchamps	Kimi Raikkonen
Italian	Monza	Juan Pablo Montoya
Chinese	Shanghai International Circuit	Fernando Alonso
Japanese	Suzuka International Racing Course	Kimi Raikkonen
Brazilian	Interlagos, Sao Paulo	Juan Pablo Montoya

2005 Formula One World Champion . . . . Fernando Alonso

2005 Constructors' title . . . . Renault

SPORT

THE 18 HOLES OF THE AUGUSTA GOLF COURSE

All 18 holes are named after flowers and plants

Hole

1	Asian Tea Olive
2	Pink Dogwood
3	Flowering Peach
4	Flowering Crab Apple
5	Magnolia
6	Juniper
7	Pampas
8	Yellow Jasmine
9	Carolina Cherry
10	Camellia
11	White Dogwood
12	Golden Bell
13	Azalea
14	Chinese Fir
15	Fire Thorn
16	Redbud
17	Nandina
18	Holly

A GOLF GLOSSARY

Ace	Alternative name for a hole in one
Air shot	Missing the ball completely when swinging the club
Albatross	Three strokes under par for any given hole
Apron	Short fringe of grass separating the green from the fairway
Birdie	One under par on any given hole
Bird's Nest	When the golf ball is lying cupped in deep grass
Bogey	One over par on any given hole
Bunker	Hazard filled by sand, known as a sand trap in the USA
Buzzard	Two strokes over par on any given hole
Dogleg	Hole in which the fairway bends sharply to the left or the right
Eagle	Two under par for any given hole
Fairway	Area of the hole between the tee and the green
Hacker	Slang term for a poor golf player
Links	Golf course near the coast
Mulligan	A free shot
19th hole	Name given to the golf course clubhouse or bar
Rough	Area of deep grass adjacent to the fairway
Mashie	Old name for a 5 iron
Niblick	Old name for a 9 iron
Scratch player	A player who has no handicap
Spade mashie	Old name for a 6 iron
Stimpmeter	Device used to measure the speed of greens
Yips	Nervous disability affecting putting

SPORT

JUDO TERMS

Chui . . . . Caution for foul play

Dan . . . . Grade of proficiency

Dojo . . . . Hall where a judo contest is held (means 'place of the way')

Goshi waza . . . . A hip throw

Hiki-wake . . . . A drawn contest

Hadaka jime . . . . A choke hold

Hajime . . . . Command to commence fighting

Hamsoku-make . . . . . . Disqualification of a contestant

Ippon . . . . Full point or full win

Judogi . . . . Garment worn by judo contestants

Kokyu . . . . Junior student grade

Kyu . . . . Senior student grade

Matte . . . . Command to stop fighting

Obi . . . . Sash that fastens the judogi jacket

Osaekomi . . . . The holding down of an opponent

Rei . . . . The bow prior to the start of a contest

Sensei . . . . Judo teacher

Shiai . . . . Judo contest

Shodan . . . . First degree black belt

Tatatmi . . . . The judo mat

Waza-ari . . . . Two waza-ari equal one full point or one ippon

HOW MANY IN A SIDE?

2 a side...... Beach volleyball

4 a side...... Polo

5 a side...... Basketball

6 a side...... Volleyball

6 a side...... Ice hockey

7 a side...... Netball

7 a side...... Water polo

9 a side...... Baseball

10 a side...... Men's lacrosse

11 a side...... Association football

11 a side...... Cricket

11 a side...... American football

11 a side...... Field hockey

12 a side...... Women's lacrosse

12 a side...... Shinty

13 a side...... Rugby league

15 a side...... Rugby union

15 a side...... Hurling

15 a side...... Gaelic football

18 a side...... Australian rules football

Beach volleyball

180!!!
A darts glossary

Annie's room . . . . A score of one

Baby ton . . . . A score of 95

Bag o' nuts . . . . A score of 45

Barrel . . . . Metal portion of the dart held in the hand

Basement . . . . Double 3

Bed and breakfast . . . . . Scoring 26 with three darts i.e. 20, 5 and 1

Bounce out . . . . When the dart hits the board and bounces out scoring 0 points

Bucket of nails . . . . When all three darts score 1

Bullseye . . . . Centre of the dartboard worth 50 points

Double top . . . . Double 20

Downstairs . . . . The lower half of the dartboard

Garden states . . . . A score of 88

Heinz . . . . Score of 57

Island . . . . Scoring area of a board. If a player misses the area completely
they are 'off the island'

Madhouse . . . . Double 1

Maximum checkout . . . . Finishing a leg by scoring 170 with 3 darts
(three treble 20s & 1 bull)

Oche . . . . The throwing line

Robin Hood . . . . Hitting a dart already in the board with another dart

Shanghai . . . . Scoring a single, a double and a treble in the same number

Three in a bed . . . . Three darts in the same number section

SCRABBLE POINTS

A	1	Q	10
B	3	R	1
C	3	S	1
D	2	T	1
E	1	U	1
F	4	V	4
G	2	W	4
H	4	X	8
I	1	Y	4
J	8	Z	10
K	5		
L	1		
M	3		
N	1		
O	1		
P	3		

The letter Z worth
10 points

SPORT

BINGO SLANG

Number 1 . . . . Kelly's eye
Number 2 . . . . One little duck
Number 5 . . . . Man alive
Number 7 . . . . The lucky seven
Number 8 . . . . The garden gate
Number 9 . . . . Doctor's orders
Number 10 . . . . Downing Street
Number 11 . . . . Legs eleven
Number 12 . . . . One dozen
Number 13 . . . . Unlucky for some
Number 16 . . . . Sweet sixteen
Number 21 . . . . Key of the door
Number 22 . . . . Two little ducks
Number 27 . . . . A duck and a crutch
Number 33 . . . . Dirty knees
Number 40 . . . . Life begins at forty
Number 45 . . . . Halfway there
Number 59 . . . . The Brighton Line
Number 66 . . . . Clickety-click
Number 77 . . . . Sunset Strip
Number 88 . . . . Two fat ladies
Number 90 . . . . Top of the shop

Bingo machine

BOOK OF LISTS

10 UNLIKELY FA CUP WINNERS

- Wanderers
- Oxford University
- Clapham Rovers
- Blackburn Olympic
- Old Etonians
- Royal Engineers
- Old Carthusians
- Bury
- Blackpool
- Wimbledon

12 FOUNDER MEMBERS OF THE FOOTBALL LEAGUE

- Accrington Stanley
- Aston Villa
- Blackburn Rovers
- Bolton Wanderers
- Burnley
- Derby County
- Everton
- Notts County
- Preston North End
- Stoke City
- West Bromwich Albion
- Wolverhampton Wanderers

SPORT

THE FORMER NAMES OF 20 FOOTBALL CLUBS

Arsenal . . . . Dial Square

Birmingham City . . . . Small Heath

Bolton Wanderers . . . . Christ Church FC

Bristol Rovers . . . . Eastville Rovers

Cambridge United . . . . Abbey United

Cardiff City . . . . Riverside Albion

Coventry City . . . . Singers FC

Everton . . . . St Domingo

Leicester City . . . . Leicester Fosse

Manchester City . . . . Ardwick FC

Manchester United . . . . Newton Heath

Oldham Athletic . . . . Pine Villa

Oxford United . . . . Headington United

Queen's Park Rangers . . . . St Jude's

Scunthorpe United . . . . Scunthorpe and Lindsey United

Stockport County . . . . Heaton Norris Rovers

Tranmere Rovers . . . . Belmont AFC

Watford . . . . West Herts

West Ham United . . . . Thames Ironworks FC

Wolverhampton Wanderers . . . . St Luke's

HISTORY

The people and events that have earned a place in historical records, from the year dot to the present day, provide rich pickings for collectors of oddball facts. Ones like these: The Red Cross was founded by Henri Dunant; the Roman goddess of motherhood is Ops; Nostradamus predicted the world will come to an end in 3755; Blackbeard's real name was Edward Teach; the *Observer* newspaper was founded in 1791; and Wyatt Earp had five brothers whose names are... (but for *that* you must read on).

THE 12 LABOURS OF HERCULES

- Skinning the Nemean Lion
- Killing the nine-headed hydra
- Capturing the hind of Ceryneia, the female pet deer of the Goddess Diana
- Capturing alive the Eyrmanthian boar
- Cleaning the stables of King Augeas
- Driving away the Stymphalian birds
- Wrestling the Cretan bull
- Capturing the man-eating horses of Diomedes
- Stealing the belt of Hippolyte, Queen of the Amazons
- Capturing the cattle of Geryon
- Stealing the golden apples of Hesperides, that belonged to Zeus
- Capturing Cerberus, the three-headed dog that guarded the entrance to Hades

Skinning the Nemean Lion

HISTORY

THE 12 DISCIPLES OF JESUS

- Simon Peter
- James
- John
- Judas (replaced by Matthias)
- Andrew
- Philip
- Bartholomew
- Matthew
- Thomas
- Simon
- James, son of Alphaeus
- Thaddeus

THE 12 TRIBES OF ISRAEL (NAMED AFTER THE SONS OF JACOB)

- Asher
- Benjamin
- Dan
- Gad
- Isaachar
- Joseph
- Judah
- Levi
- Naphtali
- Reuben
- Simeon
- Zebulun

THE 10 COMMANDMENTS

■ **The First Commandment**

Thou shalt have no other Gods before me

■ **The Second Commandment**

Thou shalt not make unto thee any graven image, or any likeness of anything that is in heaven above, or that is in the Earth beneath

■ **The Third Commandment**

Thou shalt not take the name of the Lord thy God in vain

■ **The Fourth Commandment**

Remember the Sabbath Day, to keep it holy

■ **The Fifth Commandment**

Honour thy Father and thy Mother

■ **The Sixth Commandment**

Thou shalt not kill

■ **The Seventh Commandment**

Thou shalt not commit adultery

■ **The Eighth Commandment**

Thou shalt not steal

■ **The Ninth Commandment**

Thou shalt not bear false witness against thy neighbour

■ **The Tenth Commandment**

Thou shalt not covet thy neighbour's house, thy neighbour's wife, nor his manservant, nor his maidservant, nor his ox, nor his ass, nor anything that is thy neighbour's

HISTORY

FOUNDING FATHERS

ORGANIZATION	FOUNDED BY
Alcoholic's Anonymous	Bill Wilson & Dr Robert H Smith
Amazon.com	Jeff Bezos
American Express	Henry Wells, William Fargo & John Butterfield
Amnesty International	Peter Benenson
Amstrad	Alan Sugar
Childline	Esther Rantzen
CIA	William J Donovan
FBI	J Edgar Hoover
Friends Of The Earth	David Brower
The Guardian Angels	Curtis Sliwa
Metropolitan Police Force	Sir Robert Peel
Motorola	Paul Galvin
NSPCC	Angela Burdett-Coutts
Oxfam	Canon Theodore Richard Milford
The Red Cross	Henri Dunant
The Salvation Army	William Booth
The Samaritans	Chad Varah
The Suffragettes	Emmeline Pankhurst
United Artists	Charlie Chaplin, Douglas Fairbanks Snr, Mary Pickford & DW Griffith
YMCA	George Williams

BOOK OF LISTS

GODS

GOD OF	GREEK	ROMAN
Agriculture	Cronus	Saturn
The dead	Thanatos	Mors
Fire	Hephaestus	Vulcan
Love	Eros	Cupid
The sea	Poseidon	Neptune
Sleep	Hypnos	Somnus
The Sun	Helios	Sol
War	Ares	Mars
Wine	Dionysus	Bacchus
The woods	Pan	Silvanus
Messenger of the Gods	Hermes	Mercury
King of the Gods	Zeus	Jupiter

Poseidon

HISTORY

GODDESSES

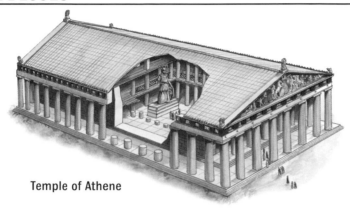

Temple of Athene

GODDESS OF	GREEK	ROMAN
Agriculture	Demeter	Ceres
The dawn	Eos	Aurora
Flowers	Hestia	Flora
Health	Hygeia	Salus
Hunting	Artemis	Diana
Love	Aphrodite	Venus
The Moon	Selene	Luna
Motherhood	Rhea	Ops
Peace	Irene	Pax
Victory	Nike	Victoria
Wisdom	Athene	Minerva
Queen of the Gods	Hera	Juno

13 PREDICTIONS OF NOSTRADAMUS

■ **Did Nostradamus predict the rise of Napoleon Bonaparte?**

Prediction – An Emperor shall be born near Italy who shall cost the Empire dear. From a simple soldier he will rise to Emperor.

■ **Adolf Hitler?**

Prediction – A captain of Germany shall come to yield himself by false hope. So that his revolt shall cause great bloodshed.

■ **The Great Fire of London?**

Prediction – The blood of the just shall be dry in London burnt by the fire of 3 times 20 and 6.

■ **The Death of Pope John Paul I?**

Prediction – When the tomb of the great Roman is found, a new Pope will be elected the following day. (Shortly after the location of St Peter's remains were officially announced Pope John Paul I died after just one month in office, to be succeeded by Pope John Paul II).

■ **The end of the world**

Prediction – In the year 3755, asteroids hit the Earth.

■ **The Death of Henry II of France?**

Prediction – The young lion will overcome the old one on the battlefield in single combat. In a cage of gold his eyes will be put out (Henry II died in a jousting tournament after a shaft was embedded In his eyes).

■ **The American War of Independence?**

Prediction – The eldest sister of the Britannic island shall be born 15 years before her brother (America gained independence in 1776, 15 years prior to the French Revolution).

HISTORY

13 PREDICTIONS OF NOSTRADAMUS

■ **The French Revolution?**

Prediction – Conflict will take place at the tile works by 500 (in 1791 a 500-strong revolutionary group attacked the Tulleries, the palace of King Louis).

■ **Submarines?**

Prediction – The fleet can swim under water. In an iron fish he will make war.

■ **The Gulf War 1990?**

Prediction – An infamous villain, tyrant of Iraq, in league with the Great Whore moves in, leaving the land horned and black.

■ **The Election of Pope Sixtus V?**

Prediction – When Nostradamus met a monk called Felix Paretti he told him he would become Pope. Two years after the death of Nostradamus, Felix Paretti took the title of Pope Sixtus V.

■ **His own death?**

Prediction – On July 1, 1566 before retiring to bed Nostradamus announced to his servant "You will not find me alive at sunrise". His servant found him dead the next day.

■ **The Desecration of his own Grave?**

Legend has it that when French revolutionary troops opened his coffin in May 1791, the remains of Nostradamus were buried with a metal plate bearing the inscription, May 1791.

BOOK OF LISTS

10 US VICE PRESIDENTS WHO BECAME PRESIDENT

- George Bush Snr
- Gerald Ford
- Theodore Roosevelt
- Lyndon B Johnson
- Richard Nixon
- John Adams
- Thomas Jefferson
- Martin Van Buren
- John Tyler
- Millard Fillmore

Richard Nixon

10 BRITISH CHANCELLORS WHO BECAME PRIME MINISTER

- Henry Pelham
- Lord Frederick North
- Spencer Perceval
- Robert Peel
- William Gladstone
- David Lloyd George
- Stanley Baldwin
- Neville Chamberlain
- James Callaghan
- John Major

HISTORY

10 HISTORICAL NOVELS

NOVEL	AUTHOR	SET DURING
All Quiet On The Western Front	Erich Maria Remarque	World War I
A Tale of Two Cities	Charles Dickens	The French Revolution
Barnaby Rudge	Charles Dickens	The Gordon Riots
Dr Zhivago	Boris Pasternak	The Russian Revolution
For Whom the Bell Tolls	Ernest Hemingway	The Spanish Civil War
Ivanhoe	Walter Scott	The reign of Richard I
Quo Vadis	Henry Sienkiewicz	The reign of Emperor Nero
The Red Badge of Courage	Stephen Crane	The American Civil War
The Three Musketeers	Alexandre Dumas	The reign of Louis XIII
War and Peace	Leo Tolstoy	The Napoleonic War

10 NOVELS SET DURING WORLD WAR II

NOVEL	AUTHOR
A Town Like Alice	Nevil Shute
Captain Corelli's Mandolin	Louis de Bernières
Catch 22	Joseph Heller
The Cruel Sea	Nicholas Monsarrat
The Eagle Has Landed	Jack Higgins
Empire of the Sun	JG Ballard
The English Patient	Michael Ondaatje
From Here to Eternity	James Jones
The Guns of Navarone	Alistair McLean
The Winds of War	Herman Wouk

BOOK OF LISTS

NICKNAMES OF PEOPLE OF THE PAST

PERSON	NICKNAME
Attila the Hun	The Scourge of God
Simon Bolivar	The Liberator of South America
William Bonney	Billy the Kid
Robert Burns	The Bard of Ayrshire
Henri Charrière	Papillon
Oliver Cromwell	Old Ironsides
The Duke of Wellington	The Iron Duke
Thomas Alva Edison	The Wizard of Menlo Park
Franz Josef Haydn	The Father of the Symphony
Helen of Troy	The Face that Launched a Thousand Ships
Joseph Holson Jagger	The Man who broke the bank at Monte Carlo
William Joyce	Lord Haw Haw
Henry Longbaugh	The Sundance Kid
Vera Lynn	The Forces' Sweetheart
Florence Nightingale	The Lady with the Lamp
Robert Leroy Parker	Butch Cassidy
Manfred von Richtofen	The Red Baron
William Shakespeare	The Bard of Avon
Charles Edward Stuart	Bonnie Prince Charlie & The Young Pretender
Edward Teach	Blackbeard

HISTORY

ASSASSINATIONS THAT SHOOK THE WORLD

YEAR	VICTIM	ASSASSINS
44BC	Julius Caesar	Brutus, Casca & other co-conspirators
1812	Spencer Perceval	John Bellingham
1865	Abraham Lincoln	John Wilkes Booth
1881	James Garfield	Charles Guiteau
1901	William McKinley	Leon Czolgosz
1914	Archduke Franz Ferdinand	Gavrilo Princip
1916	Rasputin	Felix Yussupov & other co-conspirators
1940	Leon Trotsky	Ramon Mercader
1948	Mahatma Gandhi	Nathuram Godse
1963	John F Kennedy	Lee Harvey Oswald (alleged)
1965	Malcolm X	Norman Butler, Talmadge Hayer, Thomas Johnson
1966	Henrik Verwoerd	Dimitri Tsafendas
1968	Martin Luther King	James Earl Ray
1968	Robert Kennedy	Sirhan Sirhan
1978	Aldo Moro	The Red Brigade
1979	Earl Mountbatten	IRA
1979	Airey Neave	INLA
1980	John Lennon	Mark Chapman
1981	Anwar Sadat	Islam fundamentalists
1984	Indira Gandhi	Beant Singh and Sukhwant Singh
1986	Olof Palme	Unsolved
1991	Rajiv Gandhi	Tamil Tigers
1997	Gianni Versace	Andrew Cunanan

BOOK OF LISTS

EXECUTIONS THROUGH HISTORY

1305	William Wallace
1431	Joan of Arc
1535	Thomas More
1536	Anne Boleyn
1542	Catherine Howard
1554	Lady Jane Grey
1587	Mary Queen of Scots
1606	Guy Fawkes
1618	Walter Raleigh
1649	Charles I
1739	Dick Turpin
1793	Marie Antoinette
1793	Louis XVI
1880	Ned Kelly
1915	Edith Cavell
1917	Mata Hari
1945	Vidkun Quisling
1946	William Joyce
1955	Ruth Ellis
1989	Nicolai Ceausescu

Lady Jane Grey

HISTORY

HISTORICAL EVENTS IN YEARS ENDING WITH A 6

1066	The Battle of Hastings
1206	Genghis Khan founds the Mongol Empire
1216	Henry III crowned King of England
1306	Robert the Bruce proclaimed King of Scotland
1406	Dick Whittington becomes Lord Mayor of London
1506	Leonardo da Vinci completes the Mona Lisa
1536	Henry VIII marries Jane Seymour
1606	Death of Rembrandt
1626	Charles I dissolves Parliament
1636	Harvard College founded in the USA
1666	The Great Fire of London
1756	The Seven Years War between Britain and France begins
1796	Edward Jenner discovers vaccination
1816	Argentina is granted independence from Spain
1836	The Battle of the Alamo
1846	Discovery of the planet Neptune
1856	The Crimean War ends
1876	Alexander Graham Bell invents the telephone
1886	Coca-Cola invented
1916	The Battle of the Somme
1936	Edward VIII abdicates for the love of Wallis Simpson
1956	The Suez Crisis begins

BOOK OF LISTS

BATTLE STATIONS
Historical battles pre 20th century

YEAR/BATTLE	WINNERS	LOSERS
333 BC Issus	Alexander the Great	King Darius III
31 BC Actium	Octavian	Antony & Cleopatra
1066 Stamford Bridge	Harold II	Harald III of Norway
1066 Hastings	William the Conqueror	Harold II
1297 Stirling Bridge	William Wallace	John de Warenne
1314 Bannockburn	Robert the Bruce	Edward II
1415 Agincourt	Henry V	France

Alexander the Great

HISTORY

BATTLE STATIONS
Historical battles pre 20th century

YEAR/BATTLE	WINNERS	LOSERS
1464 Hexham	Yorkists	Lancastrians
1485 Bosworth Field	Henry VII	Richard III
1513 Flodden Field	Earl of Surrey (Army of Henry VIII)	James IV of Scotland
1588 Defeat of Spanish Armada	England	Spain
1644 Marston Moor	Roundheads	Cavaliers
1645 Naseby	Roundheads	Cavaliers
1685 Sedgemoor	John Churchill (Army of James II)	Duke of Monmouth
1690 Boyne	William of Orange	James VII
1746 Culloden Moor	England	Jacobites
1798 Nile	Horatio Nelson (England)	French fleet
1801 Copenhagen	Horatio Nelson	Danish fleet
1805 Trafalgar	Horatio Nelson	French/Spanish fleet
1815 Waterloo	Duke of Wellington	Napoleon Bonaparte
1836 Alamo	General Santa Anna	Texan troops led by Colonel Travis
1863 Gettysburg	Unionists	Confederates
1876 Little Big Horn	Sitting Bull/Crazy Horse	General George Custer

FOUNDING DATES OF NEWSPAPERS

1785	*The Times* (as *The Daily Universal Register*)
1791	*The Observer*
1821	*The Guardian* (as *The Manchester Guardian*)
1825	*Le Figaro*
1827	*London Evening Standard*
1842	*The Daily Record*
1843	*The News Of The World*
1851	*New York Times*
1855	*Daily Telegraph*
1865	*San Francisco Chronicle*
1877	*Washington Post*
1881	*Los Angeles Times*
1889	*Wall Street Journal*
1896	*Daily Mail*
1900	*Daily Express*
1903	*Daily Mirror*
1912	*Pravda*
1944	*Le Monde*
1964	*The Sun* (replaced the *Daily Herald*)
1978	*Daily Star*
1982	*USA Today*
1986	*The Independent*

Typesetter

HISTORY

BIRTH AND DEATH OF 20 FAMOUS AMERICANS

NAME	BORN	DIED
Davy Crockett	1786 Grand County, Tennessee	1836 San Antonio
George Custer	1839 New Rumley, Ohio	1876 Little Big Horn, Montana
Walt Disney	1901 Chicago	1966 Los Angeles
Wyatt Earp	1848 Monmouth, Illinois	1929 Los Angeles
Dwight Eisenhower	1890 Denison, Texas	1969 Washington DC
Henry Ford	1863 Dearborn, Michigan	1947 Dearborn, Michigan
John F Kennedy	1917 Brookline, Massachusetts	1963 Dallas
Martin Luther King	1929 Atlanta, Georgia	1968 Memphis, Tennessee
Abraham Lincoln	1809 Harding County, Kentucky	1865 Washington DC
Samuel Morse	1791 Charlestown, Massachusetts	1872 New York
Richard Nixon	1913 Yorba Linda, California	1994 New York
Edgar Allan Poe	1809 Boston	1849 Baltimore
Elvis Presley	1935 Tupelo, Mississippi	1977 Memphis
Ronald Reagan	1911 Tampico, Illinois	2004 Los Angeles
John D Rockefeller	1839 New York	1937 Ormond Beach, Florida
FD Roosevelt	1882 New York	1945 Warm Springs, Georgia
Theodore Roosevelt	1858 New York	1919 Nassau County, New York
Babe Ruth	1895 Baltimore	1948 New York
Frank Sinatra	1915 Hoboken, New Jersey	1998 Los Angeles
George Washington	1732 Virginia	1799 Mount Vernon

THE WISDOM OF CONFUCIUS

- 'Never contract friendship with a man that is not better than thyself.'
- 'The strength of a nation derives from the integrity of the home.'
- 'Everything has beauty, but not everyone sees it.'
- 'Silence is a friend who will never betray.'
- 'Never give a sword to a man who can't dance.'
- 'You cannot open a book without learning something.'
- 'A journey of a thousand miles begins with a single step.'
- 'The cautious seldom err.'
- 'When anger rises, think of the consequences.'
- 'It is better to light one small candle than to curse the darkness.'
- 'If we don't know life, how can we know death?'
- 'To lead uninstructed people to war is to throw them away.'
- 'When prosperity comes, do not use all of it.'
- 'Real knowledge is to know the extent of one's ignorance.'
- 'To know what is right and not to do it is the worst cowardice.'
- 'Ignorance is the night of the mind, but a night without moon or star.'
- 'The father who does not teach his son his duties is equally guilty with the son who neglects them.'
- 'An oppressive government is more to be feared than a tiger.'
- 'To see and listen to the wicked is already the beginning of wickedness.'
- 'A man who has committed a mistake and does not correct it is making another mistake.'

HISTORY

THE WISDOM OF WINSTON CHURCHILL

- 'I am easily satisfied with the very best.'
- 'History will be kind to me, for I intend to write it.'
- 'I like a man who grins when he fights.'
- 'A sheep in sheep's clothing' (referring to Clement Attlee).
- 'Eating words has never given me indigestion.'
- 'I have nothing to offer but blood, toil, tears and sweat.'
- 'My most brilliant achievement was my ability to be able to persuade my wife to marry me.'
- 'An appeaser is one who feeds a crocodile, hoping it will eat him last.'
- 'Russia is a riddle wrapped in a mystery inside an enigma.'
- 'Before Alamein we never had a victory. After Alamein we never had a defeat.'
- 'It is a fine thing to be honest, but it is also very important to be right.'
- 'A lie gets halfway around the world before the truth has the chance to get its pants on.'
- 'I have been brought up and trained to have the utmost contempt for people who get drunk.'
- 'In a war, you can only be killed once, but in politics, many times.'
- 'Attitude is a little thing that makes a big difference.'
- 'It is more agreeable to have the power to give than to receive.'
- 'I am always ready to learn although I do not always like being taught.'
- 'No folly is more costly than the folly of intolerant idealism.'
- 'Never in the field of human conflict was so much owed by so many to so few.'
- 'If you are going through hell, keep going.'

BOOK OF LISTS

THE THINGS THEY SAID

Mohammed Ali . . . . 'I am the greatest, not only do I knock 'em out, I pick the round.'

Napoleon Bonaparte . . . . 'An army marches on its stomach.'

Bill Clinton . . . . 'I tried marijuana once, I did not inhale.'

Oliver Cromwell . . . . 'Put your faith in God and keep your powder dry.'

Walt Disney . . . . 'I loved Mickey Mouse more than any woman I've ever known.'

Elizabeth I . . . . 'I may have the body but of a weak and feeble woman; but I have the heart and stomach of a king.'

Henry Ford . . . . 'You can have any colour you want as long as it's black.'

Mahatma Gandhi . . . . 'A nation's culture resides in the hearts and in the soul of its people.'

Charles de Gaulle . . . . 'How can anyone govern a nation that has 246 different kinds of cheese.'

Alfred Hitchcock . . . . 'Actors should be treated like cattle.'

Martin Luther King . . . . . 'I want to be white man's brother, not his brother-in-law.'

Henry Kissinger . . . . 'Next week there can't be any crisis. My schedule is already full.'

Karl Marx . . . . 'Religion is the opium of the people.'

Horatio Nelson . . . . 'England expects that every man will do his duty.'

Pope John Paul II . . . . 'Social justice cannot be attained by violence. Violence kills what it intends to create.'

William Shakespeare . . . . 'Be not afraid of greatness. Some are born great, some achieve greatness, and some have greatness thrust upon them.'

Margaret Thatcher . . . . . 'I am extraordinarily patient, provided I get my own way in the end.'

George Washington . . . . . 'It is far better to be alone, than to be in bad company.'

HISTORY

20 IN LINE TO THE BRITISH THRONE IN 2004

1   The Prince of Wales, Prince Charles

2   Prince William, son of Prince Charles

3   Prince Henry, son of Prince Charles

4   The Duke of York, Prince Andrew

5   Princess Beatrice, daughter of Prince Andrew

6   Princess Eugenie, daughter of Prince Andrew

7   The Earl of Wessex, Prince Edward

8   Princess Louise, daughter of Prince Edward

9   The Princess Royal, Princess Anne

10   Peter Phillips, son of Princess Anne

11   Zara Phillips, daughter of Princess Anne

12   Viscount Linley, son of Princess Margaret

13   Charles Armstrong-Jones, son of Viscount Linley

14   Margarita Armstrong-Jones, daughter of Viscount Linley

15   Lady Sarah Chatto, daughter of Princess Margaret

16   Samuel Chatto, son of Lady Sarah

17   Arthur Chatto, son of Lady Sarah

18   The Duke of Gloucester, Prince Richard, cousin of Queen Elizabeth II

19   Alexander Windsor, son of Prince Richard

20   Lady Davina Lewis, daughter of Prince Richard

Prince Edward

BOOK OF LISTS

COLLECTIVELY SPEAKING

- **THE BIG THREE** (THE THREE LEADERS AT THE YALTA CONFERENCE)

  Winston Churchill, Josef Stalin, Franklin D Roosevelt
- **THE BIG THREE** (GOLFERS OF THE 1960s)

  Gary Player, Arnold Palmer, Jack Nicklaus
- **THE THREE KRAY BROTHERS**

  Ronnie, Reggie and Charlie
- **THE THREE GORGONS**

  Medusa, Euryale, Stheno
- **THE THREE GRACES**

  Aglaia, Euphrosyne, Thaleia
- **THE THREE NATIONS THAT SIGNED THE TRIPLE ENTENTE**

  Great Britain, France, Russia
- **THE GUILDFORD FOUR**

  Gerry Conlon, Paul Hill, Patrick Armstrong, Carole Richardson
- **THE GANG OF FOUR** (THE FOUR LABOUR MPs WHO FOUNDED THE SDP)

  Roy Jenkins, David Owen, Bill Rodgers, Shirley Williams
- **THE FOUR CREATURES SENT TO PLAGUE EGYPT IN THE BIBLE**

  Flies, frogs, gnats, locusts
- **THE FOUR GOSPEL WRITERS**

  Matthew, Mark, Luke and John
- **THE FIVE BOOKS OF THE PENTATEUCH** (FIRST FIVE OF THE OLD TESTAMENT)

  Genesis, Exodus, Leviticus, Numbers, Deuteronomy

HISTORY

COLLECTIVELY SPEAKING

■ **THE FIVE PILLARS OF ISLAM**

Faith, Prayer, Charity, Fasting, Pilgrimage (known as Hajj)

■ **THE CLASSICAL COMPOSERS KNOWN AS THE FIVE OR THE MIGHTY HANDFUL**

Alexander Borodin, Cesar Cui, Modest Mussorgsky, Nikolai Rimsky-Korsakov, Mily Balakirev

■ **THE SIX WIVES OF HENRY VIII**

Catherine of Aragon, Anne Boleyn, Jane Seymour, Anne of Cleves, Catherine Howard, Catherine Parr

■ **THE SIX PLANTAGANET MONARCHS**

Henry IV, Henry V, Henry VI, Edward IV, Edward V, Richard III

■ **THE SIX TUDOR MONARCHS**

Henry VII, Henry VIII, Edward VI, Lady Jane Grey, Mary I, Elizabeth I

■ **THE SIX HANOVERIAN MONARCHS**

George I, George II, George III, George IV, William IV, Queen Victoria

■ **THE TOLLPUDDLE MARTYRS**

James Loveless, George Loveless, Thomas Stanfield, John Stanfield, James Hammett, James Brine

■ **THE EARP BROTHERS**

Wyatt, Morgan, Virgil, Warren, Newton, James

■ **THE BIRMINGHAM SIX**

Patrick Hill, Hugh Callaghan, Richard McIlkenny, Gerard Hunter, William Power, Johnny Walker

GEOGRAPHY

Taiwan used to be called Formosa. You may have known that already, but did you know these facts: the Roman name for Paris was Lutetia; Utah is known as the Beehive State; it's against the law in California to eat oranges in a bathtub; the word 'sveiki' is Latvian for 'hello'; Toledo was once the capital of Spain; the three-legged symbol on the flag of the Isle of Man is called a 'triskellion'; and Oslo's international airport is Fornebu airport.

BOOK OF LISTS

PLACES NAMED AFTER PEOPLE

PLACE	NAMED AFTER
Alexandria	Alexander the Great
America	Amerigo Vespucci
Bolivia	Simon Bolivar
The Bronx	James Bronck
Carson City	Kit Carson
Colombia	Christopher Columbus

Christopher
Columbus

GEOGRAPHY

PLACES NAMED AFTER PEOPLE

PLACE	NAMED AFTER
Cook Islands	Captain James Cook
Everest	George Everest
Georgia, USA	King George I
Houston	Samuel Houston
Jefferson City	Thomas Jefferson
Louisiana	King Louis XIV of France
Louisville	King Louis XVI of France
Madison	James Madison
Maryland	Henrietta Maria de Bourbon, wife of Charles I
Monrovia	James Monroe
Pennsylvania	William Penn
Philippines	King Phillip of Spain
Pittsburgh	William Pitt the Elder
Queensland	Queen Victoria
Rhodesia	Cecil Rhodes
Rome	Romulus
San Francisco	St Francis
Saudi Arabia	Mohammed Bin Saud
Tasmania	Abel Tasman
Victoria Falls	Queen Victoria
Virgin Islands	Queen Elizabeth I, the Virgin Queen
Washington	George Washington

BOOK OF LISTS

WHAT TIME IS IT?

When it is 12 noon in London (Winter), it is this time in ...

Addis Ababa	15.00	Melbourne	.23.00
Adelaide	22.30	Mexico City	.06.00
Athens	14.00	Montevideo	.09.00
Bangkok	19.00	Montreal	.07.00
Barcelona	13.00	Moscow	.15.00
Beijing	20.00	New York	.07.00
Berlin	13.00	Oslo	.13.00
Boston	07.00	Paris	.13.00
Brasilia	08.00	Rio	.08.00
Buenos Aires	09.00	Rome	.13.00
Cairo	14.00	San Francisco	.04.00
Calcutta	17.15	Seoul	.21.00
Cape Town	14.00	Singapore	.20.00
Chicago	06.00	Stockholm	.13.00
Denver	05.00	Sydney	.23.00
Geneva	13.00	Tokyo	.21.00
Havana	07.00	Vienna	.13.00
Hong Kong	20.00	Tehran	.15.30
Honolulu	02.00		
Istanbul	14.00		
Lisbon	12.00		
Los Angeles	04.00		

GEOGRAPHY

CITIES BUILT ON 7 HILLS

- Amman
- Athens
- Bath
- Bergen
- Bristol
- Cincinnati
- Istanbul
- Jerusalem
- Kampala
- Kiev
- Lisbon
- Moscow
- Nimes
- Prague
- Pretoria
- Rio de Janeiro
- Rome
- Seattle

Prague

BOOK OF LISTS

FORMERLY KNOWN AS

LOCATION	FORMER NAME
Albany	Fort Orange
Atlantic City	Absecon
Bangladesh	East Pakistan
Belize	British Honduras
Benin	Dahomey
Bolivia	Upper Peru
Botswana	Bechuanaland
Burkina Faso	Upper Volta
Canada	New France
Chicago	Fort Dearborn
Cincinnati	Fort Washington
Colombia	New Granada
Djibouti	French Somaliland
Ethiopia	Abyssinia
Ghana	Gold Coast
Harare	Salisbury
Hawaii	Sandwich Islands
Ho Chi Minh City	Saigon
Iran	Persia
Iraq	Mesopotamia
Istanbul	Constantinople
Malawi	Nyasaland

Sri Lanka

GEOGRAPHY

FORMERLY KNOWN AS

LOCATION	FORMER NAME
Mali	French Sudan
Minneapolis	Fort Snelling
Montreal	Ville Marie
Mozambique	Portuguese East Africa
Myanmar	Burma
Namibia	South West Africa
New York	New Amsterdam
Oslo	Christiania
Sri Lanka	Ceylon
Surinam	Dutch Guiana
Taiwan	Formosa
Tasmania	Van Diemen's Land
Thailand	Siam
Tokyo	Edo
Tonga	The Friendly Islands
Vanuatu	The New Hebrides
Zambia	Northern Rhodesia
Zimbabwe	Southern Rhodesi

XL ROMAN PLACE NAMES

LOCATION	ROMAN NAME
Anglesey	Mona
Bath	Aquae Sulis
Budapest	Aquincum
Cambridge	Granta
Carlisle	Luguvalium
Chester	Deva
Crete	Candia
Doncaster	Danum
Dover	Dubris
England	Albion
Exeter	Isca Dumnoniorum
France	Gallia
Germany	Germania
Gloucester	Glevum
Greece	Graecia
Guernsey	Sarnia
Ireland	Hibernia
Isle of Man	Manavia
Isle of Wight	Vectis
Jersey	Caesaria
Lancaster	Lunecastrum
Lincoln	Lindum

Londinium

GEOGRAPHY

XL ROMAN PLACE NAMES

LOCATION	ROMAN NAME
Lisbon	Olisopo
Liverpool	Esmeduna
London	Londinium
Lyon	Lugdunum
Manchester	Mancunium
Newcastle	Pons Aelius
Paris	Lutetia
Portugal	Lusitania
Romania	Dacia
Scotland	Caledonia
Spain	Hispania
St Albans	Verulamium
Switzerland	Helvetia
Vienna	Vindobona
Wales	Cambria
Winchester	Venta Belgarum
York	Eboracum
Zurich	Turicum

BIRDS AND BEASTS ON FLAGS

PLACE	ANIMAL
Albania	Double-headed black eagle
Alderney	Lion
Andorra	Pair of cows
Bhutan	Dragon
California	Bear
Dominica	Parrot
Ecuador	Condor
Falkland Islands	Sheep
Idaho	Deer
Illinois	Bald eagle
Iowa	Bald eagle
Kansas	Six sheep and a horse
Louisiana	Pelican

Dominica / Parrot

GEOGRAPHY

BIRDS AND BEASTS ON FLAGS

PLACE	ANIMAL
Maine	Moose
Mexico	Eagle and snake
Michigan	Elk, moose and bald eagle
Minnesota	Horse
Missouri	Pair of grizzly bears
New Jersey	Horse
New York state	Bald eagle
North Dakota	Bald eagle
Oregon	Eagle
Pennsylvania	Two black horses and a bald eagle
Sark	Pair of lions
South Dakota	Pair of horses pulling a plough
Sri Lanka	Lion
St Helena	Wirebird
Uganda	Crested crane
Utah	Bald eagle
Vermont	Stag
Virgin Islands of the USA	Eagle
Wales	Red dragon
Wisconsin	Badger
Wyoming	Bison
Zambia	Eagle

Sri Lanka / Lion

ZIP CODES OF US STATES

Alaska	.AK
Alabama	.AL
Arkansas	.AR
Arizona	.AZ
California	.CA
Colorado	.CO
Connecticut	.CT
Delaware	.DE
Florida	.FL
Georgia	.GA
Hawaii	.HI
Idaho	.ID
Illinois	.IL
Indiana	.IN
Iowa	.IA
Kansas	.KS
Kentucky	.KY
Louisiana	.LA
Maine	.ME
Maryland	.MD
Massachusetts	.MA
Michigan	.MI
Minnesota	.MN

Hawaii / HI

GEOGRAPHY

ZIP CODES OF US STATES

Mississippi	MS	Texas	TX
Missouri	MO	Utah	UT
Montana	MT	Vermont	VT
Nebraska	NB	Virginia	VA
Nevada	NV	Washington	WA
New Hampshire	NH	West Virginia	WV
New Jersey	NJ	Wisconsin	WI
New Mexico	NM	Wyoming	WY
New York	NY		
North Carolina	NC		
North Dakota	ND		
Ohio	OH		
Oklahoma	OK		
Oregon	OR		
Pennsylvania	PA		
Rhode Island	RI		
South Carolina	SC		
South Dakota	SD		
Tennessee	TN		

BOOK OF LISTS

STATE NICKNAMES

Alabama	The Cotton State
Alaska	The Last Frontier
Arizona	The Grand Canyon State
Arkansas	The Bear State
California	The Golden State
Colorado	The Centennial State
Connecticut	The Nutmeg State
Delaware	The First State
Florida	The Sunshine State
Georgia	The Peach State
Hawaii	The Aloha State
Idaho	The Gem State
Illinois	The Prairie State
Indiana	The Hoosier State
Iowa	The Hawkeye State
Kansas	The Sunflower State
Kentucky	The Bluegrass State
Louisiana	The Pelican State
Maine	The Pine Tree State
Maryland	The Free State
Massachusetts	The Bay State
Michigan	The Wolverine State
Minnesota	The Gopher State
Mississippi	The Magnolia State
Missouri	The Show Me State
Montana	The Treasure State

Boston, Massachusetts

GEOGRAPHY

STATE NICKNAMES

Nebraska	The Cornhusker State
Nevada	The Silver State
New Hampshire	The Granite State
New Jersey	The Garden State
New Mexico	The Sunshine State
New York	The Empire State
North Carolina	The Tar Heel State
North Dakota	The Sioux State
Ohio	The Buckeye State
Oklahoma	The Sooner State
Oregon	The Beaver State
Pennsylvania	The Keystone State
Rhode Island	The Plantation State
South Carolina	The Palmetto State
South Dakota	The Coyote State
Tennessee	The Volunteer State
Texas	The Lone Star State
Utah	The Beehive State
Vermont	The Green Mountain State
Virginia	The Cavalier State
Washington	The Evergreen State
West Virginia	The Mountain State
Wisconsin	The Badger State
Wyoming	The Equality State

BOOK OF LISTS

UNUSUAL LAWS AROUND THE WORLD

In Baltimore, USA it is illegal to be accompanied by a lion to the movies

In some Swiss towns, it is illegal to flush the toilet after 10pm if living in an apartment

In Chicago a by-law states that it is illegal to fish whilst sitting on a giraffe's neck

In Swaziland, young girls are not allowed to shake hands with men

In Lee County, Alabama a law prohibits the selling of peanuts after sundown on Wednesdays

Chewing gum is outlawed in Singapore

In England, it is illegal to stand within 100 yards of a reigning monarch if not wearing socks

In Wyoming, USA it is illegal between January and April to take a photograph of rabbits without a permit

Members of parliament are forbidden to wear suits of armour in the House of Commons

In the state of Ohio, it is against the law to get a fish drunk

In England, impersonating a Chelsea pensioner is a punishable offence

In Chester, an ancient by-law states that it is legal to shoot a Welsh person with a bow and arrow within the city walls after midnight

In Israel, picking one's nose on the Sabbath is illegal

Drinking coffee in Turkey in the 17th century was punishable by death

In Louisiana, it is illegal to gargle in public

In Thailand, citizens are not allowed to leave their home without wearing underwear

In Arizona, it is against the law for donkeys to stand in bathtubs

In addition, an Arizona law forbids the hunting of camels

In California, it is against the law to eat oranges in a bathtub

GEOGRAPHY

TOP 10 HIGHEST MOUNTAINS

MOUNTAIN	HEIGHT IN METRES
Everest	8850
K2	8611
Kangchenjunga	8586
Lhotse	8516
Makalu	8462
Cho Oyu	8201
Dhaulagiri	8172
Manaslu	8156
Nanga Parbat	8125
Annapurna	8091

Everest

TOP 10 LONGEST MOUNTAIN RANGES

RANGE	LENGTH IN KILOMETRES
The Andes	7240
The Rocky Mountains	4827
The Himalayas	3861
The Great Dividing Range	3620
The Transantarctic Range	3540
The Brazilian Coastal Range	3057
The Sumatra–Java Range	2896
The Aleutians	2574
The Tien Shan	2252
The New Guinea Range	2011

BOOK OF LISTS

TOP 10 LARGEST COUNTRIES

Canada

- Russia
- Canada
- China
- USA
- Brazil
- Australia
- India
- Argentina
- Kazakhstan
- Sudan

TOP 10 LARGEST ISLANDS

- Greenland
- New Guinea
- Borneo
- Madagascar
- Baffin Island
- Sumatra
- Honshu
- Great Britain
- Victoria Island
- Ellesmere Island

Great Britain

GEOGRAPHY

TOP 10 LARGEST SEAS

- South China Sea
- Caribbean Sea
- Mediterranean Sea
- Bering Sea
- Gulf of Mexico
- Arabian Sea
- Sea of Okhotsk
- Sea of Japan
- Hudson Bay
- East China Sea

Mediterranean Sea

TOP 10 LARGEST LAKES

- Caspian Sea
- Lake Superior
- Lake Victoria
- Lake Huron
- Lake Michigan
- Aral Sea
- Lake Tanganyika
- Lake Baikal
- Great Bear Lake
- Lake Malawi

Lake Superior

BOOK OF LISTS

MOTTOS AROUND THE WORLD

COUNTRY	MOTTO
Andorra	Strength united is stronger
Argentina	In union and freedom
Bulgaria	Union is strength
Cambodia	Nation, religion, king
Canada	From sea to sea
France	Liberty, equality, brotherhood
Germany	Unity and justice and freedom
Gibraltar	Conquered by no enemy
Greece	Liberty or death
India	Truth alone triumphs
Iran	God is most great
Kenya	Let's work together
Luxembourg	We want to stay what we are
Philippines	For love of God, people, nature and country
Poland	God, honour, homeland
Swaziland	We are the fortress
Sweden	For Sweden, with the times
United Kingdom	God and my right
USA	In God we trust
Vietnam	Independence, liberty and happiness

GEOGRAPHY

10 PLACES NAMED AFTER GEORGE WASHINGTON

- Washington, D.C.
- Washington State
- George Washington Bridge, spanning the Hudson River in New York
- Washington Heights, New York
- Fort Washington, Maryland
- Washington County, Alabama
- Lake Washington, Seattle
- Washington Crossing State Park, New Jersey
- Port Washington, New York
- Mount Washington, Massachusetts

FIRST 10 STATES SET UP IN THE USA

- Delaware
- Pennsylvania
- New Jersey
- Georgia
- Connecticut
- Massachusetts
- Maryland
- South Carolina
- New Hampshire
- Virginia

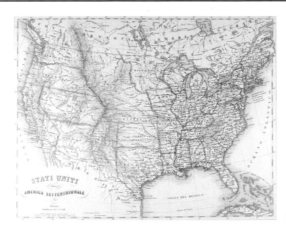

USA

BOOK OF LISTS

UNUSUAL DAYS CELEBRATED IN THE USA

January 3 . . . . Festival of Sleep

January 18 . . . . Winnie the Pooh Day

January 21 . . . . National Hugging Day

January 23 . . . . National Handwriting Day

January 31 . . . . National Popcorn Day

February 9 . . . . Toothache Day

February 26 . . . . National Pistachio Day

March 12 . . . . Alfred Hitchcock Day

March 14 . . . . National Potato Chip Day

April 4 . . . . Tell a Lie Day

April 7 . . . . No Housework Day

April 30 . . . . National Honesty Day

May 9 . . . . Lost Sock Memorial Day

May 11 . . . . Eat What You Want Day

May 28 . . . . National Hamburger Day

June 9 . . . . Donald Duck Day

June 10 . . . . National Yo Yo Day

June 26 . . . . National Chocolate Pudding Day

July 14 . . . . National Nude Day

July 22 . . . . Ratcatchers' Day

July 30 . . . . National Cheesecake Day

August 5 . . . . National Mustard Day

August 13 . . . . Blame Someone Else Day

GEOGRAPHY

UNUSUAL DAYS CELEBRATED IN THE USA

August 25 . . . . Kiss and Make up Day

September 9 . . . . Teddy Bear Day

September 13 . . . . Defy Superstition Day

September 22 . . . . Hobbit Day

September 27 . . . . Crush a Can Day

October 23 . . . . National Mole Day

November 1 . . . . Plan Your Epitaph Day

November 3 . . . . Sandwich Day

December 17 . . . . Underdog Day

December 21 . . . . Look at the Bright Side Day

September 9 – Teddy Bear Day

CITY NICKNAMES

CITY	NICKNAME
Aberdeen	The Granite City
Alexandria	The Pearl of the Mediterranean
Amsterdam	The Gateway to Europe
Bangkok	The Venice of the East
Boston	The Athens of America
Budapest	The Pearl of the Danube
Chicago	The Windy City
Christchurch	The Garden City
Dallas	The Big D
Denver	The Mile High City
Detroit	The Motor City
Edinburgh	Auld Reekie
Houston	The Magnolia City
Jerusalem	The City of David
Los Angeles	The Big Orange
Miami	Little Cuba
Montreal	The City of Saints
Nashville	The Music City
New Orleans	The Big Easy
New York	The Big Apple
Oxford	The City of Dreaming Spires
Paris	The City of Lights

GEOGRAPHY

CITY NICKNAMES

CITY	NICKNAME
Philadelphia	The City of Brotherly Love
Pittsburgh	The Steel City
Reno	The Biggest Little City in the World
Rome	The Eternal City
Salem	The City of Witches
San Antonio	The Alamo City
San Francisco	Golden Gate City
Venice	The Queen of the Adriatic

Bangkok / The Venice of the East

BOOK OF LISTS

TOP 10 US STATES FOR POPULATION

1 California
2 New York
3 Texas
4 Florida
5 Pennsylvania
6 Illinois
7 Ohio
8 Michigan
9 New Jersey
10 North Carolina

New York

BOTTOM 10 US STATES FOR POPULATION

1	Wyoming	6	South Dakota
2	Vermont	7	Montana
3	Alaska	8	Rhode Island
4	Delaware	9	Idaho
5	North Dakota	10	Nevada

Wyoming

GEOGRAPHY

THE 10 HIGHEST WATERFALLS IN THE WORLD

Angel Falls

- Angel Falls, Venezuela
- Tugela, South Africa
- Utigord, Norway
- Monge, Norway
- Mutarazi, Zimbabwe
- Yosemite, USA
- Espelands, Norway
- Mara Valley, Norway
- Tyssestrengene, Norway
- Cuquenan, Venezuela

TOP 10 MOST SPOKEN LANGUAGES IN THE WORLD

(NATIVE TONGUE)

- Chinese Mandarin
- English
- Hindustani
- Spanish
- Russian
- Arabic
- Bengali
- Portuguese
- Malay-Indonesian
- Japanese

BOOK OF LISTS

HOW TO SAY HELLO IN 40 DIFFERENT LANGUAGES

Arabic	Salaam
Bengali	Nomoskaar
Bulgarian	Zdrasti
Cantonese	Neilhou
Czech	Nazdar
Danish	God dag
Dutch	Goeiedag
Esperanto	Saluton
Fijian	Bula
Finnish	Paivaa
French	Bonjour
German	Guten Tag
Greek	Geia Sou
Hawaiian	Aloha
Hebrew	Shalom
Hindi	Namaskaar
Hungarian	Szia
Icelandic	Godan daginn
Indonesian	Selamat
Italian	Buon giorno
Japanese	Konichiwa
Korean	Annyong
Kurdish	Rozhbash
Latvian	Sveiki
Maltese	Bongu
Mandarin Chinese	Ni hao
Maori	Tena Koe
Norwegian	Goddag
Polish	Czolem
Portuguese	Ola
Punjabi	Sat siri akal
Romanian	Buna
Russian	Zdravstvuite
Spanish	Hola
Swedish	God dag
Swahili	Jambo
Thai	Sawatdi
Tibetan	Oloy
Turkish	Selam
Urdu	Adaab

GEOGRAPHY

PAST AND PRESENT CAPITALS

COUNTRY	FORMER CAPITAL	PRESENT CAPITAL
Australia	Melbourne	Canberra
Brazil	Rio de Janeiro	Brasília
Burma (Myanmar)	Mandalay	Yangon
China	Nanking	Beijing
Egypt	Alexandria	Cairo
England	Winchester	London
Finland	Turku	Helsinki
India	Calcutta	New Delhi
Japan	Kyoto	Tokyo
Netherlands	The Hague	Amsterdam
New Zealand	Auckland	Wellington
Nigeria	Lagos	Abuja
Norway	Trondheim	Oslo
Pakistan	Rawalpindi	Islamabad
Poland	Krakow	Warsaw
Russia	St Petersburg	Moscow
Scotland	Perth	Edinburgh
Spain	Toledo	Madrid
Uganda	Entebbe	Kampala
USA	Philadelphia	Washington, D.C.

BOOK OF LISTS

WHAT'S IN A NAME?
The meanings of the names of countries

COUNTRY	MEANING OF NAME
Argentina	Land of silver
Australia	Southern land
Austria	Eastern kingdom
Azerbaijan	Land of fire
Barbados	Bearded
Burkina Faso	Land of honest men
Canada	Little settlement
Costa Rica	Rich coast
Cyprus	Copper
Denmark	Flat borderland
Ecuador	Equator
El Salvador	The Saviour
Estonia	Eastern way
Faroe Islands	Sheep islands
Guyana	Land of many waters
Jamaica	Land of wood and water
Kuwait	Fortress near the water
Liechtenstein	Light stone
Luxembourg	Small castle
Maldives	Palace island
Myanmar	Fast and strong

GEOGRAPHY

WHAT'S IN A NAME?
The meanings of the names of countries

COUNTRY	MEANING OF NAME
Netherlands	Lower lands
Norway	Northern way
Panama	Place of many fish
Philippines	Lands of King Phillip
Poland	Country of fields
Portugal	Beautiful port
Puerto Rico	Rich harbour
Sierra Leone	Lion mountains
Sri Lanka	Resplendent land
Thailand	Land of the free
Ukraine	Border territory
Venezuela	Little Venice
Vietnam	Beyond the southern border
Zimbabwe	Houses of stone

BOOK OF LISTS

THE MEANINGS OF THE NAMES OF TOWNS, CITIES AND STATES

PLACE	MEANING OF NAME
Acapulco	Plain of dense reeds
Accra	Ant
Addis Ababa	New flower
Ankara	Anchor
Alaska	Great country
Arizona	Place of little springs
Baghdad	God's gift
Bangkok	Wild plum village
Baton Rouge	Red stick
Beijing	Northern capital
Belgrade	The white city
Bethlehem	House of bread
Bloemfontein	Fountain of flowers
Brussels	Of the marsh
Buenos Aires	Good winds
Canberra	Meeting place
Casablanca	White house
Chicago	Garlic place
Connecticut	On the long tidal river
Dijon	Divine
Eindhoven	End property

GEOGRAPHY

THE MEANINGS OF THE NAMES OF TOWNS, CITIES AND STATES

PLACE	MEANING OF NAME
Khartoum	Elephant's trunk
Las Vegas	The meadows
Los Angeles	City of angels
Massachusetts	Large hill place
Monte Carlo	Charles's mountain
Montevideo	I see the mountain
Montreal	Royal mountain
Munich	Home of the monks
Nebraska	Flat water
Nova Scotia	New Scotland
Oklahoma	Home of the red people
Quebec	Narrow passage
Reykjavik	Smoky bay
Rio de Janeiro	River of January
Tel Aviv	Hill spring
Tripoli	Three towns
Vermont	Green mountain
Wisconsin	The place where we live

BOOK OF LISTS

TOP 10 MOST HIGHLY POPULATED COUNTRIES IN THE WORLD

- China
- India
- USA
- Indonesia
- Brazil
- Pakistan
- Russia
- Bangladesh
- Nigeria
- Japan

WORLD POPULATION LANDMARKS

1804 . . . . 1 billion
1927 . . . . 2 billion
1960 . . . . 3 billion
1974 . . . . 4 billion
1987 . . . . 5 billion
1999 . . . . 6 billion

10 COUNTRIES THAT JOINED THE EU IN MAY 2004

- Czech Republic
- Cyprus
- Estonia
- Hungary
- Latvia
- Lithuania
- Malta
- Poland
- Slovakia
- Slovenia

GEOGRAPHY

15 COMPANIES FOUNDED IN GERMANY

- Adidas
- Agfa
- Aldi
- Audi
- BASF
- Bayer AG
- Braun
- BMW
- Grundig
- Haribo
- Hoechst
- Nivea
- Siemens
- Volkswagen
- Zeiss

20 COMPANIES FOUNDED IN JAPAN

- Canon
- Casio
- Fuji
- Hitachi
- Honda
- Kawasaki
- Konica
- Mitsubishi
- Nikon
- Nintendo
- Nissan
- Sanyo
- Sega
- Sharp
- Sony
- Subaru
- Suzuki
- Toshiba
- Toyota
- Yamaha

GSX600R Suzuki motorbike

BOOK OF LISTS

SYMBOLS ON FLAGS

COUNTRY	SYMBOL ON FLAG
Argentina	Sun of May
Barbados	Trident
Brunei	Pair of raised hands
Cambodia	Temple of Angkor
Canada	Maple leaf
Cyprus	Outline of Cyprus above a pair of olive branches
Gibraltar	Castle and a golden key
Hong Kong	Bauhinia blakensis, a species of flower unique to Hong Kong
Isle of Man	Triskellion, three-legged symbol
Israel	Star of David
Kenya	Shield and two spears
Lebanon	Cedar tree
Liechtenstein	Golden crown
Mozambique	Pair of Kalashnikov rifles
Rwanda	The letter R
Zimbabwe	Soapstone bird

GEOGRAPHY

FLAGS THAT DEPICT A UNION JACK

- Australia
- Anguilla
- British Virgin Islands
- Bermuda
- Cayman Islands
- Cook Islands
- Falkland Islands
- Fiji
- Hawaii
- Montserrat
- New Zealand
- Pitcairn Islands
- St Helena
- South Georgia
- Tuvalu
- United Kingdom

Australia

BOOK OF LISTS

AIRPORTS NAMED AFTER PEOPLE

AIRPORT	NAMED AFTER
Barbados	Grantley Adams
Caracas, Venezuela	Simon Bolivar
Genoa	Christoforo Colombo (Christopher Columbus)
Kingston, Jamaica	Norman Manley
La Paz	JF Kennedy
Liverpool	John Lennon
New Delhi	Indira Gandhi
New York	John F Kennedy
Oklahoma	Will Rogers
Paris	Charles de Gaulle
Riyadh	King Khaled
Rome	Leonardo da Vinci
San Diego	Charles Lindbergh
Santa Ana, California	John Wayne
Santiago	Arturo Marino Benitez
Tel Aviv	Ben Gurion
Toronto	Lester B Pearson
Venice	Marco Polo
Washington DC	John Foster Dulles
West Indies	FD Roosevelt

GEOGRAPHY

INTERNATIONAL AIRPORTS OF 30 CAPITAL CITIES

CAPITAL	AIRPORT	CAPITAL	AIRPORT
Addis Ababa	Bole	Paris	Orly
Amsterdam	Schipol	Prague	Ruzne
Athens	Hellenikon	Rome	Ciampino
Berlin	Tempelhof	Seoul	Kimpo
Bogota	El Dorado	Stockholm	Arlanda
Brussels	Melsbroek	Tehran	Mehrebad
Bucharest	Baneasa	Tokyo	Narita
Budapest	Serihegy	Vienna	Schwechat
Buenos Aires	Ezeica	Warsaw	Okecie
Cardiff	Rhoose		
Copenhagen	Kastrup		
Dublin	Collinstown		
Helsinki	Vantaa		
Lima	Jorge Chavez		
London	Heathrow		
Madrid	Barajas		
Mexico City	Benito Juarez		
Montevideo	Carrasco		
Moscow	Sheremetyevo		
Oslo	Fornebu		
Ottawa	Uplands		

MISCELLANEOUS

This section is a rich hunting ground for browsers
and a delight for lovers of the unexpected. Each turn
of the page may take you from the exotic names of
island capitals to the names of prisons around the
world, from memorable quotes from British Prime
Ministers to purported hangover cures, and from
suggested ways of killing vampires to the names of
the knights of the Round Table.

BOOK OF LISTS

CELEBRITY UNICEF AMBASSADORS

- Richard Attenborough
- Angela Bassett
- Harry Belafonte
- Martin Bell
- Cate Blanchett
- Pearce Brosnan
- Jackie Chan
- Judy Collins
- Mia Farrow
- Alex Ferguson
- Ralph Fiennes
- Luis Figo
- Laurence Fishburne
- Whoopi Goldberg
- Geri Halliwell
- Audrey Hepburn
- Danny Kaye
- Jemima Khan
- Nicole Kidman
- Jessica Lange
- Manchester United Football Club
- Roger Moore
- Nana Mouskouri
- Samantha Mumba
- Liam Neeson
- Leslie Nielsen
- Sarah Jessica Parker
- Vanessa Redgrave
- Isabella Rossellini
- Geoffrey Rush
- Susan Sarandon
- Claudia Schiffer
- Trudie Styler
- Liv Tyler
- Robbie Williams

MISCELLANEOUS

ACCORDING TO A 2004 SURVEY OF 9 TO 15 YEAR OLDS THESE WERE THE MOST POPULAR JOBS:

1. Builder
2. Pop star
3. Actor
4. Pilot
5. Confectionery buyer
6. Media worker
7. TV presenter
8. Policeman
9. Gardener
10. Home stylist

Pop star

ACCORDING TO THE SAME SURVEY THESE WERE THE LEAST POPULAR JOBS:

1. Prime Minister
2. Teacher
3. Doctor
4. Bus driver
5. Train driver
6. Bank manager
7. Computer worker
8. Policeman
9. Solicitor
10. Stock market trader

BOOK OF LISTS

20 FAMOUS PEOPLE WHO WERE 40 IN 2005

- Bjork
- Robert Downey Jr
- Liz Hurley
- Eddie Irvine
- Martin Lawrence
- Lennox Lewis
- Laurence Llewellyn-Bowen
- Moby
- James Nesbit
- Sarah Jessica Parker
- Joely Richardson
- JK Rowling
- Brooke Shields
- Nigel Short
- Slash
- Sophie, Countess of Wessex
- Ben Stiller
- Bryn Terfel
- Shania Twain
- Princess Stephanie of Monaco

Sarah Jessica Parker

20 FAMOUS PEOPLE WHO WERE 50 IN 2005

- Rowan Atkinson
- Tim Berners-Lee
- Ian Botham
- Kevin Costner
- Jeff Daniels
- Bill Gates
- Whoopi Goldberg
- Kelsey Grammar
- John Grisham
- Howard Jones
- Olga Korbut
- Greg Norman
- Hazel O'Connor
- Bill Paxton
- Alain Prost
- Simon Rattle
- Billy Bob Thornton
- Eddie Van Halen
- Bruce Willis
- Debra Winger

Rowan Atkinson

WHERE THERE'S A WILL
Wills of the famous

JM Barrie left the perpetual rights and royalties of the novel *Peter Pan* to the Great Ormond Street Hospital for Sick Children

Napoleon Bonaparte left his collection of swords, pistols and daggers to his son

Winston Churchill left a gold cigar case to the Earl of Birkenhead

The will of Calvin Coolidge was short and sweet and read, 'Not unmindful of my son I give all my estate, both real and personal, to my wife Grace Coolidge, in fee simple.'

Joan Crawford left the bulk of her fortune to various charities including the Muscular Dystrophy Association of America and the American Cancer Society

Princess Diana bequeathed £50,000 to her former butler Paul Burrell

The poet John Donne left his mother a poem entitled, 'The Will'

Sir Francis Drake requested that his two favourite ships should be sunk close to where his body was buried at sea. This request was not carried out

Sir Francis Drake

MISCELLANEOUS

WHERE THERE'S A WILL
Wills of the famous

Benjamin Franklin left land to his son-in-law on the provision that he freed his negro slave Bob

The German poet Heinrich Heine left his entire fortune to his wife on provision that she remarried 'Because then there will be at least one man to regret my death'

Liberace left the bulk of his fortune to the Liberace Foundation for the Performing and Creative Arts

Karl Marx died without leaving a will, however his entire estate was worth a paltry £250

Richard Nixon left his personal diaries to his daughters Patricia and Julie

Jackie Onassis left her friend Alexander Forger a copy of the inaugural presidential address of John F Kennedy

Samuel Pepys left his entire library to Trinity College, Cambridge

The Russian Tsar Peter the Great left instructions in his will advising Russian ministers to keep the country constantly at war, for the good of the nation

Babe Ruth left funds to establish the Babe Ruth Foundation for Destitute Children

William Shakespeare left his wife his second-best bed

Shakespeare also left his daughter Judith a silver bowl

Frank Sinatra left his sheet music to his son Francis Wayne Sinatra

BOOK OF LISTS

SECRET IDENTITIES OF SUPER HEROES

HERO	SECRET IDENTITY
Bananaman	Eric Twinge
Batgirl	Barbara Gordon
Batman	Bruce Wayne
Batwoman	Kathy Kane
The Bionic Woman	Jamie Summers
Captain America	Steve Rogers
Captain Marvel	Billy Batson
Daredevil	Matt Murdock
The Flash	Barry Allen
The Green Hornet	Britt Reid
He Man	Prince Adam
Hong Kong Phooey	Henry Penfold
Incredible Hulk	Dr Bruce Banner
The Lone Ranger	John Reid
The Mighty Thor	Dr Donald Blake
The Phantom	Kit Walker
Robin	Dick Grayson
The Six Million Dollar Man	Steve Austin
Spiderman	Peter Parker
Superman	Clark Kent
Wonder Woman	Diana Prince
Zorro	Don Diego De La Vega

MISCELLANEOUS

10 MEMBERS OF THE HOLE IN THE WALL GANG

- Butch Cassidy
- The Sundance Kid
- Kid Curry
- Al Smith
- Bob Smith
- Flat Nose Currie
- Bob Taylor
- Tom O'Day
- Judd Roberts
- Jesse James (reputed)

Jesse James

10 MEMBERS OF THE GREAT TRAIN ROBBERS' GANG

- Ronnie Biggs
- Bruce Reynolds
- Buster Edwards
- Charlie Wilson
- Tommy Wisbey
- Jimmy White
- Brian Field
- John Wheater
- Gordon Goody
- Bob Welch

BOOK OF LISTS

20 SAINTS' DAYS

January 20 . . . . St Fabian's Day

January 22 . . . . St Vincent's Day

February 5 . . . . St Agatha's Day

March 1 . . . . St David's Day

March 17 . . . . St Patrick's Day

March 31 . . . . St Benjamin's Day

April 4 . . . . St Isidore's Day

April 23 . . . . St George's Day

May 19 . . . . St Dunstan's Day

June 5 . . . . St Boniface's Day

July 11 . . . . St Benedict's Day

July 29 . . . . St Martha's Day

August 11 . . . . St Clare's Day

August 27 . . . . St Monica's Day

September 30 . . . . . . St Jerome's Day

October 6 . . . . St Bruno's Day

October 28 . . . . St Simon's Day

November 30 . . . . St Andrew's Day

December 26 . . . . St Stephen's Day

December 31 . . . . St Sylvester's Day

St Patrick

MISCELLANEOUS

20 TITLES HELD BY QUEEN ELIZABETH II

- Supreme Governor of the Church of England
- Head of the Commonwealth
- Head of State of the United Kingdom of Great Britain and Northern Ireland
- Commander-In-Chief of the United Kingdom Armed Forces
- Lord of Man
- Honorary Brigadier of the Women's Royal Army Corps
- Colonel-In-Chief of the 48th Highlanders of Canada
- Air-Commodore-In-Chief of the RAF
- Freeman of the City of London
- Honorary Fellow of the Royal College of Surgeons
- Defender of the Faith
- Dame Grand Cross of the Order of the Hospital of St John of Jerusalem
- Sovereign of the Order of the Thistle
- Colonel-In-Chief of the Grenadier Guards
- Honorary Doctor of Civil Law of Oxford University
- Honorary Colonel of the Queen's Own Worcestershire Hussars
- Colonel-In-Chief of the Life Guards
- Colonel-In-Chief of the Royal Malta Artillery
- Honorary Commissioner of the Royal Canadian Mounted Police
- Captain-General of the Royal Regiment of Canadian Artillery

THE LAST 20 POPES

REAL NAME	PAPAL NAME
Joseph Ratzinger	Pope Benedict XVI
Karol Wojtyla	Pope John Paul II
Albino Luciani	Pope John Paul I
Giovanni Battista Montini	Pope Paul VI
Angelo Giuseppe Roncalli	Pope John XXIII
Maria Giuseppe Pacelli	Pope Pius XII
Achille Ratti	Pope Pius XI
Giacomo della Chiesa	Pope Benedict XV
Giuseppe Melchiorre Sarto	Pope Pius X
Gioacchino Vincenzo Pecci	Pope Leo XIII
Nicholas Breakspear	Pope Adrian IV
Alberto de Morra	Pope Gregory VIII
Pierre de Tarentaise	Pope Innocent V
Bertrand de Got	Pope Clement V
Tommaso Parentucelli	Pope Nicholas V
Rodrigo Borgia	Pope Alexander VI
Maffeo Barberini	Pope Urban VIII
Annibale della Genga	Pope Leo XII
Felice Perretti	Pope Sixtus V
Giuliano della Rovere	Pope Julius II

MISCELLANEOUS

TOP 10 RANKS OF THE BRITISH ARMY

- General
- Lieutenant- General
- Major-General
- Brigadier
- Colonel
- Lieutenant Colonel
- Major
- Captain
- Lieutenant
- Second Lieutenant

In 1996, the most senior rank in the army, that of Field Marshal, was abolished

TOP 10 RANKS OF THE ROYAL NAVY

- Admiral
- Vice Admiral
- Rear Admiral
- Commodore
- Captain
- Commander
- Lieutenant Commander
- Lieutenant
- Sub-Lieutenant
- Acting Sub-Lieutenant

In 1996, the most senior rank in the Royal Navy, that of Admiral of the Fleet, was abolished

TOP 10 RANKS OF THE ROYAL AIR FORCE

- Air Chief Marshal
- Air Marshal
- Air Vice-Marshal
- Air Commodore
- Group Captain
- Wing Commander
- Squadron Leader
- Flight Lieutenant
- Flying Officer
- Pilot Officer

In 1996, the most senior rank in the Royal Air Force, that of Marshal of the Royal Air Force, was abolished

BOOK OF LISTS

JOBS IN THE HOUSEHOLD OF HENRY VIII

- Yeoman of the Cellar
- Master of the Children
- Officer of the Vestry
- The King's Barber
- Marshal of the Hall
- Purveyor of Sea Fish
- Clerk of the Spicery
- Master of the Jewels
- Officer of the Confectionery
- Sergeant of the Bake House
- Squire for the Body
- Yeoman of the Pastry
- Purveyor of Ale
- Gentlemen of the Privy Chamber
- Groom of the Privy Chamber
- Clerk of the Poultry
- Sergeant of the Larder
- Page of the King's Chambers
- Wardrober of the Robes
- Falconer
- Minstrel
- Clerk of the Green Cloth

Henry VIII

20 PEOPLE WHO SUFFERED FROM ATTENTION DEFICIT DISORDER

- Ludwig Van Beethoven
- Alexander Graham Bell
- Lewis Carroll
- Agatha Christie
- Salvador Dali
- Albert Einstein
- F Scott Fitzgerald
- Henry Ford
- Ernest Hemingway
- John Lennon
- Wolfgang Amadeus Mozart
- Sir Isaac Newton
- Louis Pasteur
- Pablo Picasso
- Babe Ruth
- George Bernard Shaw
- Vincent Van Gogh
- Jules Verne
- Woodrow Wilson
- Orville Wright

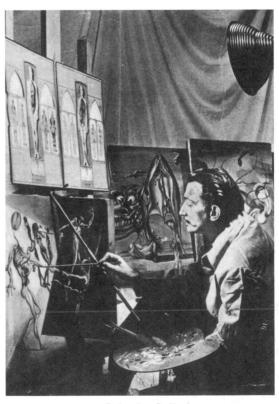

Salvador Dali

BOOK OF LISTS

STARS IMMORTALIZED ON HOLLYWOOD'S WALK OF FAME

- Julie Andrews
- Fred Astaire
- Lucille Ball
- Humphrey Bogart
- Marlon Brando
- Pierce Brosnan
- James Cagney
- Charlie Chaplin
- Gary Cooper
- Tom Cruise
- Bette Davis
- Sammy Davis Jnr
- Doris Day
- Johnny Depp
- Kirk Douglas
- Robert Duvall
- Errol Flynn
- Henry Fonda
- Harrison Ford
- Judy Garland
- Cary Grant
- Tom Hanks
- Audrey Hepburn
- Grace Kelly
- Nicole Kidman
- Jack Lemmon
- Dean Martin
- Paul Newman
- Jack Nicholson
- Leonard Nimoy
- Laurence Olivier
- Gregory Peck
- Mary Pickford
- Sidney Poitier
- Elvis Presley
- Burt Reynolds
- Edward G Robinson
- William Shatner
- Steven Spielberg
- Sylvester Stallone
- Meryl Streep
- Elizabeth Taylor
- Spencer Tracey
- Rudolf Valentino
- John Wayne
- Robin Williams

MISCELLANEOUS

10 PEOPLE WHO RECEIVED STARS ON HOLLYWOOD'S WALK OF FAME IN 2005

- Antonio Banderas
- Sandra Bullock
- Donald Duck
- Billy Joel
- Kevin Kline
- Julianne Moore
- Carly Simon
- Rod Stewart
- Ben Stiller
- Charlize Theron

IMPRINTS LEFT IN THE CEMENT OF GRAUMAN'S CHINESE THEATRE ON HOLLYWOOD BOULEVARD

- **Groucho Marx** left an imprint of his cigar
- **Betty Grable** left an imprint of her legs
- **Jimmy Durante** left an imprint of his nose
- **Al Jolson** left an imprint of his knees
- **Roy Rogers** left an imprint of his gun
- **Lassie** left a paw print
- **Champion,** Gene Autry's horse, left a hoof print
- **Harold Lloyd** left an imprint of his glasses
- **Clint Eastwood** wrote, 'You made my day.'
- **Arnold Schwarzenegger** wrote, 'I'll be back.'

20 FAMOUS PEOPLE BURIED AT WESTMINSTER ABBEY

- Clement Attlee
- Robert Browning
- Geoffrey Chaucer
- Charles Darwin
- Charles Dickens
- John Dryden
- William Gladstone
- George Frederic Handel
- Dr Samuel Johnson
- Rudyard Kipling
- David Livingstone
- John Masefield
- Isaac Newton
- Laurence Olivier
- Henry Purcell
- Ernest Rutherford
- Thomas Telford
- Alfred Lord Tennyson
- Sybil Thorndike
- William Wilberforce

Clement Attlee

MISCELLANEOUS

R.I.P.

- **Humphrey Bogart** was buried with a gold whistle inscribed by wife Lauren Bacall with the message, 'If you want anything, just whistle.'
- **Richard Burton** was buried with a copy of *The Collected Poems of Dylan Thomas*
- **Barbara Cartland** was buried in a pink chiffon gown
- **Winston Churchill** was buried next to his parents Lord and Lady Randolph Churchill
- **Henry VIII** was buried next to his favourite wife, Jane Seymour
- **Bela Lugosi** was buried in the black cape that he donned for his many film roles as Count Dracula
- **Walter Raleigh** was buried with a pipe and a tobacco box
- **Red Rum** is buried adjacent to the winning post at Aintree Racecourse
- **Frank Sinatra** was buried with a bottle of Jack Daniels whiskey

EPITAPHS ON GRAVESTONES AND MEMORIALS

Billy the Kid . . . . .He Died As He Lived

Mel Blanc . . . . .That's All Folks

Al Capone . . . . .My Jesus Mercy

Karen Carpenter . . . . .A star on Earth – A star in heaven

Bette Davis . . . . .She did it the hard way

Arthur Conan Doyle . . . . .Steel True, Blade Straight

CS Lewis . . . . .Man must endure his going hence

Dean Martin . . . . .Everybody Loves Somebody Sometime

Karl Marx . . . . .Workers of all lands unite

Edgar Allan Poe . . . . .Quoth the Raven 'Nevermore'

20 ENTERTAINERS WHO HAVE RECEIVED THE US PRESIDENTIAL MEDAL OF HONOUR

- Lucille Ball
- Count Basie
- James Cagney
- Johnny Carson
- Bill Cosby
- Doris Day
- Walt Disney
- Placido Domingo
- Kirk Douglas
- Ella Fitzgerald
- John Ford
- Samuel Goldwyn
- Audrey Hepburn
- Charlton Heston
- Bob Hope
- Danny Kaye
- Rita Moreno
- Gregory Peck
- Frank Sinatra
- John Wayne

Lucille Ball

MISCELLANEOUS

10 POLITICIANS WHO HAVE RECEIVED THE US PRESIDENTIAL MEDAL OF FREEDOM

- Jimmy Carter
- Dick Cheney
- Gerald Ford
- Hubert Humphrey
- Jesse Jackson
- Lyndon B Johnson
- John F Kennedy
- Henry Kissinger
- Ronald Reagan
- Nelson A Rockefeller

10 NON-AMERICANS WHO HAVE RECEIVED THE US PRESIDENTIAL MEDAL OF FREEDOM

- Pablo Casals
- Jacques Cousteau
- Marlene Dietrich
- Helmut Kohl
- Nelson Mandela
- Mother Teresa
- Pope John Paul II
- Anwar Sadat
- Margaret Thatcher
- Lech Walesa

Pablo Casals

BOOK OF LISTS

THE TOP 10 FILM DUOS WITH THE BEST ON-SCREEN CHEMISTRY ACCORDING TO A SURVEY BY THE ROYAL SOCIETY OF CHEMISTRY

1 Spencer Tracy and Katharine Hepburn
2 Richard Burton and Elizabeth Taylor
3 Humphrey Bogart and Lauren Bacall
4 Mel Gibson and Danny Glover
5 Paul Newman and Robert Redford
6 Jack Lemmon and Walter Matthau
7 Fred Astaire and Ginger Rogers
8 Humphrey Bogart and Ingrid Bergman
9 Stan Laurel and Oliver Hardy
10 Errol Flynn and Olivia de Havilland

THE TOP 10 DUOS OF ALL TIME ACCORDING TO A 2004 POLL OF UK WOOLWORTHS CUSTOMERS

1 Ant and Dec
2 Morecambe and Wise
3 The Two Ronnies
4 Eamonn Holmes and Fiona Phillips
5 Dawn French and Jennifer Saunders
6 Vic Reeves and Bob Mortimer
7 Richard Madeley and Judy Finnigan
8 Cannon and Ball
9 Stan Laurel and Oliver Hardy
10 Johnny Vaughan and Denise Van Outen

MISCELLANEOUS

THE 20 MOST INFLUENTIAL HAIRSTYLES OF ALL TIME ACCORDING TO A 2004 POLL BY MORPHY RICHARDS

1. Jennifer Aniston
2. Farrah Fawcett
3. Diana, Princess of Wales
4. Mary Quant
5. Marilyn Monroe
6. Twiggy
7. Cleopatra
8. Audrey Hepburn
9. Queen Elizabeth II
10. Brigitte Bardot
11. Madonna
12. Joanna Lumley
13. Sharon Stone
14. Marge Simpson
15. Joan of Arc
16. Sophia Loren
17. Lulu
18. Sinead O'Connor
19. Bjork
20. Catherine Zeta Jones

Jennifer Aniston

20 INDUCTEES INTO CANADA'S HALL OF FAME

- Bryan Adams
- Dan Aykroyd
- John Candy
- Jim Carrey
- David Cronenberg
- Celine Dion
- Linda Evangelista
- Michael J Fox
- Joni Mitchell
- Mike Myers
- Leslie Nielsen
- Mary Pickford
- Christopher Plummer
- William Shatner
- Martin Short
- Donald Sutherland
- Victoria Tennant
- Shania Twain
- Jacques Villeneuve
- Neil Young

Jim Carrey

MISCELLANEOUS

10 FOUNDING MEMBERS OF THE UK MUSIC HALL OF FAME 2004

Automatic members:

- Elvis Presley
- The Beatles
- Madonna
- U2
- Bob Marley

Members inducted after a public phone poll:

- Cliff Richard
- The Rolling Stones
- Queen
- Michael Jackson
- Robbie Williams

10 SINGERS WHO FEATURED ON THE BAND AID SINGLE, 'DO THEY KNOW IT'S CHRISTMAS' IN 2004

- Paul McCartney
- Robbie Williams
- Chris Martin
- Fran Healy
- Beverley Knight
- Natasha Bedingfield
- Justin Hawkins
- Dizzee Rascal
- Tom Chaplin
- Will Young

THE JACKSON 10

Andrew Jackson . . . . Born 1767, died 1845, the 7th President of the USA

Colin Jackson . . . . Born 1967, 110m hurdles world champion in 1999

Glenda Jackson . . . . . Born 1936, Oscar-winning actress who became a Labour MP in 1992

Gordon Jackson . . . . . Born 1923, died 1990, actor who played Hudson in *Upstairs Downstairs*

Janet Jackson . . . . . . Born 1966, youngest of the Jackson singing siblings

Jesse Jackson . . . . . . Born 1941, politician who founded PUSH (People United To Save Humanity)

Michael Jackson . . . . Born 1958, his album *Thriller* is the bestselling album of all time worldwide

Peter Jackson . . . . . . Born 1961, Oscar-winning director of *The Lord of the Rings* trilogy

Samuel L Jackson . . . Born 1948, star of the films *Pulp Fiction* and *The Long Kiss Goodnight*

Thomas Jackson . . . . Born 1824, died 1863, US soldier whose defence at the Battle of Bull Run earned him the nickname of Stonewall Jackson

Peter Jackson

MISCELLANEOUS

KEEPING UP WITH THE JONESES

Bobby Jones . . . . 1902–71, Atlanta-born golfer, winner of the British and US Open

Bruce Jones . . . . Born 1953, famed for his role as Les Battersby in *Coronation Street*

Casey Jones . . . . 1863–1900, famed train engine driver of the Cannonball Express

Chuck Jones . . . . 1912–2002, animator whose creations included *Road Runner*

Gemma Jones . . . . . . Born 1942, played the Duchess of Duke Street on TV and the mother of Bridget Jones on film

Inigo Jones . . . . 1573–1652, British architect who held the post of Surveyor General of Royal Buildings

Jack Jones . . . . Born 1938, singer of the theme for the TV show *The Love Boat*

James Jones . . . . 1921–77, US novelist who penned *From Here To Eternity*

James Earl Jones . . . Born 1931, actor who voiced Darth Vader in the *Star Wars* movies

Marion Jones . . . . . . Born 1975, winner of gold medals for 100m and 200m at the Sydney Olympics

Norah Jones . . . . Born 1979, Grammy Award-winning singing daughter of Ravi Shankar

Paul Jones . . . . Born 1942, former lead singer of Manfred Mann

Paula Jones . . . . Born 1966, state employee who accused Bill Clinton of sexual harassment

Quincy Jones . . . . . . Born 1933, record producer responsible for Michael Jackson's *Thriller*

Shirley Jones . . . . Born 1934, played the mother of the Partridge Family

Tom Jones . . . . Born 1940, enduring chart artist whose first single 'It's not Unusual' topped the charts

Tommy Lee Jones . . . Born 1946, won a Best Supporting Actor Oscar for his role in *The Fugitive*

BOOK OF LISTS

20 SCATHING COMMENTS MADE BY SIMON COWELL TO POP STAR WANNABES

- **If your lifeguard duties** were as good as your singing, a lot of people would be drowning
- **You sing like** a ventriloquist's dummy
- **I think you** just killed my most favourite song of all time
- **You sang** like you were in a dentist's chair
- **That was** distinctly average
- **My advice would be** if you want to pursue a career in the music business, don't
- **Phone up your vocal coach** and demand a refund
- **That was extraordinary**. Unfortunately extraordinarily bad
- **I can honestly** say you are the worst singer in America
- **I don't think anyone in London** is as bad as you – and London is a big city
- **You have just invented** a new form of torture
- **Did you really believe** you could become the American Idol? Well then you're deaf
- **If you would be singing** like this two thousand years ago, people would have stoned you
- **You sing like someone** who sings on a cruise ship. Halfway through I imagined the ship sinking
- **I think you invented** notes never ever heard before in music
- **We've had the musical** version of Valium
- **You sing like Mickey Mouse** on helium
- **There are only so many words** I can draw out of my vocabulary to say how awful that was
- **You had about** as much passion as a kitten mewing
- **When you stopped singing,** that was the best part

MISCELLANEOUS

10 SPORTING COMMENTATING GAFFES BY MURRAY WALKER

- **I should imagine** that the conditions in the cockpit are totally unimaginable
- **We now have exactly** the same situation as we had at the start of the race, only exactly the opposite
- **Excuse me** while I interrupt myself
- **Just under 10 seconds** for Nigel Mansell. Call it 9.5 seconds in round numbers
- **With half the race gone,** there is still half the race to go
- **How you can crash** into a wall without it being there in the first place is beyond me
- **Do my eyes deceive me,** or is Senna's Lotus sounding rough?
- **He is shedding** bucket loads of adrenaline in that car
- **Ralf Schumacher** now screaming ahead with Hakkinen breathing down his exhaust pipe
- **The lead car is unique,** except for the one behind it. Which is absolutely identical

ISLAND CAPITALS

ISLAND/ISLAND GROUP	CAPITAL
Alderney	St Annes
Bahamas	Nassau
Barbados	Bridgetown
Cayman Islands	George Town
Christmas Island	Flying Fish Cove
Comoros Islands	Moroni
Cook Islands	Ararua
Corfu	Kerkira
Corsica	Ajaccio
Crete	Khania
Cyprus	Nicosia
Easter Island	Hanga Roa
Faeroe Islands	Thorshavn
Falkland Islands	Port Stanley
Fiji	Suva
Guernsey	St Peter Port
Isle of Man	Douglas
Isle of Wight	Newport
Jersey	St Helier
Madagascar	Antananarivo
Maldives	Male

MISCELLANEOUS

ISLAND CAPITALS

ISLAND/ISLAND GROUP	CAPITAL
Malta	Valetta
Mauritius	Port Louis
Montserrat	Plymouth
Orkney Islands	Kirkwall
St Kitts	Basseterre
St Lucia	Castries
Sardinia	Cagliari
Seychelles	Victoria
Shetland Islands	Lerwick
Sicily	Palermo
Society Islands	Papeete
Solomon Islands	Honiara
Virgin Islands (British)	Road Town
Virgin Islands (USA)	Charlotte Amalie

Easter Island / Hanga Roa

BOOK OF LISTS

PRISONS AROUND THE WORLD

PRISON	LOCATION
Alcatraz	San Francisco Bay (closed 1963)
Bastille	Paris (demolished in 1789)
Chateau d'Ilf	Bay of Marseilles (closed as a prison in the 19th century)
Devil's Island	Off the coast of French Guiana (closed 1946)
Folsom State Prison	California
Lubyanka	Moscow
Robben Island	South Africa, off the coast of Cape Town
San Quentin	California
Sing Sing	New York
Spandau	Berlin

Alcatraz

MISCELLANEOUS

PRISONS IN THE UK

PRISON	LOCATION
Barlinnie	Glasgow
Dartmoor	Devon
Drake Hall	Staffordshire
Ford Prison	West Sussex
Longport	Canterbury
Marshgate	Doncaster
Maze	County Antrim (closed in 2000)
Parkhurst	Isle of Wight
Risley	Warrington
Strangeways	Manchester (now called Manchester Prison)
Winson Green	Birmingham

PRISONS IN LONDON

- Belmarsh
- Brixton
- Holloway
- Pentonville
- Wandsworth
- Wormwood Scrubs

BOOK OF LISTS

TOWERS AROUND THE WORLD

TOWER	CITY
Baiyoke Tower II	Bangkok
Bank of America Tower	Seattle
BMW Tower	Munich
Canary Wharf Tower	London
CN Tower	Toronto
Commerzbank Tower	Frankfurt
Eiffel Tower	Paris
Emirates Office Tower	Dubai
Goldman Sachs Tower	Jersey City
Hillbrow Tower	Johannesburg
Jin Mao Tower	Shanghai
Key Tower	Cleveland, Ohio
Liberation Tower	Kuwait City
Milad Tower	Tehran
Ostankino Tower	Moscow
Petronas Towers	Kuala Lumpur
Rialto Tower	Melbourne
Stratosphere Tower	Las Vegas
Trump World Tower	New York
Williams Tower	Houston

Petronas Towers

MISCELLANEOUS

10 OLDEST CITIES IN THE UK

CITY	FOUNDED	CITY	FOUNDED
Ripon	886	Oxford	1154
London	1066	Nottingham	1155
Edinburgh	1125	Winchester	1155
Chichester	1135	Exeter	1156
Derby	1154		
Lincoln	1154		

10 UK TOWNS GRANTED CITY STATUS IN THE 20th CENTURY

CITY	ACHIEVED CITY STATUS
Leicester	1919
Stoke-on-Trent	1925
Portsmouth	1926
Salford	1926
Plymouth	1928
Lancaster	1937
Cambridge	1951
Southampton	1964
Sunderland	1992
Brighton	2000

Brighton

BOOK OF LISTS

ADDRESSES OF FAMOUS BUILDINGS

BUILDING	ADDRESS
Anne Frank's home	263 Prinsengracht, Amsterdam
BT Tower	60 Cleveland Street, London
Canary Wharf Tower	1, Canada Square, London
Empire State Building	350 Fifth Avenue, New York
Football Association Headquarters	16 Lancaster Gate, London
Shakespeare's Globe Theatre	21 New Globe Walk, Bankside, London
Harrods	87–135 Brompton Road, Knightsbridge, London
Imperial War Museum	Lambeth Road, London
Kremlin	Sobornaya Ploshad, Moscow
Library of Congress	101 Independence Avenue, South East Washington
Louvre	99 Rue de Rivoli, Paris
Madison Square Garden	4 Pennsylvania Plaza, New York
Ritz Hotel, Paris	15 Place Vendome
Scotland Yard	4 Whitehall Place, London (original address)
Sears Tower	233 South Wacker Drive, Chicago
Sherlock Holmes' home	221b Baker Street, London
Sydney Opera House	Bennelong Point, Sydney, NSW 2000
Victoria and Albert Museum	Cromwell Road, Kensington, London
Vice President of the USA's home	1, Observatory Circle, Massachusetts Avenue
White House	1600 Pennsylvania Avenue, Washington DC

LIFE'S A BEACH

BEACH	LOCATION
Achravi	Corfu
Anse Lazio	Seychelles
Bondi	Sydney
Cape Hatteras	North Carolina
Chesil	Dorset
Cleopatra's Beach	Turkey
Copocabana	Rio de Janeiro
Daytona	Florida
Honda Bay	Philippines
La Diamant	Martinique
Luquillo	Porto Rico
Natadola	Fiji
Ornos	Mykonos
Palolem	Goa
Pink Beach	Bahamas
Seven Mile Beach	Jamaica
Stavros	Crete
Surfer's Paradise	Queensland
Varadero	Cuba
Waikiki	Hawaii

BOOK OF LISTS

TOP 50 PLACES TO SEE BEFORE YOU DIE ACCORDING TO A 2002 BBC SURVEY

1   The Grand Canyon
2   The Great Barrier Reef
3   Florida
4   South Island, New Zealand
5   Cape Town
6   The Golden Temple, Amritsar
7   Las Vegas
8   Sydney
9   New York
10 The Taj Mahal
11 The Canadian Rockies
12 Ayers Rock
13 Chichen Itza, Mexico
14 Machu Picchu, Peru
15 The Niagara Falls
16 Petra, Jordan
17 The Egyptian Pyramids
18 Venice
19 The Maldives
20 The Great Wall of China
21 Mutarazi (Victoria) Falls
22 Hong Kong
23 Yosemite National Park
24 Hawaii
25 Auckland

Yosemite National Park

MISCELLANEOUS

THE TOP 50 PLACES TO SEE BEFORE YOU DIE IN A 2002 BBC SURVEY

26   The Iguaçu Falls, Brazil
27   Paris
28   Alaska
29   Angkor Wat, Cambodia
30   The Himalayas, Nepal
31   Rio de Janeiro
32   The Masai Mara, Kenya
33   The Galapagos Islands
34   Luxor, Egypt
35   Rome
36   San Francisco
37   Barcelona
38   Dubai
39   Singapore
40   La Digue, Seychelles
41   Sri Lanka
42   Bangkok
43   Barbados
44   Iceland
45   The Terracotta Army
46   Zermatt, Switzerland
47   Angel Falls, Venezuela
48   Abu Simbel, Egypt
49   Bali
50   French Polynesia

Rio de Janeiro

BOOK OF LISTS

QUOTES FROM PRIME MINISTERS

Herbert Asquith . . . . 'Youth would be an ideal state if it came a little later in life.'

Clement Attlee . . . . . 'The House of Lords is like a glass of champagne that has stood for five days.'

Stanley Baldwin . . . . 'I would rather trust a woman's instinct than a man's reason.'

Arthur Balfour . . . . . 'Enthusiasm moves the world.'

James Callaghan . . . 'A leader must have the courage to act against an expert's advice.'

Winston Churchill . . . 'The best argument against democracy is a five-minute conversation with the average voter.'

Benjamin Disraeli . . . 'Patience is a necessary ingredient of genius.'

Alec Douglas-Home . 'There are two problems in life. The political ones are insoluble and the economic ones are incomprehensible.'

Anthony Eden . . . . . . 'If you have broken the eggs you should make the omelette.'

William Gladstone . . 'Justice delayed is justice denied.'

Edward Heath . . . . . . 'I owe everything to my mother.'

David Lloyd George . 'If you listen to the neverdo's it's never done.'

Ramsay Macdonald . 'We hear war called murder. It's not; it is suicide.'

Harold Macmillan . . . 'You've never had it so good.'

John Major . . . . 'The politician who never made a mistake never made a decision.'

William Pitt . . . . 'Necessity is the plea for every infringement of human freedom. It is the argument of tyrants; it is the creed of slaves.'

Margaret Thatcher . 'The lady's not for turning.'

Robert Walpole . . . . . 'Every man has his price.'

Harold Wilson . . . . . . 'A week is a long time in politics.'

MISCELLANEOUS

10 UNUSUAL POLITICAL PARTIES
These parties contested seats in the 2001 UK General Election

- Chairman of Sunrise Radio
- Church of the Militant Elvis Party
- The Extinction Club
- Fancy Dress Party
- Independent Vote for Yourself Party
- Jam Wrestling Party
- Legalise Cannabis Alliance
- Lower Excise Duty Party
- New Millennium Bean Party
- Rock and Roll Loony Party

10 UNUSUAL MANIFESTO POINTS
The Monster Raving Loony party put forward these policies in the 2001 General Election

- **Every car owner** to be given a horse in the eventuality of a fuel crisis
- **All bus shelters** to be installed with central heating
- **Flared trousers** to be made compulsory for cross-channel ferry crews
- **The closing** of the Channel Tunnel
- **Trafalgar Square** to be renamed the Official Monster Raving Loony Square
- **The National Anthem** to be replaced by 'The Funky Gibbon' by the Goodies
- **All dogs** to be fitted with nappies
- **Free Viagra** for anyone aged over 69
- **All GM foods** to be made illegal
- **Free university tuition** for all students called Grant

BOOK OF LISTS

ETIQUETTE AROUND THE WORLD

- **In South Africa** it is impolite to present gifts with one's left hand
- **Eating in the street** is considered to be the height of bad manners in Argentina
- **In India,** refrain from winking as it is interpreted as a sexual proposition
- **A gift of scissors or a knife** in China signifies the end of a relationship or friendship
- **In Greece,** raising the open palm of the hand at face level is a great insult
- **In Saudi Arabia,** displaying the sole of one's shoes to another person is considered to be insulting
- **In Egypt,** the right hand is always used for eating as the left hand is used for bodily hygiene
- **In Saudi Arabia,** it is good manners to remove your footwear when entering a building
- **Visitors to Muslim mosques** are required to remove their footwear
- **Avoid giving** red gifts in Japan, as this colour is associated with funerals
- **In Japan** it is impolite to pour your own drink
- **A gift of a clock in China** is considered to be a bad omen, as it is thought to be a symbol of death
- **In the United Arab Emirates,** men often walk hand in hand as a sign of friendship as opposed to sexual preference
- **In France,** it is frowned upon to bring wine when invited to dinner as it casts aspersions on the host's choice of wine
- **Whistling** is considered impolite in India
- **Touching the head of a child** is frowned upon in Taiwan
- **In polite circles** port is always passed to the left
- **If receiving a gift in Indonesia** do not open it immediately as this conveys a message of greed

MISCELLANEOUS

HANGOVER CURES

- **Drink large quantities of water** prior to going to sleep. Too much alcohol causes dehydration and stimulates the body to absorb water from the brain causing headaches
- **Chocolate**. Your body needs an intake of sugar as alcohol breaks down sugar stored in the liver
- **Bloody Mary** with a teaspoon of sugar and Worcestershire sauce
- **Two raw eggs**
- **Hair of the dog that bit you.** A couple of glasses of whatever caused your hangover
- **Boiled tripe**
- **Coffee** laced with honey
- **Morning walk or jog.** This causes an increased oxygen flow that aids the metabolism to break down the alcoholic toxins
- **Full English breakfast**, which helps to clear out the toxins
- **Cowboys in America's Old West** swore by a brew laced with rabbit droppings
- **Cucumber juice**
- **A medieval cure** consisted of a plate of bitter almonds and dried eels
- **In Puerto Rico,** heavy drinkers rub a cut lemon into the armpit of their drinking arm
- **Chicken soup**
- **Peanut butter**
- **Bananas**
- **Fruit cocktail**
- **Grab the flap of skin** between the thumb and forefinger of the left hand. This is an acupuncture point that relieves headaches
- **Stay in bed** as the alcohol in your system will have disrupted your sleep pattern

20 ROLES TURNED DOWN BY 20 MOVIE STARS

ACTOR	ROLE TURNED DOWN / FILM	ACTUALLY PLAYED BY
Warren Beatty	Michael Corleone / *The Godfather*	Al Pacino
Chevy Chase	Lester Burnham / *American Beauty*	Kevin Spacey
Sean Connery	Gandalf / *Lord of the Rings*	Ian McKellen
Russell Crowe	Wolverine / *X Men*	Hugh Jackman
Robert DeNiro	Jesus / *The Last Temptation of Christ*	Willem Dafoe
Kirk Douglas	Kid Shelleen / *Cat Ballou*	Lee Marvin
Harrison Ford	Jim Garrison / *JFK*	Kevin Costner
Richard Gere	John McClane / *Die Hard*	Bruce Willis
Cary Grant	James Bond / *Dr No*	Sean Connery
Tom Hanks	Jerry Maguire / *Jerry Maguire*	Tom Cruise
Burt Lancaster	Judah Ben Hur / *Ben Hur*	Charlton Heston
Anthony Newley	Alfie / *Alfie*	Michael Caine
Al Pacino	Ted Kramer / *Kramer vs Kramer*	Dustin Hoffman
Michelle Pfeiffer	Clarice Starling / *Silence of the Lambs*	Jodie Foster
Ronald Reagan	Rick Blaine / *Casablanca*	Humphrey Bogart
Robert Redford	Benjamin Braddock / *The Graduate*	Dustin Hoffman
Julia Roberts	Viola De Lesseps / *Shakespeare in Love*	Gwyneth Paltrow
George Raft	Sam Spade / *The Maltese Falcon*	Humphrey Bogart
Telly Savalas	General Patton / *Patton*	George C Scott
Frank Sinatra	Harry Callahan / *Dirty Harry*	Clint Eastwood

MISCELLANEOUS

TITLES AND POSTS HELD BY ENTERTAINERS

Richard Attenborough . . . . . Baron of Richmond-Upon-Thames

Jeremy Beadle. . . . . Honorary President of the British Quiz Association

Pierce Brosnan . . . . Freeman of Navan

Jamie Lee Curtis . . . . Lady Haden Guest

Clint Eastwood. . . . . Mayor of Carmel

Stephen Fry . . . . Rector of Dundee University

Mel Gibson . . . . Office of the Order of Australia

Charlton Heston . . . . President of the National Rifle Association

Glenda Jackson . . . . MP for Hampstead & Highgate

Hugh Laurie . . . . President of the Cambridge Footlights

James Mason. . . . . President of the Royal National Rose Society

Laurence Olivier . . . . Lord Olivier of Brighton

Peter O'Toole . . . . Associate Director of the Old Vic Theatre

Christopher Plummer . . . . . Companion of the Order of Canada

Sidney Poitier . . . . Ambassador to Japan for the Bahamas

Alan Rickman. . . . . Vice Chairman of RADA

Tony Robinson . . . . Vice President of Equity

Arnold Schwarzenegger. . . . Chairman of President Bush's Council on Physical Fitness

Shirley Temple. . . . . US Ambassador to Ghana

Peter Ustinov . . . . Chancellor of Durham University

BOOK OF LISTS

EATING DISORDERS

Pica	Condition of craving and eating non-food substances
Geophagia	Compulsive urge to eat soil
Plumbophagia	Compulsive urge to eat lead
Trichophagia	Compulsive urge to eat hair
Pagophagia	Compulsive urge to eat ice
Amylophagia	Compulsive urge to eat washing powder
Lithophagia	Compulsive urge to eat stones
Cautopyreiophagia	Compulsive urge to eat burnt matches
Acuphagia	Compulsive urge to eat sharp objects
Coprophagia	Compulsive urge to eat faeces
Xylophobia	Compulsive urge to eat wood
Geomelophagia	Compulsive urge to eat raw potatoes
Mucophagy	Compulsive urge to eat mucus
Gooberphagia	Compulsive urge to eat peanuts
Anorexia nervosa	Disorder characterized by voluntary starvation
Bulimia	Binge-eating followed by induced vomiting
Dipsophobia	Morbid fear of drinking
Geumatophobia	Morbid fear of taste
Ortharexia nervosa	An obsession with eating healthy foods
Phagophobia	Morbid fear of swallowing

MISCELLANEOUS

CHRISTMAS DISHES AROUND THE WORLD

COUNTRY	CHRISTMAS DISH
Brazil	Turkey marinated in rum and ham, with coloured rice
Czech Republic	Fish soup, salad, carp and eggs
Denmark	Roast duck
Finland	Turkey casserole with carrots, macaroni, potatoes & rutabaga
Germany	Roast goose
Greenland	Seabirds wrapped in the skin of a seal
Hungary	Fish soup and fried fish
Iceland	Smoked lamb
Jamaica	Curried goat, rice and gungo peas
Latvia	Sausage, cabbage and brown peas in a pork sauce
Luxembourg	Venison, hare and black pudding
Nicaragua	Chicken stuffed with fruit and vegetables
Norway	Cod or haddock and Christmas meat loaf
Portugal	Salted codfish and potatoes
Romania	Bread-based Christmas cake called turta
Russia	Goose and suckling pig
Sweden	Herring, ham and meatballs
Ukraine	Meat broth

BOOK OF LISTS

THE PC WORLD

POLITICALLY CORRECT TERM	TRADITIONAL ALTERNATIVE
Alternative dentation	False teeth
Assistant referee	Linesman
Chalkboard	Blackboard
Conversationally selective	Shy
Cosmetically challenged	Ugly
Domestic engineer	Housewife
Economically deficient	Poor
Flight attendant	Stewardess
Hearing impaired	Deaf
Home invader	Burglar
Humankind	Mankind
Intellectually challenged	Stupid
Metabolically challenged	Fat
Motivationally deficient	Lazy
Nasally inferior	Smelly
Non-traditional shopper	Looter
Optical illuminator enhancer	Window cleaner
Terminally inconvenienced	Dead
Utility hole	Manhole
Vertically challenged	Short

MISCELLANEOUS

TEXTING ABBREVIATIONS

ABBREVIATION	STANDS FOR
AFAIK	As far as I know
BCNU	Be seeing you
BRB	Be right back
BTW	By the way
CID	Consider it done
CUL8R	See you later
D8	Date
DNR	Dinner
DUR	Do you remember?
EZ	Easy
4e	Forever
FWIW	For what it's worth
GTG	Got to go
HAND	Have a nice day
HHOJ	Ha ha only joking
IAC	In any case
IDK	I don't know
ILU	I love you
IMHO	In my humble opinion
ISWYM	I see what you mean
IYSS	If you say so
KIT	Keep in touch

ABBREVIATION	STANDS FOR
LOL	Laughing out loud
MYOB	Mind your own business
NE1	Anyone
NRN	No reply necessary
oxoxoxoxo	Hugs and kisses
PLS	Please
SRY	Sorry
SWDYT	So what do you think?
t+	Think positive
2MORO	Tomorrow
THX	Thanks

BOOK OF LISTS

WORDS ACROSS THE OCEAN
American counterparts of English words

ENGLISH	AMERICAN
Autumn	The fall
Biscuit	Cookie
Bonnet (car)	Hood
Boot (car)	Trunk
Braces	Suspenders
Bum (backside)	Fanny
Candyfloss	Cotton candy
Chips	French fries
Courgette	Zucchini
Crisps	Chips
Curtains	Drapes
Drawing pin	Thumbtack
Dummy (baby's)	Pacifier
Estate car	Station wagon
Frying pan	Skillet
Full stop	Period
Grill	Broil
Jam	Jelly
Jumble sale	Rummage sale
Ladybird	Ladybug
Love bite	Hickey

Courgette (zucchini)

MISCELLANEOUS

WORDS ACROSS THE OCEAN
American counterparts of English words

ENGLISH	AMERICAN
Nappy	Diaper
Noughts & Crosses	Tic Tac Toe
Paraffin	Kerosene
Pavement	Sidewalk
Petrol	Gas
Pimple	Zit
Post code	Zip code
Primary school	Grade school
Ring road	Beltway
Semi-detached house	Duplex
Solicitor	Attorney
Spanner	Wrench
Suitcase	Valise
Toffee	Candy
Toilet	Restroom
Truncheon	Nightstick
Undertaker	Mortician
Waistcoat	Vest
Wallet	Billfold

PROVERBIALLY SPEAKING

- A bird in the hand is worth two in the bush
- A chain is no stronger than its weakest link
- A dog always returns to its own vomit
- A fool and his money are easily parted
- All that glisters is not gold
- A rolling stone gathers no moss
- A stitch in time saves nine
- Birds of a feather flock together
- Blood is thicker than water
- Cowards die many times, but a brave man only dies once
- Cut your coat according to your cloth
- Don't burn down your bridges before they're crossed
- Don't count your chickens before they hatch
- Don't put all your eggs in one basket
- Early to bed and early to rise makes a man healthy, wealthy and wise
- Empty barrels make the most noise
- Every rule has its exception
- Everything comes to him who waits
- Familiarity breeds contempt
- Fine words butter no parsnips
- Good fences make good neighbours
- Great oaks from little acorns grow
- Half a loaf is better than none

MISCELLANEOUS

PROVERBIALLY SPEAKING

- Hell hath no fury like a woman scorned
- He who laughs last laughs longest
- In the land of the blind, the one-eyed man is king
- Laughter is the best medicine
- Look before you leap
- Many hands make light work
- No man can serve two masters
- Once bitten twice shy
- People who live in glass houses shouldn't throw stones
- Pride comes before a fall
- Rome wasn't built in a day
- Starve a fever, feed a cold
- The grass is always greener on the other side of the fence
- The pen is mightier than the sword
- The proof of the pudding is in the eating
- The road to hell is paved with good intentions
- To err is human, to forgive divine
- Too many cooks spoil the broth
- Two heads are better than one
- Two's company, three's a crowd
- Variety is the spice of life
- What goes around comes around
- Where there's a will, there's a way

A chain is no stronger than its weakest link

MYTHS AND LEGENDS
Origins of superstitions

■ **Throwing salt over the left shoulder**

In the Middle Ages salt was used for medicinal purposes. It was believed that throwing spilt salt over one's shoulder would strike evil spirits in the eye, thus preventing sickness

■ **Break a leg**

This theatre term for good luck derives from the practice of bending down on one knee in deference to someone. Actors therefore wished fellow actors to break a leg in the hope that they would be bowing down before an appreciative audience

■ **Friday the thirteenth**

It is believed that Adam and Eve were expelled from the Garden of Eden on Friday 13th

■ **Throwing rice at a wedding**

This custom is to wish the bride and groom fertility and prosperity

■ **Unlucky third light**

Originating in the Boer War, when lighting a cigarette with a match. A sniper saw the flame on the first light, took aim on the second light and fired on the third light

■ **Bad luck to kill a ladybird**

Said to be bad luck as a ladybird represents the Virgin Mary

■ **God bless you**

During the Great Plague the Pope passed a law whereby people were required to bless the sneezer

■ **Lucky seven**

Considered to be a number of perfection in deference to the seven days of creation

MISCELLANEOUS

MYTHS AND LEGENDS
Origins of superstitions

■ **Lucky horseshoes**

Made by blacksmiths, considered to be a lucky trade. Hanging horseshoes with the ends pointing upwards symbolises a receptacle for storing good luck

■ **Walking under a ladder**

The triangle formed by a ladder when leaning against a wall represents the Holy Trinity. By walking through the triangle it signifies that the person is in league with the devil

■ **Seven years' bad luck for breaking a mirror**

Ancient Romans believed that a mirror reflected the soul of the person looking into it. They also believed that the soul was renewed every seven years, therefore breaking a mirror would require a recovery period for the soul, lasting for seven years

■ **Touch wood for good luck**

In Pagan times, trees were held in high esteem and were believed to be the homes of wood spirits that provided protection against evil forces

■ **Lucky rabbit's foot**

As long ago as 600BC it is believed that rabbits were immune to evil forces and a symbol of fertility

■ **Unlucky thirteen**

Thirteen is considered an unlucky number as there were thirteen diners present at the Last Supper

■ **Holding your hand over your mouth when you yawn**

Not just good manners, but also a barrier to prevent the spirit of the devil from entering your body

GHOSTLY GOINGS ON

- **The Santa Maria del Popolo Church** in Rome is said to be haunted by Emperor Nero
- **On Hollywood Boulevard** a number of sightings have been reported of the ghost of Lon Chaney sitting on a bus bench
- **Gawsworth Hall** in Macclesfield, Cheshire, is haunted by Mary Fitton, the Maid of Honour of Elizabeth I
- **According to legend** the ghost ship *The Flying Dutchman* haunts the Cape of Good Hope
- **Caligula** the Roman Emperor, is said to haunt the Lamian Gardens in Rome
- **Don't stay in suite 928** at the Hollywood Roosevelt Hotel. Allegedly the ghost of Montgomery Clift haunts the room where he stayed whilst filming the movie *From Here To Eternity*
- **At the same hotel,** a mirror is said to reflect the ghostly image of Marilyn Monroe
- **The Gun Inn Pub** in London is said to be haunted by Horatio Nelson
- **Sightings of the ghost of Boris Karloff** have been reported in Bramshott Village, where the actor resided in later life
- **It is believed** that the ghost of Ivan the Terrible haunts the Kremlin
- **Abraham Lincoln** is said to haunt the White House
- **The great lover** and movie icon Rudolph Valentino is said to haunt the Paramount Studios in Hollywood
- **Durwood Street** in Whitechapel, London, is haunted by Mary Nicholls. She was one of the unfortunate victims of Jack the Ripper and this street was the scene of her murder
- **According to legend** Thomas Becket haunts Traitors' Gate
- **Charles Dickens** expressed the desire to be buried in the castle graveyard of Rochester Castle. This request was never fulfilled and consequently Dickens is said to haunt the castle grounds

GHOSTLY GOINGS ON

- **Several sightings** of the ghost of Marie Antoinette have been reported at Versailles Palace
- **Sweet Lady Jane's Restaurant** in Los Angeles was one of the favourite haunts of Orson Welles when he was alive. It is now said to be haunted by the actor since his death
- **According to legend** Windsor Castle is said to be haunted by Elizabeth I
- **Hampton Court** is said to be haunted by Catherine Howard
- **The Tower of London** is apparently overrun with ghosts, including the spectres of Anne Boleyn, Edward V, Guy Fawkes and Sir Walter Raleigh

Caligula

HOW TO REPEL OR KILL A VAMPIRE

- Garlic is a repellent
- A stake through the heart kills them
- Sunlight kills them
- Burying their corpse at a four-way crossroads prevents them from leaving their coffin
- Decapitation kills them
- Holy water burns them
- A crucifix is a repellent
- A vampire cannot cross running water
- The sprinkling of salt is a repellent
- A vampire can only be invited into a home by a person living there. So don't let them in!

10 ACTORS OF VAMPIRES ON FILM

- David Bowie in *The Hunger*
- Kiefer Sutherland in *The Lost Boys*
- Geoffrey Lewis in *Salem's Lot*
- Grace Jones in *Vamp*
- Eddie Murphy in *Vampire In Brooklyn*
- Jonathan Lipnicki in *The Little Vampire*
- Wesley Snipes in *Blade*
- Tom Cruise in *Interview With The Vampire*
- Brad Pitt in *Interview With The Vampire*
- Antonio Banderas in *Interview With The Vampire*

MISCELLANEOUS

WEDDING-DAY SUPERSTITIONS
10 good omens on a wedding day

- Seeing a rainbow
- Meeting a chimney sweep
- Seeing a lamb
- Seeing a dove
- A cat sneezing in front of you
- The bride crying as it signifies she has cried all her tears away
- Marrying in June, life will be one long honeymoon
- Seeing a spider
- Snow on the wedding day is a symbol of future fertility and wealth
- Seeing a nanny goat

CHOOSE YOUR WEDDING DAY CAREFULLY

- Monday for health
- Tuesday for wealth
- Wednesday best of all
- Thursday for losses
- Friday for crosses
- Saturday for no luck at all

BOOK OF LISTS

10 ARGONAUTS
The following accompanied Jason on his quest for the Golden Fleece

- Amphion
- Calais
- Castor
- Euphemus
- Heracles
- Orpheus
- Philoctetes
- Polyphemus
- Telamon
- Zetes

10 KNIGHTS OF KING ARTHUR'S ROUND TABLE

- Bedevere
- Sir Bors
- Cador
- Sir Gawian
- Sir Galahad
- Sir Geraint
- Sir Kay
- Sir Lancelot
- Palemades
- Tristram

Excaliber

MISCELLANEOUS

TAROT CARDS

- **76 cards** in a pack
- **The 76 cards are divided** into two sets, the Major Arcana and the Minor Arcana
- **The four suits** in a pack of tarot cards are called Cups, Swords, Wands and Pentacles

22 TRUMP CARDS OF THE MAJOR ARCANA

- The Chariot
- Death
- The Devil
- The Emperor
- The Empress
- The Female Pope, also known as the High Priestess
- The Fool
- The Hanged Man
- The Hermit
- Judgement
- Justice
- Lovers
- The Magician
- Moon
- The Pope, also known as the Hierophant
- Star
- Strength
- Sun
- Temperance
- Tower
- Wheel of Fortune
- World

12 DAYS OF CHRISTMAS

1st Day . . . . A partridge in a pear tree

2nd Day . . . . Two turtle doves

3rd Day . . . . Three French hens

4th Day . . . . Four calling birds

5th Day . . . . Five gold rings

6th Day . . . . Six geese a laying

7th Day . . . . Seven swans a swimming

8th Day . . . . Eight maids a milking

9th Day . . . . Nine ladies dancing

10th Day . . . Ten lords a leaping

11th Day . . . Eleven pipers piping

12th Day . . . Twelve drummers drumming

WHAT THE GIFTS OF THE 12 DAYS OF CHRISTMAS REPRESENT

Partridge . . . . Jesus Christ

Two turtle doves . . . . The Old and New Testament

Three French hens . . . . . . Faith, hope and charity (the three theological virtues)

Four calling birds . . . . Four Gospels

Five gold rings . . . . First five books of the Old Testament

Six geese . . . . Six days of creation

Seven swans . . . . Seven sacraments

Eight maids . . . . Eight beatitudes

Nine ladies . . . . Nine fruits of the Holy Spirit

Ten lords . . . . The Ten Commandments

Eleven pipers . . . . The eleven faithful Apostles

Twelve drummers . . . . The twelve points of doctrine in the Apostles' Creed

MISCELLANEOUS

IF AT FIRST YOU DON'T SUCCEED

- **Albert Einstein** failed his first college entrance exam

- **"Can't act, can't sing,** slightly bald, can dance a little." A famous verdict given by a movie executive on an unknown struggling actor by the name of Fred Astaire

- **Michael Jordan** was dropped from his high school basketball team

- **Lucille Ball** was asked to leave drama school, as she was too shy

- **The Beatles** were turned down by Decca Records after a company executive informed them that, "Guitar groups are dead."

- **Stephen King's first novel,** *Carrie*, met with the following comment from a publisher, "We are not interested in science fiction which deals with negative utopias. They do not sell"

- **Henry Ford** was declared bankrupt five times

- **Thomas Alva Edison** carried out approaching 10,000 separate experiments before perfecting the light bulb

- **The telephone** patented by Alexander Graham Bell was initially dismissed as a useless electronic toy

- **Napoleon Bonaparte** finished rock bottom of his class at military school

- **A Hollywood executive** told Clint Eastwood he would never make it as a movie star as he talked too slowly

- **The Pepsi Cola Company** was declared bankrupt three times

- **Before becoming an actor** Sean Connery worked as a coffin polisher, a male model, a bricklayer and a lifeguard

- **Colonel Harland Sanders** received hundreds of rejections from various restaurants whilst attempting to introduce his new style of chicken onto the market

- **The supermodel** Claudia Schiffer was bullied at school for being ugly

A SUIT OF ARMOUR

Ailettes . . . . .Small square shields protecting the shoulders

Aventail . . . . .Chainmail bib protecting the neck

Bascinet . . . . . . .Type of helmet

Beaver . . . . .Cup-shaped piece protecting the chin

Besagew . . . . . .Small round plate protecting the armpits

Cervellaire . . . . .Skull cap

Chamfron . . . . . .Metal plate protecting the head of a horse

Colf . . . . .Hooded chainmail protecting the head

Couter . . . . .Rounded cup protecting the elbow

Cuirass . . . . . . .The part of the armour that consists of the breastplate and backplate

Gauntlet . . . . . .Large glove

Gorget . . . . .Metal plate protecting the neck

Grille . . . . .Metal visor protecting the face

Pauldron . . . . . .Metal plate protecting the shoulders

Poleyn . . . . .Cup-shaped piece protecting the knee

Rerebrace . . . . .Metal plates protecting the upper arms

Sabaton . . . . . . .Armour for the feet

Surcoat . . . . . . .Cloth covering worn outside a suit of armour

Tasset . . . . .Metal plate protecting the hips

Vambrace . . . . . .Rounded iron armour protecting the lower arms

MISCELLANEOUS

THE *TITANIC*

- Built in the Harland & Wolff shipyard in Belfast
- Owned by White Star Line
- 269m long
- 899 crew on board
- Accommodated 3300 passengers
- 2252 passengers on board when it sank
- Hit the iceberg on April 14, 1912 and finally sank at 2.20 a.m. the next morning
- Survivors 705
- Fatalities 1547
- Captain of the ship was Edward Smith
- Wreck discovered September 1, 1985

10 PASSENGERS WHO SURVIVED THE SINKING

- Margaret Brown who became known as the Unsinkable Molly Brown
- Mary Wilburn
- Daniel Buckley
- Marshall Drew
- Michael Navratil
- Edith Russell
- Charles Lightoller
- Douglas Spedden
- Violet Jessop
- Lady Lucille Wallace Sutherland Duff Gordon

BOOK OF LISTS

HOW MANY?

- 2 hulls on a catamaran
- 3 holes in a ten-pin bowling ball
- 4 strings on a violin
- 7 spikes on the Statue of Liberty's crown
- 8 bits in a byte
- 9 symphonies composed by Beethoven
- 10 legs on a lobster
- 13 witches in a coven
- 14 lines in a sonnet
- 27 books in the New Testament
- 39 books in the Old Testament
- 40 days and 40 nights in Lent
- 50 stars on the American flag
- 63 dots in the Braille alphabet
- 64 squares on a chessboard
- 67 islands in the Orkneys
- 88 keys on a standard piano (52 white, 36 black)
- 142 staircases at Hogwart's School
- 144 in a gross
- 158 verses in the Greek national anthem
- 168 hours in a week
- 294 steps in the Leaning Tower of Pisa
- 6500 windows in the Empire State Building

Violin

MISCELLANEOUS

FAN CLUBS

Gerry Anderson	Fanderson
Buster Keaton	Damfinos (stands for damned if I know)
Laurel & Hardy	Sons of the Desert
The Marx Brothers	The Marx Brotherhood
Marilyn Monroe	Marilyn Lives Society
Monty Python	FOUL (stands for Friends Of Unnatural Llamas)
The Prisoner	The Number Six Club
Prisoner Cell Block H	Blockies
Sherlock Holmes	The Baker Street Irregulars
Star Trek	Starfleet International

10 FAN CLUBS OF ELVIS PRESLEY

- Graceland's Rising Sun
- Elvis's Teddy Bears
- Always on my Mind in Ohio
- From A Jack To A King
- Blue Hawaiians
- The Memphis Mafia
- Elvis in the Heart of Dixie Fan Club of Alabama
- Rock a Hula Girls
- Jailhouse Rockers of California
- Friends of Elvis Treat Me Nice

'WOOD' YOU BELIEVE IT?

- **Petrified wood** is the official state fossil of Arizona
- **George Washington** had a set of false teeth made of wood, later replaced by an ivory and gold set
- **During World War II,** film Oscars were made out of wood, due to the scarcity of metal
- **Wood** is the 5th wedding anniversary
- **Coal** is formed from trees that lived in pre-historic times
- **Old superstition** tells us to knock three times on wood after mentioning good fortune so that evil spirits will not ruin it
- **Plywood** was invented and patented by Immanuel Nobel, the father of Alfred Nobel
- **Maine** is the most heavily forested state of the USA, with approximately 90% of its area covered by forest
- **The last tennis player** to win a Grand Slam tournament using a wooden racket was Bjorn Borg, when he lifted the French Open title in 1981
- **In medieval times,** the floors of houses were covered in straw, also known as thresh. The piece of wood placed in the doorway to stop the straw spilling out became known as the threshold.
- **Less well-off people** used dirt instead of thresh, hence the saying, dirt poor

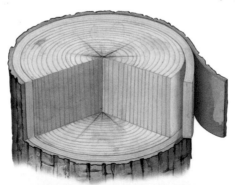

MISCELLANEOUS

ALL THE THREES

The Three Stooges	Curly, Larry & Moe
West Indian cricketers known as the 3 Ws	Frank Worrell, Clyde Walcott, Everton Weekes
The three British Kings of 1936	George V, Edward VIII, George VI
Three instruments in a string quartet	Viola, cello, violin (2 violins)
The Three Tenors	Luciano Pavarotti, Jose Carreras, Placido Domingo
The original *Charlie's Angels* actresses	Farrah Fawcett, Jaclyn Smith, Kate Jackson
The three middle names of Prince Charles	Philip, Arthur, George
The three deities in the Hindu trinity	Brahma, Vishnu, Shiva
The three categories of Shakespeare plays	Tragedies, histories, comedies
The three methods of heat energy transference	Convection, conduction, radiation
The three saint's crosses on the Union Jack	George, Andrew, Patrick
The three classification groups for diamonds	Flats, stones, cleavages
The three countries ruled by King Canute	Denmark, Norway, England
The three J's that the city of Dundee is famed for	Jute, jam, journalism
The three composers known as the Three Bs	Beethoven, Bach, Brahms
The three fire signs of the zodiac	Leo, Aries, Sagittarius
The three Earth signs of the zodiac	Taurus, Virgo, Capricorn
The three air signs of the zodiac	Gemini, Libra, Aquarius
The three water signs of the zodiac	Cancer, Scorpio, Pisces

BOOK OF LISTS

SCREEN FAREWELLS
The last cinema releases of some famous movie stars

Fred Astaire	1981	*Ghost Story*
Dirk Bogarde	1990	*Daddy Nostalgia*
Humphrey Bogart	1956	*The Harder they Fall*
Charles Bronson	1994	*Death Wish V*
Yul Brynner	1980	*Lost To The Revolution*
Richard Burton	1984	*1984*
James Cagney	1981	*Ragtime*
Charlie Chaplin	1966	*A Countess from Hong Kong*
Joan Crawford	1970	*Trog*
Bette Davis	1989	*Wicked Stepmother*
Marlene Dietrich	1978	*Just a Gigolo*
Errol Flynn	1959	*Cuban Rebel Girls*
Henry Fonda	1981	*On Golden Pond*
Clark Gale	1961	*The Misfits*
Greta Garbo	1941	*Two-Faced Woman*
Judy Garland	1963	*I Could Go on Singing*
John Gielgud	1998	*The Titchbourne Claimant*
Cary Grant	1966	*Walk Don't Run*
Audrey Hepburn	1989	*Always*
Katharine Hepburn	1994	*Love Affair*
William Holden	1981	*S.O.B.*
Buster Keaton	1966	*Sergeant Deadhead*

MISCELLANEOUS

SCREEN FAREWELLS
The last cinema releases of some famous movie stars

Grace Kelly	1956	*High Society*
Vivien Leigh	1965	*Ship Of Fools*
Jack Lemmon	2000	*The Legend Of Bagger Vance*
Bela Lugosi	1956	*Plan 9 From Outer Space*
Lee Marvin	1986	*The Delta Force*
James Mason	1984	*The Shooting Party*
Steve McQueen	1980	*The Hunter*
Robert Mitchum	1997	*Waiting for Sunset*
Marilyn Monroe	1961	*The Misfits*
David Niven	1983	*The Curse of the Pink Panther*
Laurence Olivier	1989	*War Requiems*
Oliver Reed	2000	*Gladiator*
Edward G Robinson	1973	*Soylent Green*
Robert Shaw	1979	*Avalanche Express*
Rod Steiger	2002	*Poolhall Junkies*
Spencer Tracy	1967	*Guess Who's Coming to Dinner*
Rudolph Valentino	1926	*The Son of Sheikh*
John Wayne	1976	*The Shootist*
Johnny Weissmuller	1976	*Won Ton Ton the Dog that Saved Hollywood*
Mae West	1977	*Sextet*
Natalie Wood	1983	*Brainstorm*

BOOK OF LISTS

THE COCKTAIL MENU

COCKTAIL	INGREDIENTS
B and B	Brandy and Benedictine
Between the sheets	Cointreau, rum, brandy, lemon juice
Black Russian	Vodka, kahlua, coke
Black velvet	Stout, champagne
Bloody Mary	Vodka and tomato juice
Blue Lagoon	Vodka, Malibu, Curacao, lemonade
Blue Hawaii	White rum, blue Curacao, pineapple juice, coconut cream
Bronx	Gin and vermouth
Bucks Fizz	Champagne and orange juice
Cosmopolitan	Vodka, triple sec, cranberry juice, lime juice
Gibson	Gin, vermouth, cocktail onion
Gimlet	Gin, lime juice
Green Dragon	Champagne, midori
Harvey Wallbanger	Vodka, Galliano, orange juice
Horse's Neck	Whisky and ginger ale
Kamikaze	Vodka, triple sec, lime juice
Long Island Iced Tea	Vodka, gin, Cointreau, white rum, lemon juice, cola
Macaroni	Pernod, vermouth
Mai Tai	White rum, triple sec, grenadine, lime juice
Manhattan	Bourbon whisky, vermouth
Margarita	Tequila, Cointreau, lime juice
Moscow Mule	Vodka, ginger beer, lime juice

MISCELLANEOUS

THE COCKTAIL MENU

Pina Colada. . . . . White rum, coconut milk, pineapple juice

Pink gin. . . . . Gin, angostura bitters

Rossini . . . . Sparkling wine, pureed strawberries

Rusty Nail . . . . Whisky, drambuie

Screwdriver . . . . Vodka, orange juice

Sex On The Beach. . . . . Vodka, peach schnapps, orange juice, cranberry

Sidecar . . . . Brandy, Cointreau, lemon juice

Tequila Sunrise . . . . Tequila, grenadine, orange juice

Tom Collins. . . . . Gin, lemon juice, sugar, soda

White Lady. . . . . Gin, vermouth, lemonade

Zombie . . . . White rum, dark rum, grenadine, pineapple juice

CHAMPAGNE BOTTLE SIZES

Quarter bottle. . . . . Split

Two bottles . . . . Magnum

Four bottles . . . . Jeroboam

Six bottles . . . . Rehoboam

Eight bottles . . . . Methuselah

Twelve bottles. . . . . Salmanazar

Sixteen bottles . . . . Balthazar

Twenty bottles . . . . Nebuchadnezzar

Twenty-four bottles . . . . Melchior

Sixty-seven bottles. . . . . Sovereign

HOW TO SAY GOODBYE IN 30 LANGUAGES

Amharic	Selam	**Norwegian**	Farvel
Arabic	M'Asselema	**Polish**	Czesc
Bengali	Bidai	**Portuguese**	Ate a vista
Bulgarian	Doskoro	**Punjabi**	Salam
Czech	Ahoj	**Russian**	Dosvi'daniya
Danish	Farvel	**Spanish**	Hasta la vista
Dutch	Vaarwel	**Swedish**	Adjo
Farsi	Khoda hafaz	**Turkish**	Hoscakal
Finnish	Heippa	**Welsh**	Hwyl
French	Au revoir		
German	Auf Wiedersehen		
Greek	Geia		
Hebrew	Shalom		
Hindi	Namaste		
Hungarian	Viszlat		
Italian	Ciao		
Japanese	Sayonara		
Latin	Vale		
Latvian	Ata		
Maltese	Sahha		
Mandarin Chinese	Zai hui		

MISCELLANEOUS

LAST WORDS OF 20 FAMOUS PEOPLE

Anna Pavlova . . . ."Get my swan costume ready."

Pablo Picasso . . . ."Drink to me."

George V . . . ."Bugger Bognor."

Cecil Rhodes . . . ."So little done, so much to do."

Bing Crosby . . . ."That was a great game of golf, fellas."

Julius Caesar . . . ."Et tu Brute?"

Archimedes . . . ."Wait till I have finished my problem."

Oscar Wilde . . . ."Either that wallpaper goes or I do."

Charles II . . . ."Let not poor Nelly starve."

PT Barnum . . . ."How were the receipts today at Madison Square Garden?"

WC Fields . . . ."On the whole, I'd rather be in Philadelphia."

Elizabeth I . . . ."All my possessions for a moment of time."

Lou Costello . . . ."That was the best ice cream soda I ever tasted."

Humphrey Bogart . . . ."I should never have switched from Scotch to Martinis."

Henry VIII . . . ."All is lost. Monks, monks, monks!"

Noel Coward . . . ."Goodnight my darlings, I'll see you tomorrow."

Beethoven . . . ."I shall hear in heaven."

Lady Nancy Astor . . . ."Am I dying or is this my birthday?"

Franklin D Roosevelt . . . ."I have a terrific headache."

Karl Marx . . . ."Last words are for fools who haven't said enough."

Acknowledgements

All artworks are from the Miles Kelly Artwork Bank

The Publishers would like to thank the following picture sources
whose photographs appear in this book:

PictorialPress.com (Pages 26, 29, 31, 32, 37, 48, 57, 69, 78, 87, 92, 94, 96, 218, 223,
229, 231, 252, 259, 262, 265, 273, 278, 279, 289, 290, 292, 295, 296, 297, 298, 313,
315, 318, 343, 380, 456, 457, 459, 460, 462)

45 Hanna-Barbera; 52 Volkswagen; 81 FOX/pictorialpress.com; 199 MGM/Selznick
International/pictorialpress.com; 200 UA/Mirisch-Alpha/pictorialpress.com;
202 Walt Disney/pictorialpress.com; 206 LUCASFILMS/pictorialpress.com;
214 Warner/Morgan/pictorialpress.com; 221 Anabasis Investments NV/Buzz
Feitshans/pictorialpress.com; 222 Buena Vista/Touchstone/Valhalla/pictorialpress.com;
226 Buena Vista/Tiger Moth/Miramax/pictorialpress.com;
227 CBS/Warner/pictorialpress.com; 232 Polygram/Channel 4/Figment/Noel
Gay/pictorialpress.com; 238 UA/Mirisch/Alpha/pictorialpress.com;
240 DANJAQ S.A./pictorialpress.com; 248 Fox TV; 269 BBC; 320 Sony Computer
Entertainment; 327 Thames TV; 329 David Wolper/pictorialpress.com;
431 Suzuki; 440 Mayer/pictorialpress.com; 441 Polygram/pictorialpress.com; 485 Nokia

All other images from:

Castrol, Corbis, Corel, digitalSTOCK, digitalvision, Dover
Hemera, ILN, John Foxx, Nasa, PhotoAlto, PhotoDisc